D0083155

Women, Minorities,
and Unions
in the Public Sector

Recent Titles in
Contributions in Labor Studies

Confrontation, Class Consciousness, and the Labor Process: Studies in Proletarian Class Formation
Michael Hanagan and Charles Stephenson, editors

We Offer Ourselves as Evidence: Toward Workers' Control of Occupational Health
Bennett M. Judkins

Between Class and Nation: The Formation of the Jewish Working Class in the Period Before Israel's Statehood
Amir Ben-Porat

Solidarity or Survival? American Labor and European Immigrants, 1830–1924
A. T. Lane

Comparable Worth, Pay Equity, and Public Policy
Rita Mae Kelly and Jane Bayes, editors

The Politics of Right to Work: The Labor Federations as Special Interests, 1943–1979
Gilbert J. Gall

Social Workers and Labor Unions
Howard Jacob Karger

Capitalist Development and Class Capacities: Marxist Theory and Union Organization
Jerry Lembcke

Occupation and Class Consciousness in America
Douglas M. Eichar

Our Own Time: A History of American Labor and the Working Day
David R. Roediger and Philip S. Foner

Women, Minorities, and Unions in the Public Sector

Norma M. Riccucci

Contributions in Labor Studies, Number 28

Greenwood Press
New York · Westport, Connecticut · London

Copyright Acknowledgments

The author and publisher want to thank the following for permission to use material from:

Employment Discrimination Law, 2d. ed. by Schlei & Grossman, BNA Books, 1983, © 1983 by the American Bar Association Section of Labor and Employment Law;

Policy Paper No. 10, *Equal Apprenticeship Opportunities: The Nature of the Issue and the New York Experience*, by F. Ray Marshall and Vernon M. Briggs, Jr., Institute of Labor and Industrial Relations, The University of Michigan;

William Gould, "Labor Relations and Race Relations," in *Public Workers and Public Unions*, ed. Sam Zagoria, New York, The American Assembly;

William Sylvis, "A Union's Position," in *America's Working Women*, ed. Rosalyn Baxandall, Linda Gordon and Susan Reverby, copyright by Random House, Inc.;

Norma M. Riccucci, "Union Liability for Wage Disparities Between Women and Men," in *University of Detroit Law Review*, vol. 65, issue 3, Spring 1988;

Grune and Reder, "Pay Equity," in *Public Personnel Management*, International Personnel Management Association;

Jacobs and Crotty, "Guard Unions and the Future of the Prisons," August 1978, IPE Monograph No. 9, Ithaca, NY: New York State School of Industrial and Labor Relations, Cornell University.

Library of Congress Cataloging-in-Publication Data

Riccucci, Norma M.
    Women, minorities, and unions in the public sector / Norma M.
Riccucci.
        p.   cm. — (Contributions in labor studies, ISSN 0886-8239 ;
    no. 28)
        Includes bibliographies and index.
        ISBN 0-313-26043-5 (lib. bdg. : alk. paper)
        1. Trade-unions—Government employees—United States. 2. Women in
    the civil service—United States. 3. Civil service—United States—
    Minority employment. 4. Pay equity—United States. 5. Affirmative
    action programs—United States. 6. Discrimination in employment—
    United States. I. Title. II. Series.
    HD8005.2.U5R53 1990
    331.4'781135'0000973—dc20   89-7481

British Library Cataloguing in Publication Data is available.

Library of Congress Catalog Card Number: 89-7481
ISBN: 0-313-26043-5
ISSN: 0886-8239

First published in 1990

Greenwood Press, Inc.
88 Post Road West, Westport, Connecticut 06881

Printed in the United States of America

The paper used in this book complies with the
Permanent Paper Standard issued by the National
Information Standards Organization (Z39.48-1984).

10 9 8 7 6 5 4 3 2 1

In loving memory of my parents,
Tosca and George Riccucci

CONTENTS

Tables   xi

Acknowledgments   xiii

1 INTRODUCTION   1

The Role of Unions in Female and Minority Employment
in the Public Sector   1

The Significance of Public Sector Union Involvement   2

Purpose of This Book   4

Organization of the Book   5

2 WOMEN AND MINORITIES IN PUBLIC SECTOR UNIONS   11

Female and Minority Membership in Public
Sector Unions   14

Membership and Leadership Patterns in Individual Public
Sector Unions   22

Conclusions   28

3 THE LEGAL OBLIGATIONS OF UNIONS   33

Duty of Fair Representation   34

   DFR for Unions Representing State and Local
   Government Workers   37

DFR for Unions Representing Federal
Government Workers   40

Union Liability Under Title VII   43

Seniority Systems: Questions of Law and Equity
under Title VII   44

Affirmative Action, Layoffs and Seniority in the
Public Sector   54

Conclusions   61

**4 WOMEN, MINORITIES, AND JOINT LABOR-MANAGEMENT
COOPERATION   67**

Joint Labor-Management EEO/AA Committees   68

How Desirable and Useful Is Cooperation
over EEO/AA?   68

A Cursory Review of Some Joint EEO/AA Committees   69

Joint Apprenticeship Programs/Committees   74

Historical Overview of Apprenticeships   74

General Barriers That Women and Minorities Face in
Entering Apprenticeships   78

Unions as a Barrier to Women and Minorities   80

Public Sector Apprenticeship Training   84

Female and Minority Representation in Public
Sector Apprenticeship Programs: A Preliminary
Look at Potential Union Involvement   90

Conclusions and Policy Recommendations   94

**5 WOMEN IN UNIFORMED SERVICE JOBS: THE ROLE
OF UNIONS   103**

Female Employment in the Uniformed Services   105

Fire   109

Police   116

Corrections   124

Sanitation   129

Conclusions   133

6 UNIONS AND COMPARABLE WORTH 141

What Is Comparable Worth? 142

Unions and Pay Equality 143

Unions and Pay Equity 147

    Collective Bargaining 147

    Job Evaluation Studies 150

    Union Organizing 156

    Official Union Policies 158

    Political Activities 160

    Litigation 162

    Conclusions 166

7 CONCLUSIONS AND SUMMARY 171

Directions for Future Research 172

Epilogue 175

Table of Cases 177

Index 183

TABLES

2.1 Women and Minorities in Public Sector Work
Forces, 1977, 1980   14

2.2 Female and Minority Union Membership as a Percentage
of Females and Minorities in the Work Force, 1977, 1980   15

2.3 Female and Minority Union Membership as a Percentage
of Employed Females and Minorities, Sample Data,
1985   18

2.4 Female and Minority Share of Union Membership in
the Public Sector, 1977, 1980   20

2.5 Female and Minority Share of Union Membership in
the Public Sector, Sample Data, 1985   20

2.6 Female and Minority Union Membership as a Percentage
of the Total Public Sector Work Force, All Levels,
1977, 1980   22

2.7 Female Members, Officers and Officials of Selected
International and National Unions, 1972, 1978   23

4.1 Female and Minority Apprentices in the
United States, 1978, 1979, 1987   77

4.2 Number and Size of Public Sector Apprenticeship
Programs Registered with the BAT or SACs as of
December 31, 1987   86

4.3 Joint and Nonjoint Apprenticeship Programs in the
Public Sector, Registered with the BAT or SACs as of
December 31, 1987   88

4.4 Women and Minorities in Public Sector
Apprenticeship Programs Registered with the BAT or SACs
as of December 31, 1987   90

4.5 Distribution of Women and Minorities to Joint and Nonjoint
Public Sector Apprenticeship Programs Registered with
the BAT or SACs as of December 31, 1987   91

4.6 Apprentices in Jointly Run Firefighting Programs,
California, 1982, 1986   93

4.7 Apprentices in Jointly Run Firefighting Programs,
Washington, December 1987   93

4.8 New York State Stationary Engineer Apprentices
in Office of General Services, 1981, 1982   95

5.1 Female Representation in Uniformed Services,
1975, 1980, 1985   106

6.1 Federal Government Employees' Annual Salaries
by Gender, 1919   146

6.2 Summary of Case Law on Pay Equity   163

ACKNOWLEDGMENTS

I am indebted to a number of persons who not only were instrumental in my work on this book but also made the experience invaluable. First, I thank my family members, Margherita Catani, John Riccucci and Nancy Dame, for their unyielding support. I also wish to thank the following colleagues for their encouragement, criticism, and input, without which this book could not have been written: Stephen L. Wasby, David H. Rosenbloom, Phillip J. Cooper, Sally Friedman, Carolyn Ban, Frank J. Thompson, James L. Perry, Chris E. Bose, David P. McCaffrey, Sue R. Faerman, Bruce Hamm, Judy Avner, Steven Moskowitz, and Sarah Phillips. Of course, the author is solely responsible for the final content of this book. ·

I also thank Jeanne E. Gullahorn, Vice President for Research and Dean of Graduate Studies at the State University of New York at Albany, for the very useful research assistance she provided.

I thank the staff members of several organizations who provided prompt and efficient responses to my requests for information. These persons come from the U.S. Bureau of Apprenticeship and Training, Equal Employment Opportunity Commission, the Demography Center and the Center for Women in Government of the State University of New York at Albany, Cornell University's Labor-Management Documentation Center, New York State Department of Labor, California Department of Industrial Relations, Washington Department of Labor and Industries, Bureau of National Affairs and a number of other state personnel agencies.

Finally, I wish to express thanks to the New York State/United University Professions Joint Labor-Management Committee for providing me with a Dr. Nuala McGann Drescher Affirmative Action Leave, which enabled me to complete this book.

Women, Minorities, and Unions in the Public Sector

1
INTRODUCTION

The Role of Unions in Female and Minority Employment in the Public Sector

Affirmative action and other policy tools aimed at promoting the equal employment of women and minorities in public sector work forces have received much scholarly attention in the past decade or so. Recently, the interest in these mechanisms has peaked in light of new judicial developments. Specifically, the U.S. Supreme Court in the last few years has upheld the legality and constitutionality of affirmative action in hiring and promotion decisions[1] in order to remedy past employment discrimination and, perhaps of greater significance, racial and gender imbalances in the work force.[2] These decisions have resolved ambiguities over the legality and constitutionality of affirmative action in the public sector that arose with the U.S. Supreme Court's rulings in *Regents v. Bakke* (1978) and *United Steelworkers v. Weber* (1979).

Despite the attention given to affirmative action or, more generally, the employment patterns of women and minorities in the public sector, little attention has been placed on union involvement in these employment patterns. This is interesting for a number of reasons one being that the role of unions in female and minority employment patterns in the *private* sector has been of concern to policy makers and scholars for many decades. Overlooking public sector union involvement has ultimately left gaps in the policy processes targeted at enhancing the employment status of women and minorities and also the scholarly literature on female and minority employment in government work forces. This book is intended to fill some of these gaps.

The Significance of Public Sector Union Involvement

The premise of this book is that unions in the public sector are important, yet overlooked, participants in the decision- and policy-making processes that affect the employment of women and minorities. They are overlooked actors largely because their formal powers tend to be circumscribed by statutory or case law, which stems from their operation in the *government* as opposed to private sector sphere.

There is a long history of debate over the appropriateness of unionism in the public sector (Nigro and Nigro 1986; Klingner and Nalbandian 1985; Perry 1985; Rosenbloom and Shafritz 1985; Kearney 1984; Bent and Reeves 1978; Wellington and Winter 1969). The controversy revolves around such issues as the propriety of government employees to share in political, social and economic decisions that have traditionally fallen solely within the province of the government or sovereignty. In addition, questions have arisen regarding whether public employees, if allowed the right to participate in governmental decision making, could effectively discharge their duties as protectors and stewards of the public interest, which includes the public till. The right of public employees to strike has also generated a good deal of controversy, particularly for uniformed service employees such as police, firefighters, correctional officers and sanitation workers.

Today, many government leaders, government workers and members of the general citizenry, particularly in the South, continue to believe that unions should not operate in the public sector. These attitudes and beliefs have not only retarded the advent and further development of the public sector labor movement but also have resulted in severe limitations on the formal or statutory powers of unions, especially those representing federal government employees.

A corollary of the research presented in this book suggests, however, that unions in the public sector often possess de facto power to influence the employment progress of women and minorities in government work forces. Depending upon the circumstances, unions can directly or indirectly exert their control at the bargaining table through meet-and-confer conferences with management, by filing lawsuits, by lobbying political officials and by mobilizing public support.

Then, despite efforts to limit their formal powers, public sector unions are able to influence female and minority employment progress (Gerhart 1969). The next question becomes, Are unions hindering or facilitating this progress? Unions, in some cases, have promoted equal employment opportunity (EEO) and even affirmative action (AA) for women and minorities.[3] Importantly, these are the cases that have shaped general beliefs about the behaviors and attitudes of public sector unions toward women and minorities. That is, there appears to be a popular belief that public sector unions have very progressive female and minority employment records (Gould 1972). As this volume will show, however, the generalizations about public sector unions' support for EEO and AA from these isolated cases have been overstated. There are, in fact, many instances where unions have set up salient barriers to the employment of women and minorities. These cases are seldom scrutinized or documented in any scholarly fashion.

The problem of making generalizations is a serious one, which stems from a number of factors including the tendency to blur the boundaries of the different levels of unions—federation, national and local. Assumptions are often made, for example, that because the AFL-CIO at the federation level has expressed support for at least EEO, its affiliates also support EEO.[4] Similarly, it is assumed that because a union at the national or international level supports EEO and AA, all affiliated locals will likewise support EEO and AA.

Assumptions such as these are misguided, as can be seen with the experiences of the American Federation of State, County and Municipal Employees (AFSCME), one of the largest public employee unions in the United States. This union has indeed shown its support for women and minorities in various arenas, the most recent being its battle for equal pay for comparable worth. It must be kept in mind, however, that although AFSCME at the national level as well as some of its locals may support comparable worth and other female and minority employment issues, not *all* AFSCME locals support EEO and AA. For example, as will be discussed in Chapter 6, there are instances where AFSCME locals do not support comparable worth. In addition, AFSCME's position on EEO and AA comes into question when we consider that, in New York State alone, AFSCME locals within the past several years have faced over one hundred charges of discrimination before the state's Division of Human Rights. It is inappropriate and erroneous to assume that because AFSCME at the national level supports EEO and AA, all AFSCME locals do as well.

Another reason for generalizing about public sector unions' support for EEO and AA relates to a failure to account for the presence of "craft" unions in the public sector.[5] Craft unions represent workers in a specific skilled trade or craft, which generally requires some form of training or apprenticeship to learn the trade. In the public sector, such professions as police, firefighting and corrections can be viewed as crafts, since special training is required for entry into the profession. Because the work is specialized, craft unions often have a relatively good deal of control over their own employment. For example, they can exert control over wage rates as well as who can enter the occupation (Riccucci 1988; Methé and Perry 1980).

Craft unions in the public sector, similar to those operating in the private sector, have not been very receptive to the presence of women and minorities in their particular crafts. Perhaps the primary reason for this is that these unions are comprised mostly of white males. In any event, a full and thorough assessment of the position of public sector unions on EEO and AA cannot ignore the policies and practices of these unions.

Also contrary to common belief, not all industrial or "noncraft" unions operating in the public sector support EEO and AA. Rather, industrial unions' positions seem to vary depending upon a number of factors. Just as is the case with craft unions, one reason relates to the social characteristics of an industrial union's constituency. If a union representing industrial workers in the public sector is comprised mainly of white males, it may show little support for EEO and AA.

In sum, public sector unions do not always facilitate the employment progress of women and minorities. In many cases, they hinder such progress. To the extent that we overlook unions as barriers to female and minority employment in the public sector, we omit them from policy formulas and alternatives aimed at not only dismantling discrimination in the workplace but also promoting AA measures. On the other hand, to the extent that unions support EEO or AA, we overlook them as viable components of the policy process.

Purpose of This Book

The purpose of this book, then, is to examine, through legal, political and historical frameworks, the pattern of union involvement in the employment of women and minorities in public sector work forces. In addition, the potential motivations for their support as well as opposition will be assessed in order to provide insight into union behaviors toward the equal employment of women and minorities in the government sector. An understanding of unions' motivations is critical for determining their proper role in the development and implementation of female and minority employment policies.

The case law on female and minority employment will be heavily relied upon not only as a source of law but also as an indication of public sector unions' positions on EEO and AA. Previous studies, although few, have taken an explanatory approach to examine union involvement in female and minority employment patterns.[6] These studies are important, but may not capture the full picture because of their reliance on surrogate measures of unionism. Such measures tend to obscure unions' true positions on EEO and AA. More clearly, because unions are such closed and guarded organizations, it is usually impossible to gain access to union records or union officials for interviewing purposes. If one is granted an interview with union officials, the union's position on EEO and AA may be revealed only if the union supports such issues. It is unlikely that union officials will publicly state opposition to EEO and AA.

As such, explanatory studies tend to rely on such measures as the presence or absence of unions in a particular work force. This may not reflect unions' true positions on EEO and AA. An examination of the case law, however, although not as systematic, will illustrate unions' actual positions because the unions are required to legally justify them. Case law, then, serves as the major source of data for the analyses presented in this book. Descriptive statistics are also relied upon to support the themes of various chapters. It should further be noted that although the primary focus of this book is on public sector unions, comparisons are made to the practices of private sector unions toward women and minorities. Such comparisons are useful in examining the role of public sector unions in female and minority employment.

Finally, educational unions receive minimal attention in this book because of their unique qualities. For example, there are important differences between the governing structures of public school employees as compared to local government employees. Because of these differences, educational unions, at least for research purposes, are seldom lumped into the general category of "public sector unions." Yet, it is important to point out that where educational unions are discussed (Chapters 3 and 4) some interesting patterns emerge regarding their support for EEO and AA, particularly at the higher education level where women and minorities are not well represented on teaching staffs (Menges and Exum 1983). Future studies should examine these patterns and also compare the practices and policies of educational unions toward women and minorities with those of other unions.

Organization of the Book

Public sector unions play an important role in the employment of women and minorities. They can thwart or promote EEO and AA measures aimed at the equitable employment of these groups in state, local and federal government work forces. There are many factors that can contribute to a union's position on EEO and AA. As noted earlier, one relates to the social composition of the union, which will be presented in Chapter 2. In addition, the values and beliefs of union officials may also influence the union's position on EEO and AA. As will be illustrated in Chapter 2, union hierarchies tend to be dominated by white males. The lack of women and minorities in union leadership positions is especially revealing for those unions that support EEO and AA because it reflects assumptions about the competency of women and minorities to govern and run unions.

Chapter 3 looks at the legal obligations of unions to protect and promote the employment interests of women and minorities. Attention is placed on two critical legal doctrines. One is the *duty of fair representation*, which requires unions to fairly represent all of its members, notwithstanding such characteristics as race and sex. The other doctrine is *union liability* for its own discrimination as well as employer discrimination against women and minorities.

Chapter 3 also examines the legality of seniority systems and the effects of seniority on the employment of women and minorities. Employment decisions based on seniority, which is almost always prescribed by the collective bargaining contract, take their worst toll on women and minorities since these groups are systematically the last to enter the work force. Despite the effects, the courts in recent years have upheld the use of seniority, providing that its use is "bona fide," that is, it does not *intend* to discriminate under Title VII of the Civil Rights Act of 1964, as amended. This represents a serious setback to the employment progress of women and minorities in both public and private sector work forces.

Chapter 4 examines joint labor-management cooperation over EEO and AA. Cooperative efforts are strongly recommended when both labor and management genuinely support EEO and AA. However, when the parties oppose EEO and AA, labor-management cooperation works against the equal employment of women and minorities. The best illustration of this can be seen in the policies and practices of joint apprenticeship committees (JACs) which are examined in this chapter.

Chapter 5 looks at the history of women's employment in such nontraditional occupations as firefighting, police, corrections and sanitation. The chapter begins with a general overview of the underrepresentation of women as well as minorities in these occupations. It then points to the institutionalized discrimination against women seeking entry, promotion or retention in these craft jobs,[7] and then points to union involvement in the discriminatory practices. In particular, it points to the problems associated with the continued reliance on physical agility exams to measure "merit" for entry into these professions. These exams adversely affect women and are seldom job related, but unions insist upon their use.

Union involvement in the comparable worth or pay equity debate is examined in Chapter 6. Specifically, the chapter looks at the attempts of unions to either facilitate or hinder efforts across the country aimed at paying women the same wages as men when performing different jobs of comparable value to employers. Unions have exerted their influence over comparable worth policy in many ways, including at the bargaining table, through union policies, through political activities and by filing lawsuits.

Each of the strategies is presented separately in order to demonstrate the breadth and depth of alternatives available to unions to affect comparable worth measures. The motivations of unions to support or oppose comparable worth are also examined in order to determine their proper role in this policy process.

Chapter 7 provides conclusions and policy recommendations for the role of unions in female and minority employment in the public sector. Suggestions for future research are also presented.

It is important to note at the outset that this book, as the title suggests, addresses issues related to both women and minorities; however, some chapters tend to place greater emphasis on only one protected class group.[8] For example, Chapters 3 and 4 emphasize minority concerns, specifically those of male minorities. Various union legal obligations in the field of equal opportunity arose out of challenges by male minorities to discriminatory union behaviors. Chapter 4 focuses heavily upon the activities of JACs, which have historically worked against male minorities seeking entry into apprenticeship programs. It is only more recently that women have sought entry into apprenticeship programs and have thereby encountered obstacles set up by unions.

Chapters 5 and 6, on the other hand, place more attention on women. Women receive greater attention in Chapter 5 because of its emphasis on union involvement in the use of physical ability exams as selection devices for entry into uniformed service jobs such as firefighting and law enforcement. In general, those exams tend to adversely affect women of all colors rather than minority men. Finally, Chapter 6 looks solely at women because the issue of comparable worth involves pay inequities mainly between women and men.[9] In sum, although some chapters devote more attention to only one protected class group, on the whole, this book addresses issues that are pertinent to both women and minorities.

Notes

1. The Court, however, seems unwilling to uphold the use of affirmative action in layoff decisions. This will be further addressed in Chapter 3.

2. See, for example, *Sheet Metal Workers v. EEOC* (1986); *Firefighters v. Cleveland* (1986); *Wygant v. Jackson Board of Education* (1986); *United States v. Paradise* (1987); and *Johnson v. Transportation Agency* (1987). But, compare with *City of Richmond v. Croson Company* (1989). For a further discussion, see Chapter 3, in particular text accompanying note 26. Also see, Nalbandian (1989), for an excellent analysis of the U.S. Supreme Court's affirmative action rulings. It is also important for the reader to consult the Epilogue which briefly addresses the U.S. Supreme Court decisions that were handed down while this book was in press.

3. For the purposes of this book, EEO refers to refraining from discrimination

while AA refers to proactive measures aimed at enhancing the employment progress of women and minorities.

4. These assumptions seem to be more prevalent for public as compared to private sector unions.

5. Labeling particular public sector unions as craft as opposed to industrial is difficult because some unions represent specialized as well as less specialized workers. For example, AFSCME is often viewed primarily as industrial, but many AFSCME locals often represent specialized or skilled workers. Indeed, AFSCME represents the largest number of correctional officers in the United States (Potter 1981). Hence, the use of the term "craft" union does not refer to any specific union but rather to any union representing skilled craft workers.

6. See, for example, Riccucci (1986); Leonard (1985); Davis (1984) and Beyer, Trice and Hunt (1980).

7. Sanitation is labeled a "craft" because it shares characteristics with other crafts, as will be further addressed in Chapter 5.

8. The classification "women" includes women of all colors and the use of "minorities," unless otherwise indicated, refers to male minorities.

9. See, however, Scales-Trent (1984), which looks specifically at the utility of a comparable worth theory for blacks.

References

Bent, Alan Edward and T. Zane Reeves. *Collective Bargaining in the Public Sector.* Menlo Park, California: The Benjamin/Cummings Publishing Co., Inc., 1978.

Beyer, Janice M., Harrison M. Trice, and Richard Hunt. "The Impact of Federal Sector Unions on Supervisors' Use of Personnel Policies." *Industrial and Labor Relations Review* 33 (1980) 2:212–231.

City of Richmond v. Croson Company 57 *Law Week* 4132, January 24, 1989.

Davis, Charles. "Equity vs. Fairness: The Impact of State Collective Bargaining Policies on the Implementation of Affirmative Action Programs." *Journal of Collective Negotiations in the Public Sector* 13 (1984), 3:225–234.

Firefighters Local No. 93 v. Cleveland 106 S.Ct. 3063, _U.S._ (1986).

Gerhart, Paul F. "Scope of Bargaining in Local Government Labor Negotiations." *Labor Law Journal* 20 (August 1969), 545–552.

Gould, William B. "Labor Relations and Race Relations." In Sam Zagoria (ed.), *Public Workers and Public Unions.* Englewood Cliffs, New Jersey: Prentice-Hall, Inc., 1972:147–159.

Johnson v. Transportation Agency, Santa Clara County, California 107 S. Ct. 1442, _U.S._ (1987).

Kearney, Richard C. *Labor Relations in the Public Sector.* New York: Marcel Dekker, Inc., 1984.

Klingner, Donald E. and John Nalbandian. *Public Personnel Management: Contexts and Strategies.* Englewood Cliffs, New Jersey: Prentice-Hall, Inc., 1985, 2d ed.

Leonard, Jonathan S. "The Effect of Unions on the Employment of Blacks, Hispanics, and Women." *Industrial and Labor Relations Review* 39 (1985), 1:115–132.

Menges, Robert J. and William H. Exum, "Barriers to the Progress of Women and Minority Faculty." *Journal of Higher Education* 54 (1983), 2:123–144.

Methé, David T. and James L. Perry. "The Impacts of Collective Bargaining on Local Government Services: A Review of Research." *Public Administration Review* 40 (1980), 4:359–371.

Nalbandian, John. "The U.S. Supreme Court's 'Consensus' on Affirmative Action." *Public Administration Review* 49 (1989), 1:38–45.

Nigro, Felix A. and Lloyd G. Nigro. *The New Public Personnel Administration.* Itasca, Illinois: F. E. Peacock Publishers, Inc., 1986, 3d. ed.

Perry, James L. "The 'Old Testament': A Litany of Beliefs about Public Sector Labor Relations—A Symposium." *Review of Public Personnel Administration* 5 (1985), 2:1–4.

Potter, Joan, "Guard Unions: The Search for Solidarity." In Robert R. Ross (ed.), *Prison Guard/Correctional Officer.* Toronto, Canada: Butterworth & Co., 1981:321–336.

Regents v. Bakke 98 S.Ct. 2733, 438 U.S. 265 (1978).

Riccucci, Norma M. "Female and Minority Employment in City Government: The Role of Unions." *Policy Studies Journal* 15 (1986), 1:3–15.

———. "A Typology for Union Discrimination: A Public Sector Perspective." *Public Personnel Management* 17 (1988), 1:41–51.

Rosenbloom, David H. and Jay M. Shafritz. *Essentials of Labor Relations.* Reston, Virginia: Reston Publishing Co., Inc., 1985.

Scales-Trent, Judy, "Comparable Worth: Is This a Theory for Black Workers?" *Women's Rights Law Reporter* 8 (1984), 1/2:51–58.

Sheet Metal Workers Local 28 v. EEOC 106 S. Ct. 3019, _U.S._ (1986).

United States v. Paradise 107 S. Ct. 1053, _U.S._ (1987).

United Steelworkers v. Weber 99 S. Ct. 2721, 443 U.S. 193 (1979).

Wellington, Harry H. and Ralph K. Winter. "The Limits of Collective Bargaining in Public Employment." *Yale Law Journal* 78 (1969), 7:1107–1127.

Wygant v. Jackson Board of Education 106 S. Ct. 1842, _U.S._ (1986).

2
WOMEN AND MINORITIES IN PUBLIC SECTOR UNIONS

Women and minorities have historically had lower rates of unionization than white males (Freeman and Leonard 1987). This has been attributed to a number of factors including a desire by unions to keep women and minorities completely out of certain segments of the work force (Wertheimer 1984). Quite simply, women and minorities at one time represented a competitive source of cheap labor, which posed a serious threat to unions. As such, many unions would not foster the presence of women and minorities in the work force by organizing them; indeed, many were openly hostile to them. It was not difficult for unions to bar women and minorities from their ranks, particularly in the 1800s and early 1900s, given the position that women and minorities held in society.

Union leaders, like society in general, had very traditional views about women and hence about female participation in the labor force. Women's calling was in the home, serving the needs of a husband and children (Kenneally 1978). Even relatively progressive unions, such as the National Labor Union (NLU) which beginning in the 1860s permitted women to join with full membership status, saw women's participation in the work force and, hence, labor movement as an "unfortunate necessity" (Baxandall, Gordon and Reverby 1976, 77). For example, William Sylvis, head of the NLU between 1868 and 1869, made it clear that

females should not labor outside the domestic circle. Being forced into the field, the factory, and the workshop . . . they come in direct competition with men in the great field of labor; and being compelled of necessity, from their defenceless condition, to work for low wages, they exercise a vast influence over the price of labor in almost every department . . . But there is another reason, founded upon moral principle and common humanity, far above and beyond this, why they should not be thus employed. Woman was created and intended to be man's companion, not his slave. Endowed as she is with all her loveliness and powers to please, she exercises an almost unlimited influence over the more stern and unbending disposition of man's nature (Sylvis 1976, 77-78).

Unions' exclusion of minorities was grounded in societal discrimination or racism. As Marshall (1965, 5) has pointed out "[l]ike most other racial problems, the Negro-union relationship had its roots in slavery and Reconstruction. Slavery not only caused the American Negro to be regarded as an inferior person, but produced other lasting effects on race relations." Although some labor federations such as the NLU and the Knights of Labor (KL) attempted to solve race problems in the labor movement, racial prejudices at the local level perpetuated the exclusion of racial minorities. Moreover, as Marshall (1965) notes, integrating racial minorities into unions was difficult due to fundamental political differences between blacks and white union leaders.

When unions recognized that women and minorities were a growing part of the labor force, they allowed these groups to become members, but treated them differently or as separate classes of workers (Steinberg and Cook 1981).[1] For example, it was common for some unions to impose higher membership dues on women. Alternatively, unions would establish a reduced membership rate for women, but then would require any gains won by the union (e.g., wage increases) to be distributed to union members proportionate to their dues contribution. It was also common for unions to place women and minorities in segregated locals or divisions which perpetuated the existing occupational segregation of these workers. Moreover, because collective bargaining was conducted by the parent white male union and not the segregated local, the needs and interests of women and minorities were never fully served.

A notable example of maintaining segregated locals in the public sector can be seen in the postal service. Many postal service unions would admit blacks to their ranks but segregated them into "colored" locals (Spero 1927). The National Association of Letter Carriers (NALC), for example, would issue separate charters to white and "colored" carriers (*The Postal Record* 1935).

There was at least one postal union, the Railway Mail Association, that barred black clerks altogether (Gould 1972; Spero 1927). To cope with the ostracism of the white postal union, black clerks in 1913 formed the National Alliance of Postal Employees.[2] The Postal Alliance, as it is also referred to, was composed predominantly of black railway mail clerks, but other classes of postal employees were also welcomed. In fact, for many years, a faction of the NALC attempted to require black letter carriers to join the Postal Alliance in order to completely rid the NALC of black carriers. One resolution at the 1927 NALC convention stated:

Whereas the conditions in the south, as well as the entire Association of the United States, in respect to the colored members of the National Association of Letter Carriers, in that in many of the Branches the colored members have come to majority, and, therefore, places them in authority, causing a disruption in the ranks of the membership . . .

Whereas their strength in voting has proved without question in these Branches that white letter carriers have been compelled to either withdraw their membership or take the embarrassment of being defeated to positions of local officers and representation in our National Conventions, and

Whereas the higher-minded and considerate colored carriers have recognized these conditions, and desiring to avoid any future trouble have instituted an organization for the colored civil service employees, which is known as the Postal Alliance, its purposes are for the protection of the colored employees and improvement of the service; therefore be it

Resolved, That this convention goes on record as endorsing this organization, and appeals to all colored carriers to avail themselves in its membership in order that peace may be preserved in the service . . . (The Postal Record 1927, 408).[3]

In sum, women and minorities did not readily join unions for a number of reasons, one being that they were not welcomed by such institutions. To the extent that they did or were allowed to join, they were often treated as inferiors. Certain sociopolitical and socioeconomic shifts, however, eventually brought changes to union attitudes and behaviors. For example, societal attitudes towards women and minorities gradually improved. In addition, certain employment protections for women and minorities were created or strengthened through statutory and case law. Such changes, along with the increased labor participation of women and minorities and their growing assertiveness led many unions to target these workers for unionization.

Today, the rate of unionization for women and minorities looks considerably different as compared to even a few decades ago. What follows is an examination of female and minority membership rates in public sector unions. Such an examination will allow us to make inferences about the popularity of unions among women and minorities and, related, the position of unions toward these workers. Also addressed in this chapter is the represention of women and minorities in union leadership positions, which reflects, among other things, unions' position on the ability of women and minorities to serve in upper-level union policy-making positions.

Female and Minority Membership in Public Sector Unions

To better examine union membership of women and minorities, the employment patterns of these groups are first presented. Table 2.1 shows percentages of women and minorities in public sector work forces for 1977 and 1980. The data are broken down by race and gender in order to provide a richer picture of female and minority employment and ultimately female and minority union membership patterns. As the data show, the employment of white and minority women in public sector jobs increased between 1977 and 1980. The employment of minority males decreased slightly and white male employment dropped by 1.8 percent. As the figures further indicate, changes in the employment of these groups vary by level of government.

It should be noted at this point that these data do not reflect the job levels of public employees. They do not show, for example, that women tend to be concentrated in secretarial and clerical positions and social and health services (Steinberg and Cook 1981). As such, an increase in female

Table 2.1 Women and Minorities in Public Sector Work Forces, 1977, 1980

Employment Sector	Total (1,000)	White Male (%)	Minority Male (%)	White Female (%)	Minority Female (%)
Public (all levels)					
1977	4,978	57.7	8.8	28.2	5.1
1980	5,361	55.9	8.1	29.1	6.9
Federal					
1977	1,559	52.9	9.7	30.2	7.1
1980	1,798	50.0	8.6	31.2	10.2
Postal					
1977	690	64.6	14.5	15.2	5.6
1980	691	61.9	13.3	17.4	7.4
State					
1977	846	55.0	5.6	34.4	5.3
1980	973	55.9	4.3	34.3	5.6
Local					
1977	1,876	60.8	7.3	28.3	3.4
1980	1,905	59.2	7.5	28.8	4.5
Private					
1977	76,261	51.9	5.8	37.1	5.4
1980	82,009	50.1	5.9	38.5	5.7

SOURCE: Calculated from the U.S. Department of Labor, Bureau of Labor Statistics. *Earnings and Other Characteristics of Organized Workers*, 1979 and 1981.

employment is not necessarily indicative of improvements in the status and salary of women. It simply suggests that more women entered the public sector labor force between 1977 and 1980. Likewise, since white males tend to dominate upper-level, higher-paying positions (Cayer and Sigelman 1980), a decrease in white male employment does not necessarily imply that their overall employment status was lowered. Rather, the decrease suggests that fewer white males, for a variety of reasons, entered or remained in the public service during this time period.

As noted earlier, the interest here is to compare female and minority employment in the public sector to female and minority membership in unions. Table 2.2 illustrates female and minority membership in public sector unions between 1977 and 1980. Although the percentage changes are relatively small, there are several noteworthy observations when the data from Tables 2.1 and 2.2 are compared. For example, the growth rate of white female employment in the total public sector work force does not keep pace with white female union membership. White female employment increased by not even 1 percent, but union membership for this group increased by 3.7 percent. This suggests that unions became popular

Table 2.2 Female and Minority Union Membership as a Percentage of Females and Minorities in the Work Force, 1977, 1980

Employment Sector	Total Unionized	White Male	Minority Male	White Female	Minority Female
Public (all levels)					
1977	32.1	37.6	43.3	17.5	31.5
1980	33.8	39.2	42.9	21.2	32.3
Federal					
1977	16.1	15.4	30.9	11.9	18.2
1980	19.3	21.4	28.3	12.3	22.9
Postal					
1977	72.3	78.0	74.3	45.7	74.4
1980	73.7	78.1	83.6	50.0	76.5
State					
1977	26.7	28.6	36.2	22.7	20.1
1980	26.0	28.5	21.4	22.2	27.3
Local					
1977	33.1	41.5	37.3	14.1	34.4
1980	36.9	43.7	39.3	23.5	29.4
Private					
1977	23.3	28.3	34.5	14.4	23.0
1980	22.3	27.0	33.0	14.3	23.3

SOURCE: Calculated from the U.S. Department of Labor, Bureau of Labor Statistics. *Earnings and Other Characteristics of Organized Workers*, 1979 and 1981.

with white women at least between 1977 and 1980. Or, looking at it another way, perhaps as white female employment increased in certain occupations, albeit slightly, certain unions started to target this group for unionization in order to bolster union strength.

A somewhat different picture seems to emerge for minority women. For example, the percentage of minority women in unions is much higher than their percentage in public sector jobs. Minority women comprised only 6.9 percent of the public sector work force in 1980, but 32.3 percent of the minority women were unionized. Viewing the data another way, however, shows that between 1977 and 1980 minority women's total public sector employment increased by almost 2 percent, but their union membership increased by only a little over one-half of a percent. This could suggest that the popularity of unions was declining among minority women. It could also suggest that unions were not exerting enough effort to attract minority women, despite their growing presence in public sector work forces. It may be that the policies, programs and directions of unions were not geared toward serving the interests of minority women and, so, this group of workers was uninterested in unionization.

Public sector unions may also be declining in popularity among minority males. Although the rate of unionization of minority males decreased at only a slightly lower rate than the decline in minority male employment, this was the only group of workers whose union membership declined. The decline may be due to a number of factors, one being a lack of attention on the part of unions to the needs and interests of minority males.

Interestingly, white males increased their union membership despite a drop in their employment between 1977 and 1980. This differs from the pattern for minority males who, as noted above, also lost a share of public sector jobs. It also differs from the private sector picture, where white male union membership declined with an almost comparable drop in white male employment. Perhaps unions shifted their organizing efforts to the public sector, even though white males, overall, declined in government employment. If this was a deliberate strategy on the part of unions, however, it must be questioned as to why union membership did not increase for minority males in the public sector between 1977 and 1980.

The picture in the private as compared to public sector differs for other groups as well. As the data show, the rate of unionization remained more stable for white and minority women. There was a slight increase in minority female employment in the private sector accompanied by a comparable increase in their rate of unionization. For white women, there was a small increase in their employment and a negligible change in their union membership. Minority male employment was relatively stable between 1977 and 1980 but their rate of unionization dropped between the two time periods.

Unlike in the public sector, then, union growth for minority females in the private sector kept pace with the increase in minority female employment during this time period. Also, unlike in the public sector, white female union membership did not keep pace with the growth of white female employment in the private sector work force. For minority males, the picture in the private sector did not differ from that in the public.

The differences in patterns for at least white and minority women as well as white men may reflect differences between public and private sector unions in terms of priorities and, hence, organizing drives. The position of both public and private sector unions toward minority males, however, is interesting, suggesting that unions may not have been as attentive to the needs of this group of workers, whether public or private sector.

A breakdown of the data by level of government for 1977 and 1980 also shows some interesting patterns. For example, despite the loss of minority male employment in the postal service there was about a 10 percent increase in minority male union membership. It may be that some postal unions were making an effort to organize minority workers. Indeed, although not reflected in these data, the Postal Alliance has a very progressive record in terms of minority membership. Importantly, however, since enactment of the Postal Reorganization Act in 1970, the Postal Alliance can no longer bargain with the postal service. Today, it serves mainly as a coalition for blacks in the postal service, working to improve their employment status.

Union membership of minority males also increased at the local level of government and at a higher rate than the small growth in minority male employment in local government work forces. The area where unions lost the highest rate of minority male members was in state government. There was a 1.3 percent decrease in minority male employment at the state level of government, but a 14.8 percent decrease in male minority union membership. This was the largest drop in union membership for any group of workers at any level of government.

For white women, unionization seemed to increase most in local government—there was minimal change in their employment in local government work forces, but a 9.4 percent increase in their union membership. On the other hand, minority female employment increased by 1.1 percent in local government, but there was a 5 percent decrease in union membership of minority women.

Union membership seemed to grow most for minority women in state government. There was only a small increase of 0.3 percent in minority female employment between the two time periods, but a 7.2 percent increase in minority female union membership. It may be that unions were appealing to minority women in certain public sector work forces but

Table 2.3 Female and Minority Union Membership as a Percentage of Employed Females and Minorities, Sample Data, 1985

Item	Total	White Male	Minority Male	White Female	Minority Female
Public Sector (all levels)					
Unionized	34.9	35.8	37.5	34.4	31.3
In Work Force	—	51.3	7.9	31.9	8.9
Private Sector					
Unionized	14.4	19.0	21.6	7.2	14.0
In Work Force	—	47.6	8.7	37.4	6.3

SOURCE: Tabulated from the Current Population Survey (CPS), U.S. Bureau of the Census, March 1985. The Census Bureau collects data on labor union membership from only 25 percent of the workers surveyed in each CPS. These data, then, represent only a small sample. (The base used for employed persons is the number of persons unionized + the number of persons not unionized.)

not others. This is important because it points to the special needs and interests that minority women may have apart from white women.[4] Perhaps only certain unions operating in certain government sectors are recognizing this.

The most interesting pattern seems to emerge for white males. Just as the data for overall government work forces indicate, white male employment decreased at almost every level, yet their rate of unionization increased at virtually every level. At only the state level of government was there a slight increase in white male employment and a negligible decrease in white male union membership. Perhaps unions will continue to be popular with white males in the public sector, despite their loss in employment.

Table 2.3 presents more recent data on female and minority membership in public sector unions. It should be stressed, however, as noted in the table, that these data represent a small sample of workers who are unionized. Notwithstanding, the data may be useful for estimating membership trends. As the data show, 34.9 percent of the public employees sampled were unionized in 1985. This represents a slight increase in public sector union membership since 1980. Interestingly, the sample data show a decrease in unionization between 1980 and 1985 for every group except white females (compare with Table 2.2). The biggest drops were for white and minority men, with only a slight drop of 1 percent for minority women. On the other hand, white women increased their union membership by 13.2 percent. This is relatively high considering that white women increased their share of public sector jobs by only 2.8 percent (compare with Table 2.1).

It is also useful to compare the rate of unionization for the various groups to their concentration in the work force, as illustrated in Table 2.3. Notwithstanding the fluctuations between time periods as discussed earlier, both female and male minorities have disproportionately high rates of unionization as compared to their share of public sector jobs. For whites, the picture is somewhat different. The percentage of white women unionized is almost the same as the percentage of white women in public sector work forces and the rate of unionization of white males does not keep up with the percentage of white males in public sector work forces.

It is important to note that these data cannot be broken down by level of government, which might show a slightly different picture. In addition, it may be that this particular sample is not representative of the total population, which would make conclusions about female and minority membership in public sector unions tenuous.

Data for the private sector, as illustrated in Table 2.3, show that 14.4 percent of the work force was unionized in 1985. This represents a 7.9 percent drop in total workers unionized from 1980 to 1985. In addition, the data show a drop in union membership for every category of worker. Comparing unionization rates to work force concentration in 1985 shows that female and male minorities, just as in the public sector, are unionized at a higher rate than their representation in the work force. White males, on the other hand, had a much lower rate of unionization in comparison to their concentration in the work force. And, unlike in the public sector, there is a much larger disparity between the percentage of white women unionized and the percentage of white women in the private sector work force. Again, however, it must be kept in mind that these data may not be representative of the total population.

Table 2.4 presents females' and minorities' share of union membership in the public sector for 1977 and 1980. As we might expect, white males constituted the largest share of union members for the overall government sector as well as for each level of government. The data also show that in the total public sector work force, white and minority females' share of union membership grew between 1977 and 1980 and white and minority males' share dropped. The same pattern exists in the private sector for at least white and minority women and white males; however, minority males' share of union membership in the private sector remained relatively stable.

A breakdown by level of government shows that minority females' share of union membership grew at every level, with the biggest change in the federal government (an increase of 4.1 percent). White women decreased their share of union membership at the federal level, but there was a slight

Table 2.4 Female and Minority Share of Union Membership in the Public Sector, 1977, 1980

Employment Sector	Total Unionized (1,000)	White Male (%)	Minority Male (%)	White Female (%)	Minority Female (%)
Public (all levels)					
1977	1,598	67.6	11.9	15.4	5.0
1980	1,812	64.8	10.3	18.3	6.6
Federal					
1977	251	50.6	18.7	22.7	8.0
1980	347	55.3	12.7	19.9	12.1
Postal					
1977	499	69.7	14.8	9.7	5.8
1980	509	65.6	15.1	11.8	7.6
State					
1977	226	58.8	7.5	29.2	4.0
1980	253	61.3	3.6	29.2	5.9
Local					
1977	621	76.2	8.2	12.1	3.5
1980	703	70.1	8.0	18.3	3.6
Private					
1977	17,737	63.2	8.6	22.9	5.3
1980	18,283	60.6	8.7	24.7	6.0

SOURCE: Calculated from the U.S. Department of Labor, Bureau of Labor Statistics. *Earnings and Other Characteristics of Organized Workers,* 1979 and 1981.

Table 2.5 Female and Minority Share of Union Membership in the Public Sector, Sample Data, 1985

Employment Sector	White Male	Minority Male	White Female	Minority Female
Public (all levels)	38.3	9.9	41.4	10.4
Private	60.4	13.3	18.8	7.5

SOURCE: Tabulated from the Current Population Survey (CPS), U.S. Bureau of the Census, March 1985. The Census Bureau collects data on labor union membership from only 25 percent of the workers surveyed in each CPS. These data, then, represent only a small sample. (The base is total unionized for sampled workers.)

increase in their share at the postal service and an increase of 6.2 percent at the local level of government.

The picture for minority males is similar to that portrayed in Tables 2.1 and 2.2. Minority males' share of union membership declined at every level except the postal service, where there was only a slight increase of 0.3 percent. The decrease in minority male union membership is extremely small at the local level but relatively large at the federal and state levels of government. At the federal level, male minorities lost 6 percent of their share of union membership and almost 4 percent at the state level. Again, this could reflect the popularity of unions among black workers in the public sector as well as unions' failure to adequately represent the interests of male minorities.

Changes in white males' share of union membership seem to vary by level of government. Their share increased at the federal and state levels but decreased in the postal service and at the local level of government. Notwithstanding, white males, at least in the aggregate, continued to dominate union ranks between 1977 and 1980.

More recent sample data on females' and minorities' share of union membership is presented in Table 2.5. The data show that white females' share of public sector union membership was 41.4 percent, which represents a 23.1 percent increase from 1980. Minority women also increased their share of union membership between 1980 and 1985 but by only 3.8 percent. Minority males sustained a slight drop in their share (0.4 percent), but white males dropped by 26.5 percent. This pattern suggests that as unions in the public sector became less popular with white males, they may have become more popular with white women.

In the private sector, a different picture emerges. White males' union membership remained relatively stable, but white females dropped by 5.9 percent. On the other hand, the share of union membership for both female and male minorities increased. Again, however, these data represent a small sample, which may not be reflective of the total population.

Table 2.6 provides percentages of female and minority union members within the total public sector work force for 1977 and 1980. As the data show, unions seemed to be most popular with white males, who accounted for 21.9 percent of the union membership in 1980, representing a slight increase from 1977. White and minority women, on the other hand, accounted for a much smaller percentage of union membership but, importantly, the increase between the two time periods reflects a growing popularity of unions, *overall,* for women of all races. For minority males, the popularity appears to be decreasing, which is consistent with the data presented earlier.

In sum, the descriptive statistics on female and minority union membership in the public sector between 1977 and 1985 suggest that some

Table 2.6 Female and Minority Union Membership as a Percentage of the Total Public Sector Work Force, All Levels, 1977, 1980

Year	Total	White Male	Minority Male	White Female	Minority Female
1977	32.1	21.7	3.8	4.9	1.6
1980	33.8	21.9	3.5	6.2	2.2

NOTE: Sums of each item may not equal totals due to rounding.

SOURCE: Calculated from the U.S. Department of Labor, Bureau of Labor Statistics. *Earnings and Other Characteristics of Organized Workers*, 1979 and 1981.

workers may be better targeted by unions than others. White women seem to be receiving a good deal of attention by public sector unions but minority women, despite their growth in employment, may be receiving attention by unions in only some sectors, most notably the state level of government.

White male union membership grew between 1977 and 1980, notwithstanding the loss in white male employment in the public sector. By 1985, however, there was a slight drop in white male union membership. Overall, and across time, it seems that public sector unions are least responsive to minority males and yet, for any given time period, minority males are disproportionately unionized as compared to their concentration in public sector work forces.

Importantly, more comprehensive, recent data are needed here, especially by level of government. More encompassing data on public sector employees would enable us to make more accurate predictions of the future trends of female and minority membership in public sector unions.

Membership and Leadership Patterns in Individual Public Sector Unions

Table 2.7 shows a breakdown of union membership by gender for individual public sector unions. In addition, the representation of women in the leadership structures of these unions is presented. It should be noted at the outset that more recent data are not available. In addition, data exist solely for women, and so a breakdown by race cannot be made. Also, similar data are not available for minority males.[5] This is a serious problem because it prevents an examination not only of minority membership

Table 2.7 Female Members, Officers and Officials of Selected International and National Unions, 1972, 1978

Union	Total Members	Female Members (%)	Total Officers & Officials	Female Off/Ofc. (%)	Total Governing Board	Females on Governing (%)
International Association of Fire Fighters (IAFF)						
1972	160,258	0	8	0	18	0
1978	176,474	1,740* (1.0)	10	0	16	0
American Federation of Government Employees (AFGE)						
1972	292,809	N.A.	9	0	18	0
1978	265,506	130,000* (49.0)	10	1 (10.0)	18	0
National Association of Letter Carriers (NALC)						
1972	220,000	8,800 (4.0)	7	0	28	0
1978	227,005	11,350 (5.0)	9	0	28	0
American Postal Workers Union (APWU)						
1972	238,763	107,443 (45.0)	6	0	48	0
1978	245,826	80,454 (32.7)	8	0	52	0
American Federation of State, County & Municipal Employees (AFSCME)						
1972	529,035	195,743 (37.0)	9	0	23	1 (4.3)
1978	1,020,000	408,000 (40.0)	10	0	25	1 (4.0)
American Federation of Teachers (AFT)						
1972	248,521	129,231 (52.0)	8	0	21	5 (23.8)
1978	500,000	300,000 (60.0)	8	2 (25.0)	31	8 (25.8)

Table 2.7 (Continued)

Union	Total Members	Female Members (%)	Total Officers & Officials	Female Off/Ofc. (%)	Total Governing Board	Females on Governing (%)
National Federation of Federal Employees (NFFE)						
1972	85,000	42,500 (50.0)	7	1 (14.3)	8	3 (37.5)
1978	51,000	25,500 (50.0)	10	3 (30.0)	11	2 (18.2)
National Association of Government Employees (NAGE)						
1972	100,000	30,000 (30.0)	8	0	7	0
1978	200,000	60,000 (30.0)	10	2 (20.0)	9	0
Postal Alliance (NAPFE)						
1972	20,000**	8,000** (40.0)	8	0	15	4 (26.7)
1978	20,000	5,268* (26.3)	10	2 (20.0)	16	4 (25.0)
National Treasury Employees Union (NTEU)						
1972	33,000	14,850 (45.0)	6	1 (16.7)	15	1 (6.7)
1978	70,000*	N.A.	9	2 (22.2)	19	3 (15.8)
American Nurses Association (ANA)						
1972	156,665	N.A.	11	8 (72.7)	16	15 (93.8)
1978	187,000	181,390 (97.0)	9	4 (44.4)	15	11 (73.3)
Fraternal Order of Police (FOP)						
1972	125,000	625 (.5)	4	0	28	0
1978	140,000	1,470** (1.1)	6	0	37	1 (2.7)

24

Page 154 contains an inadvertent reprint of page 152. The correct page 154 is reprinted below:

inantly by white males. At the same time, the plan recommended upgrading a total of 239 titles. It is important to note, however, that *incumbent* employees would neither be downgraded nor sustain a pay cut; rather, pay grades would be lowered when normal turnover brought in new employees. PEF's support for this plan shifted sharply. The union contended that downgrading would have deleterious effects on the future of PEF membership because it would create a two-tier wage system where employees at the same grade would be paid different wages.

Two-tier wage systems have been popular in the private sector—supported by employers and many unions—as a way to reduce labor costs without hurting incumbent workers. Two-tier wage systems, however, have created problems which outweigh their cost-saving benefits. Many companies and unions have cited such problems as friction between lower- and upper-level workers, high turnover, and difficulties in recruitment. The outcome has hurt productivity as well as public relations (Salpukas 1987). Nonetheless, many organizations continue to rely on two-tier wage systems in order to cut or redistribute costs. Indeed, a 1982 contract between CSEA and New York State called for such a system. CSEA officials have admitted that they can be effective, but PEF remains opposed.

Parenthetically, two-tier wage systems are legal under the Equal Pay Act. Lowering the salaries of existing male employees to increase the salaries of female employees would clearly be illegal under the Act. But, the state's plan falls within those exceptions enumerated in the Act which permit employers to pay employees performing the same or similar work unequal wages, if the wages are based on seniority or "any factor other than sex." PEF threatened to file a legal challenge, but has not yet done so. It has, however, attempted to thwart the implementation of the pay plan in other ways. For example, PEF lobbied the state legislature, albeit unsuccessfully, to kill the bill which would appropriate monies for the upgrades (Picchi 1987b). It also filed a grievance charging that the pay plan exceeds the authority of PEF's contract with the state.

Interestingly, there were also concerns that CSEA might not have supported the implementation of the study's recommendations, even though the majority of the titles upgraded were CSEA-represented. The opposition actually came from the female rank-and-file who were not upgraded, which includes many stenographers and similar types of clerical and data processing workers (Picchi 1987a). They objected to the upgrading of lower-level female employees to their level or beyond without having to work for it (e.g., pass civil service exams). This opposition points to a lack of understanding of what comparable worth is and is intended to achieve.

Comparable worth in a very narrow sense is a "women's" issue and, as such, it has become a red herring. But comparable worth, broadly

Table 2.7 (Continued)

Union	Total Members	Female Members (%)	Total Officers & Officials	Female Off/Ofc. (%)	Total Governing Board	Females on Governing Board (%)
Amalgamated Transit Union (ATU)						
1972	130,000	10,400 (8.0)	6	1 (16.7)	9	0
1978	154,242	2,800** (1.8)	6	0	25	0
Amer. Assoc. Univ. Profs. (AAUP)						
1972	85,614	17,123 (20.0)	8	0	38	8 (21.1)
1978	68,100	15,663 (23.0)	9	3 (33.3)	30	9 (30.0)
Nat'l Ed. Assoc. (NEA)						
1972	1,165,617	736,670 (63.2)	8	1 (12.5)	118	25 (21.2)
1978	1,696,469	1,239,452* (73.1)	10	2 (20.0)	121	56 (46.3)
State Employee Association						
California						
1972	103,000	41,200 (40.0)	9	0	800	N.A.
1978	105,000	N.A.	8	1 (12.5)	27	3 (11.1)
Maine						
1972	10,580	3,121** (29.5)	6	2 (33.3)	292	N.A.
1978	9,529	N.A.	4	0	15	1 (6.7)
Washington						
1972	4,110	1,370 (33.3)	5	2 (40.0)	0	0
1978	2,515	1,006 (40.0)	9	2 (22.2)	18	4 (22.2)

SOURCE: <u>Directory of National Unions and Employee Associations</u>. U.S. Dept. of Labor, Bureau of Labor Statistics, 1974 and 1980.

* 1976 data   ** 1974 data   N.A. Not Available

in certain unions but also of minority representation in union leadership positions. Such an examination would complement the findings presented earlier that unionization appears to be declining in popularity among minority workers in public sector work forces.

As the data show, female membership in public sector unions varies. Women represent an extremely small portion of the union members in such unions as the International Association of Firefighters (IAFF), the National Association of Letter Carriers (NALC), and the Fraternal Order of the Police (FOP). This is not surprising, given the relatively small percentages of women in the professions represented by such unions (see Chapter 5).[6] On the other hand, women comprise a large portion of the membership in such unions as the American Nurses Association (ANA) and the National Education Association (NEA). In 1978, women comprised 97 percent of ANA's membership and 73.1 percent of NEA's membership. In several other unions, such as the American Federation of State, County and Municipal Employees (AFSCME), the National Association of Government Employees (NAGE), and the National Treasury Employees Union (NTEU), women represented a sizable percentage of union members.

Several interesting observations can be made from the data in Table 2.7. First, there appear to be patterns of sex segregation which were not evident in Tables 2.1 through 2.6. For example, females are not well represented by unions in male-dominated professions such as police and fire. On the other hand, they are well represented by unions in professions that they tend to dominate such as nursing and teaching. They are also well represented by those postal unions that target clerks, for example, the American Postal Workers Union (APWU), as compared to letter carriers, jobs traditionally held by men. Then, the unionization of women is sex-segregated, reflecting the sex segregation of jobs in the public sector by occupation and profession. In effect, women continue to be treated as a separate class of workers, but not necessarily by unions.

Another interesting observation is that women are not well represented in union leadership positions,[7] even in those unions that are comprised predominately of female members. In unions such as AFSCME this is particularly surprising, given the popular belief that AFSCME has a very progressive gender relations record. In other unions such as the APWU, NAGE, NTEU, the National Federation of Federal Employees (NFFE) and the American Federation of Teachers (AFT), where they comprise sizable portions of union membership, women are extremely underrepresented in leadership positions. This comports with the private sector picture, where women as well as minorities hold few union leadership positions (Wertheimer 1984; U.S. Commission on Civil Rights 1982; Gould 1977).

These patterns are very revealing. They suggest that unions may be responding at least to the increase of women in certain public sector jobs and professions by organizing them. Unions are not elevating them, however, to positions of leadership and responsibility within unions.[8] Although not illustrated in Table 2.7, it also appears that racial minorities are underrepresented in the upper levels of union hierarchies (U.S. Commission on Civil Rights 1982; Gould 1977, 1972; Lucy 1974). Gould (1972, 151) points out that "some unions in the public sector with an increasingly large black membership retain lily-white leadership. . . . An example of this situation is the Amalgamated Transit Union (ATU) which includes drivers and mechanics for public transit. Some of the tensions between that organization's leadership and the rank and file are undoubtedly attributable to the absence of black representation for the union's black members." Gould further notes that the American Federation of Government Employees (AFGE) also has a growing number of black members, yet the leadership positions are held mostly by whites.[9]

The lack of female and minority representation in leadership positions may be due to a number of factors.[10] For example, Koziara and Pierson (1981) have pointed out that women are underrepresented in union office because the persons generally selected as union leaders hold upper-level high-status jobs in the organization, and these jobs tend to be dominated by white men. This may also explain the lack of racial minorities in union office. Perhaps of greater significance, some men as well as women simply view women and minorities as inappropriate for leadership positions (Koziara and Pierson 1981; Twentieth Century Fund 1975).

The perception that women and minorities are inappropriate for union office may stem in part from negative gender and racial stereotypes. Research on sex stereotypes, for example, characterizes men as more aggressive, competitive, assertive and intelligent than women (Koziara and Pierson 1981; Masengill and DiMarco 1979; Schein 1975; Rosen and Jerdee 1974). Similarly, racial stereotypes portray whites as being more competent, intelligent and motivated than minorities (McConahay and Hough 1976; Ashmore 1970; Karlins, Coffman and Walters 1969). These stereotypic characteristics of white males, then, may lead union members to favor white males in positions of union power. In addition, union members may believe that because white males share characteristics with management, white males may be perceived more as "equals" by management. Ultimately, according to union members, white males would make better leaders (Koziara and Pierson 1981).

The exclusion of women and minorities from leadership positions for whatever reasons has serious implications. Perhaps the most critical is that without female and minority representation, the interests of these groups may not be adequately served. As the U.S. Commission on Civil Rights (1982, 26) has found, "[w]ithout increased representation within the union leadership, the problems of women and minorities may be overshadowed by the interests and concerns of the majority."

Of course, it must be questioned whether female and minority union leaders would push for the needs of their counterparts within union ranks. It may be that these groups would be co-opted by the group in power (i.e., white males).[11] Indeed, the body of literature on the social representativeness of bureaucratic institutions points to the uncertainty around whether persons in policy-making positions will retain the values and beliefs associated with their cultural backgrounds, or if organizational socialization processes will destroy them (Mosher 1982; Krislov and Rosenbloom 1981; Thompson 1976).

Notwithstanding the potential dissonance between cultural background and current attitudes and values, many women and minorities believe that their interests will not be fully served without representation in union office. Then, the presence of women and minorities in leadership positions would seem to have political as well as pragmatic significance.

To cope with the lack of female and minority representation in leadership roles, various caucuses and coalitions have been formed. For example, the Labor Council on Latin American Advancement, founded in 1973, has been very effective in encouraging unionized Hispanic workers to become more vocal in union politics (U.S. Commission on Civil Rights 1982). In addition, the Negro American Labor Council was formed in the 1950s to promote the status of blacks in the labor movement. The newer organization, the Coalition of Black Trade Unionists (CBTU), formed in 1972, has been even more effective in addressing the interests of unionized black workers (Gould 1972). Also, the Coalition of Labor Union Women (CLUW), founded in 1974, has been instrumental in enhancing the status of unionized women.[12] One important goal of CLUW is to elevate women to policy-making positions within unions (U.S. Commission on Civil Rights 1982).

In sum, women do not hold leadership positions proportionate to their share of union membership. Although the data are incomplete, the same pattern seems to exist for racial minorities. Breaking down negative stereotypes of women and minorities may help to redress the problem. Until they are better integrated into the upper levels of union structures, the needs and interests of women and minorities may not be adequately addressed. Ultimately, organizing drives and union policies aimed at attracting and retaining female and minority union members may not be entirely successful.

Conclusions

It would appear that white female membership in public sector unions was on the rise, at least between 1977 and 1985. The rate of minority female unionization appeared more stable overall, but, between 1977 and

1980, it showed some notable increases at certain levels of government. White males in the public sector also increased their membership in unions between 1977 and 1980, despite their drop in employment. By 1985, however, white male union membership was on the decline, as was their concentration in the work force. Minority males lost a share of public sector jobs between 1977 and 1985 and also experienced a decline in unionization. Some of the potential underlying reasons for these patterns were discussed in this chapter. Importantly, however, until more comprehensive and recent data become available, future trends in the unionization of women and minorities in the public sector cannot be estimated.

Although union membership may be increasing for at least women in certain government sectors, women continue to be underrepresented in leadership positions. Even those unions which are comprised of at least a majority (if not an overwhelming majority) of women have not elevated women to positions of power within union hierarchies. The data also show that minorities are not well represented in the upper levels of union administrations. The lack of women and minorities in upper-level union posts may reflect unions' perceptions about the abilities of these groups to run unions as well as to make policy. This is particularly noteworthy for those unions which claim to be very committed to the enhancement of female and minority employment in the public sector.

Notes

1. Of course, this excludes those few unions such as the International Ladies Garment Workers Union (ILGWU) that organized specifically around women.

2. The Postal Alliance still exists today, but, as Gould (1972) points out, does not have bargaining rights with the Postal Service given the way in which units are determined under the Postal Reorganization Act of 1970. It also expanded its scope to incorporate other workers and, so, is now known as the National Alliance of Postal and Federal Employees. Although the Postal Alliance cannot bargain with the Postal Service, it can and does legally bargain with other federal agencies. The Postal Alliance or Alliance has been headed by a black male, Robert L. White, since 1970 (Turner 1988).

3. Although this particular resolution did not pass, it indicates the sentiment among a faction of letter carriers regarding black membership in the NALC.

4. See Brown (1988), for example, who addresses the special problems faced by and needs of black female firefighters.

5. For information on the representation of minorities in selected unions, see, for example, Gould (1972, 1977).

6. According to the Affirmative Action Office of the U.S. Postal Service, 17.7 percent of the letter carriers for city and special delivery at the end of Fiscal Year 1987 were women. Between January 1988 and March 11, 1988, 18.5 percent of the

letter carriers for city and special delivery were women. (These data are not presented in Chapter 5.)

7. Leadership positions are defined in accordance with definitions set forth by the Bureau of Labor Statistics (1980). Leadership positions include, for example, president, executive secretary, treasurer, research director, and heads of organizing and legal departments.

8. It should be noted that women as well as minorities are also not well represented at the federation level. The AFL-CIO Executive Council, for example, is comprised predominantly of white males. For a discussion, see, for example, U.S. Commission on Civil Rights (1982).

9. It should be noted that a black male, John N. Sturdivant, was recently elected president of AFGE (Swoboda 1988).

10. Much of the research focuses on the reasons why women are absent from union leadership positions, but many of the reasons apply equally to racial minorities.

11. Or, if males allow women into leadership positions, they may select women who are viewed as mainstream or conformist.

12. Also noteworthy, in the early 1900s, the National Women's Trade Union League (WTUL) was formed, with the goal of organizing women and improving their status within the labor movement. The WTUL was disbanded in 1950. For a discussion, see, for example, Kenneally (1978).

References

Ashmore, R. D. "Prejudice: Causes and Cures." In B.E. Collins, *Social Psychology.* Reading, Massachusetts: Addison-Wesley, 1970:245–339

Baxandall, Rosalyn, Linda Gordon and Susan Reverby (eds.). *America's Working Women.* New York: Random House, 1976.

Brown, Roxanne. "Black Women Firefighters." *Ebony* 43 (1988), 5:132–137.

Bureau of Labor Statistics, U.S. Department of Labor. *Directory of National Unions and Employee Associations, 1979.* Washington, D.C: BLS, 1980.

Cayer, N. Joseph and Lee Sigelman. "Minorities and Women in State and Local Government: 1973-1975." *Public Administration Review* 40 (1980), 5:443–450.

Freeman, Richard B. and Jonathan S. Leonard. "Union Maids: Unions and the Female Work Force." In Clair Brown and Joseph A. Pechman (eds.), *Gender in the Workplace.* Washington, D.C.: The Brookings Institution, 1987:189–212.

Gould, William B. *Black Workers in White Unions.* Ithaca, New York: Cornell University Press, 1977.

————. "Labor Relations and Race Relations." In Sam Zagoria (ed.), *Public Workers and Public Unions.* Englewood Cliffs, New Jersey: Prentice-Hall, Inc., 1972:147–159.

Karlins, M., T. Coffman and G. Walters. "On the Fading of Social Stereotypes: Studies in Three Generations of College Students." *Journal of Personality and Social Psychology* 13 (1969), 1:1-16.

Kenneally, James J. *Women and American Trade Unions.* St. Albans, Vermont: Eden Press Women's Publications, Inc., 1978.

Koziara, Karen S. and David A. Pierson. "The Lack of Female Union Leaders: A Look at Some Reasons." *Monthly Labor Review* 104 (1981), 5:30–32.

Krislov, Samuel and David H. Rosenbloom. *Representative Bureaucracy and the American Political System.* New York: Praeger Publishers, 1981.

Lucy, William. "The Black Partners." *The Nation* 219 (September 7, 1974), 6:177–180.

Marshall, Ray. *The Negro and Organized Labor.* New York: John Wiley & Sons, Inc., 1965.

Masengill, Douglas and Nicholas DiMarco. "Sex-Role Stereotypes and Requisite Management Characteristics." *Sex Roles* 5 (1979), 5:561–570.

McConahay, John B. and Joseph C. Hough, Jr. "Symbolic Racism." *Journal of Social Issues* 32 (1976), 2:23–45.

Mosher, Frederick C. *Democracy and the Public Service.* New York: Oxford University Press, 1982, 2d ed.

The Postal Record. Convention of the National Association of Letter Carriers (NALC), vol. 40, October 1927.

———. Convention of the National Association of Letter Carriers (NALC), vol. 48, October 1935.

Rosen, Benson and Thomas H. Jerdee. "Sex Stereotyping in the Executive Suite." *Harvard Business Review* 52 (1974), 2:45–58.

Schein, Virginia E. "Relationships Between Sex Role Stereotypes and Requisite Management Characteristics Among Female Managers." *Journal of Applied Psychology* 60 (1975), 3:340–344.

Spero, Sterling Denhard. *The Labor Movement in a Government Industry.* New York: The MacMillan Co., 1927.

Steinberg, Ronnie and Alice Cook. *Women, Unions and Equal Employment Opportunity.* Albany, New York: Center for Women in Government, State University of New York at Albany, January 1981.

Swoboda, Frank. "Organization Man Takes Helm of Shaky Federal Union." *The Washington Post,* 26 August 1988, A4.

Sylvis, William. "A Union's Position." In Rosalyn Baxandall, Linda Gordon and Susan Reverby (eds.), *America's Working Women.* New York: Random House, 1976:77–78.

Thompson, Frank J. "Minority Groups in Public Bureaucracies: Are Passive and Active Representation Linked?" *Administration and Society* 8 (1976), 2:201–226.

Turner, Renee D. "The Civil Rights Crusader of the Labor Movement." *Ebony* 43 (1988), 4:76–80.

Twentieth Century Fund. *Exploitation from 9 to 5.* Report of the Twentieth Century Fund Task Force on Women and Employment. Lexington, Massachusetts: Lexington Books, 1975.

U.S. Commission on Civil Rights. *Nonreferral Unions and Equal Employment Opportunity.* Washington, D.C., March 1982.

Wertheimer, Barbara Mayer. "The United States of America." In Alice H. Cook, Val K. Lorwin and Arlene Kaplan Daniels (eds.), *Women and Trade Unions in Eleven Industrialized Countries.* Philadelphia: Temple University Press, 1984: 286–307.

3

THE LEGAL OBLIGATIONS OF UNIONS

Judicial and legislative bodies have long recognized the pervasiveness of union discrimination against women and minorities. This is evident in the legal obligations placed on unions not only to refrain from discrimination but also to promote the interests of all the workers they represent without regard to social characteristics. If unions fail to do so, depending upon the circumstances, they can be held liable to the victims of the discriminatory practices for any damages a court may award.

The legal obligations of unions are derived either explicitly or implicitly from various statutes. Perhaps the most explicit as well as significant and comprehensive piece of legislation proscribing union discrimination against women and minorities is Title VII of the Civil Rights Act of 1964, as amended by the 1972 Equal Employment Opportunity Act to cover public employment. Section 703(c) provides:

It shall be an unlawful employment practice for a labor organization—
(1) to exclude or expel from its membership, or otherwise to discriminate against, any individual because of his race, color, religion, sex, or national origin;
(2) to limit, segregate, or classify its membership or applicants for membership, or to classify or fail or refuse to refer for employment any individual, in any way which would deprive or tend to deprive any individual of employment opportunities, or would limit such employment opportunities or otherwise adversely affect his status as an employee or as an applicant for employment, because of such individual's race, color, religion, sex, or national origin; or
(3) to cause or attempt to cause an employer to discriminate against an individual in violation of this section.

Judicial interpretation of Section 703(c) as well as other statutes has generated two closely related doctrines that create implicit legal obligations for unions.[1] They are the duty of fair representation (DFR) and union liability.[2] They apply to both public and private sector unions but there are differences in the statutory bases for at least the DFR.

These implicit legal obligations of unions are important in the battle against gender and racial discrimination. For one thing, they broaden the legal rights of and remedies available to women and minorities under statutory and/or common law. Also, although the mere existence of legislation will not encourage unions to refrain from discrimination or promote the interests of women and minorities, the enforcement of certain doctrines emanating from the legislation may in time circumscribe the *behaviors* of some unions.

Because the DFR and union liability have been analyzed extensively, they will not be reexamined here. Rather, a review of the literature and leading cases will provide the reader with a general framework of the legal obligations of unions operating in the public sector. Also of interest in the discussion of unions' legal obligations is the legality of seniority systems and their effects on women and minorities, which will be addressed later in this chapter.

Duty of Fair Representation

The duty of fair representation (DFR) refers in general to a union's obligation to represent all members of its bargaining unit "without hostility or discrimination toward any, to exercise its discretion with complete good faith and honesty, and to avoid arbitrary conduct" (Schlei and Grossman 1983, 628). The DFR requirement is not explicitly stated in any statute but rather is implied by the courts under various statutes, including the Railway Labor Act (RLA), the National Labor Relations Act (NLRA), as amended by the Labor Management Relations Act (LMRA),[3] Title VII, and Section 1981 of the 1866 Civil Rights Act. It applies to a union's negotiation and administration of contracts as well as its handling of grievances (Schlei and Grossman 1983).

The DFR was initially created to protect black workers from the potential adverse effects of exclusive recognition requirements of various labor statutes (Simon 1980). Exclusive recognition essentially guarantees a union jurisdiction over an entire designated group of employees; these employees form what is known as the bargaining unit. All employees in this unit are required to rely on the union as their sole or *exclusive* bargaining agent. Employees cannot bargain individually with their employer, nor can they rely on any other organization or bargaining agent to promote their interests.

Exclusive recognition is important to unions because it assures them exclusive power and control over a group of employees. The rationale behind exclusive recognition is that a union can better represent its constituents if it need not expend time and energy competing with rival unions. Exclusive recognition requirements, however, raise several critical questions: Who are the union's constituents? Are they the majority of workers who elected the union? If the majority of workers happens to be white male, are women and minorities viewed by the union as constituents? Are the constituents members of the *union* as opposed to members of the *unit?* Unit members may not necessarily be union members but, if the union is legally recognized as the unit's exclusive bargaining representative, do all members of the unit not deserve equal and *fair* representation? Or, are race, gender and/or membership status the controlling factors for unions in fulfilling their charge as exclusive representatives?

When unions are elected or designated as exclusive representatives, they are expected to promote and protect the interests of *all* employees in the bargaining unit. Employees in unionized shops have no other alternative but to rely on their union.[4] This creates the potential for a good deal of abuse, which was recognized and feared by black workers in the middle part of this century.

Steele v. Louisville & Nashville Railroad, the 1944 U.S. Supreme Court decision that first established the DFR, illustrates that black workers' fears over exclusive representation were justified (Simon 1980). In *Steele*, the union proposed changes to the collective bargaining contract that would have demoted black workers to lower-paying, more arduous jobs. The demotions, in turn, would have created vacant positions to be filled by less-senior white workers. Steele argued that the union's actions here were racially motivated. (It is also worth noting that only white workers were allowed to join the union; black workers were explicitly barred from union membership.)

The Court ruled for Steele, asserting that unions have a duty under the RLA to represent all members of the bargaining unit fairly. It reasoned that

the representative is clothed with power not unlike that of a legislature which is subject to constitutional limitations on its power to deny, restrict, destroy or discriminate against the rights of those for whom it legislates and which is also under an affirmative constitutional duty equally to protect those rights (*Steele* 1944, 198).

The Court emphasized a union's duty under the RLA, saying that Congress "did not intend to confer plenary power upon the union to sacrifice, for the benefit of its members, rights of the minority of the craft, without imposing on it any duty to protect the minority" (*Steele* 1944, 199).

The Court ruled that the exclusive representative requirement of the

RLA could not and should not interfere with a union's duty to protect the interests of *all* members of the unit equally. In *Wallace Corp. v. National Labor Relations Board* (1944), which was decided on the same day as *Steele,* the Supreme Court also implied a DFR under the NLRA, but it was not until several years later that the Court attempted to define the parameters of that duty (Simon 1980).

Today, the DFR is relied upon not only by women and minorities who feel their interests are not being served by their union but also by any member of the unit who is not a union member. The remedies available under the RLA, NLRA, LMRA and Title VII include injunctive relief, attorney's fees and back pay.[5] DFR suits are not always successful, but they place an enormous financial burden on unions in terms of time, energy and legal fees (McKelvey 1985).

One of the reasons why DFR suits are difficult to win is that there is little agreement by the courts over standards for measuring the parameters of the DFR. Aaron (1977, 18) succinctly makes the point that "the Supreme Court has spoken with such impenetrable ambiguity that the federal courts, which bear the burden of construing the nature and scope of the duty, are understandably in disagreement as to what the law is."

Perhaps the most guidance thus far on whether a union has violated its duty comes from the U.S. Supreme Court's 1967 *Vaca v. Sipes* ruling. In this case, the Court advanced a three-prong test for determining whether a union operated within a "zone of reasonableness." The Court declared that a union violates its duty to fairly represent all members of the unit if it acts in a manner that is "arbitrary, discriminatory, or in bad faith" (*Vaca* 1967, 190). Importantly, this ruling was made under the NLRA, but courts have relied upon the *Vaca* standards in DFR claims arising from other statutes as well.

More recently, the courts have implied a DFR under Title VII as well as Section 1981. This is especially important for public sector employees. With the exception of postal workers, who are covered by amendments to the NLRA, the RLA and the NLRA apply only to private sector employees. This has limited the scope of the DFR. If a state employee, for example, felt that a union was not fairly representing her interests, her only recourse, up until recently, was either to file an unfair labor practice before the state's public sector labor relations agency or to sue the union under the state collective bargaining law.

Although courts often read a DFR requirement in state collective bargaining laws, the choice of forum and statute—Title VII, Section 1981 or state law—may affect both the procedural and substantive law. For example, Title VII imposes a very stringent obligation on unions to fairly represent all members of the unit. Schlei and Grossman (1983, 629) point out that "Title VII imposes upon a union an affirmative duty to insure that employers comply with equal employment opportunity statutes with respect to employees which the union represents." Then, a stricter duty may be implied under Title VII as compared to state collective bargaining law.

What follows is a discussion of the application of the DFR to public sector employees. A cursory review of a sample of cases will point to the use of the DFR in state and local government employment. In addition, the application of the DFR to federal workers—including postal workers—under Title VII and Section 1981 will be discussed. Compared to state and local governments, where a DFR for unions has generally been found, there appear to be some unresolved questions as to the legal responsibilities and obligations of federal unions under Title VII and Section 1981 to protect female and minority workers.

DFR for Unions Representing State and Local Government Workers

It would appear that DFR cases that do not involve a charge of race or sex discrimination are predominately brought before, and settled by, public sector labor relations agencies. (These agencies parallel the National Labor Relations Board, which oversees labor relations for private sector and postal employees.) These cases are filed by members of the unit alleging that the union is not representing them fairly because they are not members of the union. The charges are often brought as an unfair labor practice, and the administrative bodies will generally read a DFR requirement into a union's duty not to commit an unfair labor practice (Newman 1985).[6] This is the case in New York State, for example, where the Public Employment Relations Board views a union's violation of its DFR as an unfair labor practice (Riccucci and Ban 1989).

Depending upon the jurisdiction, unfair labor practice proceedings can represent a powerful remedy for DFR breaches. When an unfair labor practice has been found, it will result in a cease and desist order. When enforced by the courts, that order is backed by the courts' contempt powers. Refusing to abide by the order can ultimately result in stiff penalties and/or imprisonment (Sovern 1966).[7]

It seems that DFR breaches that turn on race and/or sex discrimination by unions are brought before the courts rather than labor relations agencies.[8] Moreover, with few exceptions,[9] they seem to be brought under state collective bargaining laws or fair employment practices laws as opposed to Title VII or Section 1981. It should be noted that even though courts read a DFR requirement into state law, the choice of statute may nonetheless affect the outcome of the case. As pointed out earlier, Title VII, for example, imposes strict DFR requirements on unions. Given that most cases are brought under state law, however, and there is a paucity of cases here in any event, it may be too soon to determine the motivations as well as possible advantages (e.g., better remedies) of filing DFR suits under state law as opposed to Title VII or Section 1981.

Importantly, in implying a DFR requirement from state law, courts rely heavily on the body of case law addressing the DFR for private sector unions. For example, in *Allen v. Seattle Police Officers Guild* (1983), Washington's Public Employees Collective Bargaining Act was likened to the NLRA in construing a DFR requirement.

In *Allen,* a collective bargaining agreement between the city and the Seattle Police Guild, the police officers' exclusive bargaining agent, required that any changes to past personnel practices be made with notification to and, in some instances, involvement of the union. Prior to 1976, and at the Guild's insistence, the city had a practice of hiring and promoting employees on a rank-ordered basis. Recognizing the adverse impact rank-ordered systems had on women and minorities, the city not only abandoned this practice, but also adopted a goal of hiring and promoting one female or minority for every white male hired or promoted (Reynolds 1984).

The Guild filed several suits challenging the city's actions on the grounds that the collective bargaining clause guaranteeing the retention of past practices had been violated. The union's challenges, and their costs of over $35,000, led black officers to file suit against the union for breaching "its duty to fairly represent their interests, and act[ing] arbitrarily, in bad faith, and with hostility or discrimination toward them" (*Allen,* Wash. App. 1982, 1116).

In applying a DFR requirement under Washington state law, some deference was paid to federal statutory and case law. The Washington Appellate Court, for example, stated that

[t]he Guild's duty of fair representation is an adjunct to its authority as exclusive bargaining representative for all officers up to and including the rank of sergeant. The Guild derives this authority from [Washington's Public Employees Collective Bargaining Act, which] is similar to the National Labor Relations Act.... In construing state labor acts which are similar to federal labor legislation, decisions under federal labor law, while not controlling, are persuasive.... Therefore, we look to federal cases and commentary on those cases to clarify the issues before us (*Allen,* Wash. App. 1982, 1118).

The Washington Supreme Court, in affirming the appellate court's decision, also acknowledged the importance of federal case law, but went even further to conclude that *explicit* reference in the state collective bargaining law imposed a duty on unions. The law states that "the representative 'shall be required to represent . . . all the public employees within the unit without regard to membership in said bargaining representative.' " The court went on to say that "[c]ertainly, if the unions are forbidden from discriminating on the basis of union membership, they should also be prohibited from discriminating on the basis of race or on other grounds" (*Allen* 1983, 252).

Once it determined that the state law imposed a DFR on unions, the court then examined whether the union had in fact breached its duty. The Washington Supreme Court disagreed with the appellate court's finding that the duty applied only to union activities in negotiating, administering and enforcing collective bargaining agreements, thus precluding grounds for action in this case. The supreme court said that "collective bargaining is a continuing process which involves, among other things, day-to-day adjustments in the contract and other working rules, resolution of new problems and protection of employee rights already secured by contract" (*Allen* 1983, 253).

Thus, the higher court supported an expansive view of the DFR. But, although the court found that the DFR *applied* to the union's conduct in this case, the court concluded that the union did not actually breach its duty. Interestingly, the court set forth standards similar to those developed in *Vaca v. Sipes*, yet the court did not judge the issues presented in *Allen* against those standards. Rather, because of the court's "limited experience in the duty of fair representation area . . . [it left] further development of the doctrine to future cases" (*Allen* 1983, 254) and turned instead to the facts presented in this case.

Specifically, the court ruled on these facts: (1) the past and current contract requiring that hiring and promotions be made from the upper quarter of eligible applicants; (2) the retention of benefits and past practices clause in the current contract; (3) the past practice of using a rank-ordered system for hiring and promotions; (4) hiring or promoting out-of-rank had been opposed by the union, regardless of race or sex (Reynolds 1984). In considering these facts, the court concluded that "the Guild's decisions to litigate the validity of the City's affirmative action program was a good faith, nonarbitrary attempt to represent all its members by seeking enforcement of the contract" (*Allen* 1983, 255).

The *Allen* decision established the applicability of a DFR to public sector unions under Washington's labor law, but it did little to strengthen the parameters of this duty. The court seemed to be creating standards for future cases, standards which, as in *Allen*, may or may not be applied. So, while Washington law obligates public sector unions to fairly represent all bargaining unit members without consideration of race and sex, the *enforcement* of that obligation or duty remains in question.

There are other cases where courts have implied a DFR from state law,[10] but the decisions, similar to *Allen*, provide little guidance as to what actually constitutes a breach. For example, in *Golden v. Local 55, Firefighters* (1980), black firefighters claimed that their union violated the California Fair Employment Practice Act by failing to fairly represent them in their grievances against the fire department. The U.S. Court of Appeals for the Ninth Circuit alluded to the *Vaca* standards but did not seem to apply them. The court ultimately concluded that the union did not breach its duty.

Then, a DFR will be read into state collective bargaining legislation, but the scope of this duty seems unclear. Perhaps the boundaries would be clearer if the charges were brought under Title VII or Section 1981.[11] As the case law continues to unfold, we may be in a better position to determine, first, the motivations for filing under certain statutes and, second, whether there are differences between and advantages to filing a DFR claim under Title VII or Section 1981 as compared to state law.

DFR for Unions Representing Federal Government Workers

As noted earlier, postal workers, for all practical purposes, are governed by the NLRA, as amended by the Labor Management Relations Act (LMRA).[12] Thus, with the exception of the right to strike, postal workers enjoy all the same rights and privileges as private sector union members (Rosenbloom and Shafritz 1985; Fossum 1982). Other federal workers are covered by the Civil Service Reform Act (CSRA) of 1978.

Because of these jurisdictional issues, it is certain that postal unions have a DFR requirement imposed on them by the Labor Management Relations Act (*Bowen v. U.S. Postal Service* 1983). In addition, the CSRA creates a duty for federal unions through its unfair labor practice provisions (*Karahalios v. National Fed. of Federal Employees* 1989; Wood 1988; Aaron 1986).[13] It is unclear, however, whether Title VII or Section 1981 of the Civil Rights Act of 1866 create a DFR for federal unions, including those operating in the postal sector. The uncertainty revolves around whether Title VII provides a cause of action against (i.e., a right to sue) federal sector labor unions for employment discrimination.

An important aspect of Title VII's coverage of labor unions is its requirement that unions represent "employees." And, an employee, as defined in Section 701(f) of Title VII, is "an individual employed by an employer." Because Title VII's Section 701(b) explicitly excludes the federal government from the definition of an "employer," it is questionable as to whether Title VII has jurisdiction over federal government employee unions. Quite simply federal employees do not work for an "employer" within the meaning of Title VII and, as such, are not represented by labor unions within the meaning of the Act (Schlei and Grossman 1983). This has resulted in very ambiguous judicial interpretations over rights of action against federal employee unions.

It should be noted, however, that Title VII does provide federal employees with protection from employment discrimination. Section 717 (added to the Act with the 1972 amendments) prohibits the heads of federal departments, agencies or units from discriminating on the basis of race, color, religion, sex or national origin. But, labor organizations are not explicitly named in Section 717's language.

Some courts have held that there is no cause of action against labor organizations in the federal sector under Title VII. Moreover, these courts have further held that because Title VII is intended to provide an "exclusive" remedy for employment discrimination, federal sector unions cannot be sued under Section 1981 either.[14] This was the case in *Newbold v. U.S. Postal Service* (1980), where a postal employee filed suit under Title VII and Section 1981 against the postal service and the American Postal Workers Union (APWU) on the grounds that he was discriminated against because of his race. The U.S. Court of Appeals for the Fifth Circuit ruled that the plaintiff "could not have sued APWU . . . under [Section 717], providing for suit against the head of a department or agency or unit, as it is not a proper defendant under that section (*Newbold* 1980, 47).

The court went on to say that a suit could neither be brought against federal agencies nor *unions* under Section 1981 because "Title VII is 'an exclusive preemptive administrative and judicial scheme for the redress of federal employment discrimination' " (*Newbold* 1980, 47; citing *Brown v. General Services Administration* 1976, 1966).

Interestingly, the *Newbold* court made no reference to *Allen v. Butz* (1975), a DFR decision issued five years earlier. In *Butz*, the district court clearly found a cause of action against a federal employee union under Section 1981. In this case, a federal employee of the Agriculture Department filed suit against his union, the American Federation of Government Employees (AFGE), and the Secretary of Agriculture, on the grounds that he was the victim of various racial discriminatory practices. He specifically charged the AFGE with refusal to fairly represent him in a grievance over his suspension from work. The district court ruled that "the complaint adequately charges that the alleged refusal to represent was the result of racial discrimination. Such an allegation clearly states a cause of action under 42 U.S.C. 1981" (*Allen v. Butz* 1975, 841).

These two cases, taken together, point to the ambiguity over the rights of federal employees to sue their unions under Title VII and Section 1981. Perhaps some clarification can be found in *Jennings v. American Postal Workers Union* (1982). In this case, a postal employee charged her union with discrimination on the basis of race and sex for not representing her fairly in a grievance against the postal service. Relying on *Newbold,* the lower court rejected the plaintiff's claims. The Eighth Circuit Appellate Court, however, reversed. Referring to Section 703(c) of the Act, the court said that "[i]t is clear that Title VII provides a cause of action against labor organizations for unlawful employment practices. . . . The fact that the defendant in this case is a labor organization representing federal employees is not controlling" (*Jennings* 1982, 715).

The court reasoned that

[i]n *Newbold v. United States Postal Service* . . . the court held that the American Postal Workers Union could not be sued under Section 717 (c) of Title VII . . . which provides for suit against a *federal department or agency*. The court, however, made no mention of the applicability of Section 703(c) . . . which concerns labor organizations. Section 717(c) is the exclusive remedy against federal agencies as employers for . . . discrimination, but it does not limit the rights of employees against unions representing federal employees (*Jennings* 1982, 715 at note 6, emphasis in original).

Then, the court found a cause of action against federal employee unions not under Section 717 but instead under 703(c).

The court also found a cause of action under Section 1981.[15] In so doing, the court, again, referred to the *Newbold* decision, where, as noted earlier, the Fifth Circuit ruled that unions could not be sued under Section 1981. The *Newbold* court, in framing its ruling here, relied primarily on the U.S. Supreme Court's decision *Brown v. General Services Administration* (1976). In *Brown*, the Court held that Section 717 of Title VII precludes redress of federal employment discrimination under Section 1981.

The *Jennings* court, however, ruled that reliance on *Brown* was misplaced, because the action in that case was not brought against a union, but rather a federal agency. Moreover, the *Jennings* court said that "[t]he Supreme Court has held that the existence of [Section 703], which includes labor organizations, does not bar an action under Section 1981" (*Jennings* 1982, 716). The court, drawing a distinction between Sections 717 and 703(c), went on to say that Section 717

speaks only of actions against federal departments, agencies, or units. Apparently the . . . plaintiff in *Newbold* . . . relied exclusively on Section 717. The Fifth Circuit's brief [in *Newbold*] . . . does not mention the possible applicability of Section 703(c) to the union defendant. We are not sure that the Fifth Circuit, if squarely presented with a Section 703(c) theory, would adhere to its apparent view that a federal-employee union cannot be liable under Section 1981. In any event, we hold that such a union, like a labor organization representing nonfederal employees, is subject to 42 U.S.C. Section 1981 as well as to [Section 703(c)] (*Jennings* 1982, 716).

Finally, the *Jennings* court ruled that the plaintiff also had a cause of action against her union under the Labor Management Relations Act for a DFR breach.[16] The important point to be made here is that, given the ambiguity surrounding the question of cause of action under Title VII against federal employee unions, at least postal workers should rely on the LMRA for protection under the DFR doctrine.

There are still a good deal of unanswered questions regarding the application of the DFR to federal sector unions. The *Jennings* court provides some clarification on cause of action under Title VII and Section 1981 but the breadth and depth of this ruling are yet uncertain. It is at least hoped that future rulings will turn on the *Jennings* decision as opposed to *Newbold,* because federal employee unions should not be allowed to escape the legal obligations that are imposed on unions operating in every other sector. Congress could not have intended this exemption, indeed disparity, with amendments to the Civil Rights Act.

Union Liability Under Title VII

This section addresses union liability under Title VII because this law imposes perhaps the strictest standards on unions for their involvement in practices that discriminate against women and minorities.[17] Unions will be consistently found jointly liable with employers for injunctive relief and back pay when the practices are embodied in the collective bargaining contract. Moreover, unions face the possibility of individual liability if they encourage an employer to discriminate. Because the courts do not afford unions a good faith defense, unions cannot escape responsibility for the discriminatory practices.

In assessing union liability under Title VII, the courts will first determine whether a union has violated the Civil Rights Act. In general, the courts will examine the post-Act behaviors and policies of unions to determine if they have an adverse impact on protected class members. Or, they will examine the past histories of unions because courts "view such evidence as illustrative of the purpose and effect of present policies, or as proof of the existence of long-standing patterns of discrimination whose effects have a current adverse impact on a protected class of workers" (Willenborg 1984, 146).

Once unions are found guilty of discrimination, they will be held liable for injunctive relief as well as monetary damages in the form of back pay (Volz and Breitenbeck 1984). Perhaps the pivotal issue in Title VII suits is the *level* of involvement in discriminatory practices because it determines whether the union will be jointly or individually liable. For example, if a union discriminates against women and minorities on its own, it will be held individually liable. Unions will also be held individually liable when they induce employers to discriminate. Schlei and Grossman (1983, 634) point out that a "union is unquestionably liable and may be forced to pay full back pay when it takes the initial action and induces an employer to discriminate." Unions have also been held liable on their own for failing to process employees' racial discrimination claims in grievances (*Goodman v. Lukens Steel Co.* 1987).

If the union discriminates with the employer, however, the union will be found jointly liable. A typical source of discrimination by both union and employer is the collective bargaining agreement. If a union is a signatory to a collective bargaining contract that contains discriminatory provisions, the union will be found jointly liable with the employer. Similarly, unions may be jointly liable for acquiescing to discriminatory practices of the employer. If the practices are contained in the collective bargaining contract, the courts have uniformly held unions liable. Unions may also be jointly liable for acquiescing to employer discrimination not prescribed by the collective bargaining agreement, providing the noncontractual discriminatory policy or conduct is within the union's scope of bargaining. The courts' rationale in holding unions jointly liable under such circumstances is that Title VII imposes a responsibility on unions to protect women and minorities at the bargaining table. Thus, if a union has legal access to the discriminatory policies of the employer, it is obligated to correct them.

A final area in which unions will be held jointly liable for injunctive relief and monetary damages in the form of back pay is when a union rejects an employer's offer to eliminate discriminatory provisions embodied in the collective bargaining agreement. Again, unions as bargaining agents have an obligation to protect women and minorities from discriminatory treatment.

International and national unions may also be held jointly liable with their local affiliates and employers if they are "sufficiently connected" to the discriminatory practices or policies. For example, if the parent union was a direct participant to the negotiated agreement, indirectly influenced the agreement, or even authorized the local's agreement, the parent union will be held jointly liable with the employer.

As noted earlier, good faith defenses are normally unavailable to unions under Title VII. Although some courts have taken good faith efforts into account in assessing the amount of back pay to be awarded, other courts have looked only at the actual provisions of the contract and not at the circumstances for their development, hence, precluding a union's escape from monetary liability on good faith grounds.

One of the most common types of joint liability lawsuits involves seniority provisions. As such, the legality of seniority systems deserves further attention especially since the use of seniority appears to be a significant problem for women and minorities in public sector employment. (This issue will be further addressed in Chapter 5 in the context of female employment in nontraditional jobs.)

Seniority Systems: Questions of Law and Equity under Title VII

Unions have historically supported the use of seniority in such employment decisions as promotion, transfer and retention. The use of seniority, however, whether measured by total length of service in an organization (i.e., plant seniority), or length of service in a department, line of progression or job, hinders the employment opportunities of women and minorities. Let's say, for example that employment decisions such as promotions are based on total length of service in an organization. If women and minorities, because of past discriminatory practices, were barred from employment, they will lack the seniority needed to compete equally with white males for promotions. In short, employment decisions based on seniority systematically favor white males. Despite this apparent inequity, Congress, in constructing Title VII, protected the use of "bona fide" seniority systems. Section 703(h) provides:

Notwithstanding any other provision of this title, it shall not be an unlawful employment practice for an employer to apply different standards of compensation, or different terms, conditions, or privileges of employment pursuant to a bona fide seniority or merit system . . . provided that such differences are not the result of an intention to discriminate because of race, color, religion, sex or national origin.

Section 703 (h) was incorporated in the Act as a compromise to critics of the proposed civil rights legislation. Critics argued that existing seniority rights would be destroyed by the bill. Proponents of the bill consistently rebutted this argument. Senators Clark of Pennsylvania and Case of New Jersey, for example, stated that

Title VII would have no effect on established seniority rights. Its effect is prospective and not retrospective. Thus, for example, if a business has been discriminating in the past and as a result has an all-white working force, when the title comes into effect the employer's obligation would be simply to fill future vacancies on a non-discriminatory basis. He would not be obliged—or indeed, permitted—to fire whites in order to hire Negroes, or to prefer Negroes for future vacancies, or once Negroes are hired, to give them special seniority rights at the expense of the white workers hired earlier (*Congressional Record* 1964, 7213).

Senator Clark, voicing a statement of the Justice Department, further stated:

Title VII would have no effect on seniority rights existing at the time it takes effect. If, for example, a collective bargaining contract provides that in the event of layoffs, those who were hired last must be laid off first, such a provision would not be affected in the least by Title VII. This would be true even in the case where owing to discrimination prior to the effective date of the title, white workers had more seniority than Negroes (*Congressional Record* 1964, 7207).

So, the inclusion of Section 703(h) was imperative for the passage of Title VII. Its purpose was to ensure that "bona fide" seniority systems would not be unlawful under Title VII. Judicial interpretation of Section

703(h) and the meaning of "bona fide" has led to different conclusions of law and, hence, liability for unions and/or employers. The differences are particularly apparent when we compare the legality of departmental and job seniority systems to plant seniority systems.

Between 1968 and 1977, the courts uniformly found facially neutral departmental, progression-line, and job seniority systems as a perpetuation of the effects of past discrimination and, hence, in violation of Title VII.[18] The leading case here is *Quarles v. Philip Morris, Inc.* (1968), where the district court said that a seniority and transfer system represented present discrimination in violation of Title VII, if it locked protected class members into the inferior positions that they were originally hired into as a result of discrimination.

It was very common at one time for organizations to operate departmental seniority systems. Departmental seniority, as noted earlier, is computed by total length of service within a particular department. The use of this type of seniority system was particularly harmful to blacks, who, prior to the Civil Rights Act, were generally hired (if hired at all) into low-paying, unskilled jobs in segregated departments. If a black worker had accumulated any seniority, that worker could compete for promotions within the segregated department. If that black worker sought to transfer to a better paying job in a "white" department, however, that worker would lose her/his accumulated departmental seniority rights and protections. The black worker would essentially be permanently disadvantaged as a result of past discriminatory practices. The *Quarles* court acknowledged the discriminatory effects of such a system and, therefore, found the use of seniority here in violation of Title VII.

The case law on departmental seniority systems further evolved with *Papermakers, Local 189 v. United States* (1969). In this case, the Fifth Circuit Court of Appeals was faced with the question of a proper remedy for victims of discriminatory seniority provisions.

Prior to 1964, the labor union and employer in *Papermakers* maintained racially segregated departments, mainly through the use of segregated progression lines within departments. After Title VII was enacted, the company merged black and white progression lines within single departments. The effect was to place all blacks (with one exception) beneath all whites in each department. After passage of the Act, blacks could also transfer into the progression line of any department without loss of seniority. Because black progression lines were merged below white lines, however, and transferring to other departments meant being placed at the bottom of a progression ladder, black employees were lower than whites on integrated ladders, even though many whites were less senior in terms of total length of service with the organization.

The Fifth Circuit, consistent with the *Quarles* court, ruled that the seniority and transfer policies were in violation of Title VII because they perpetuated pre-Act discrimination into the present. In setting forth a remedy, the court looked at three alternatives. One approach, known as the "freedom now" theory, would require the employer to undo the effects of past discrimination by allowing black employees to displace or bump white employees who might not be in the more desirable positions if it were not for the past discrimination. A second alternative would be to maintain the "status quo." Under this theory, the employer would not be in violation of the Act if it simply ended the explicit racially discriminatory policies.

The third alternative, known as the "rightful place" theory, falls somewhere in the middle of the first two. Under this approach, minority employees could not bump less senior whites but could use their accumulated *plantwide* seniority to bid for new openings in "white" departments. The court opted for the "rightful place" remedy on the grounds that it "accords with the purpose and history of the [Act]" (*Papermakers* 1969, 988), which, as stated above, is prospective rather than retrospective.

Then, the Fifth Circuit in *Papermakers,* consistent with the *Quarles* court, set forth a remedy for discriminatory departmental seniority systems which included the use of a plant seniority system. As will be seen shortly, later court interpretations of the use of such a remedy proved to be detrimental for the bona fides of plant seniority.

The *Franks v. Bowman Transportation Co.* (1976) case also addressed appropriate remedies but not for discriminatory seniority systems per se. Rather, the *Franks* Court set forth a proper remedy in terms of seniority for victims of discrimination in hiring. More clearly, the *Franks* Court questioned, If an individual challenges hiring practices as being discriminatory and is later hired as a result of a successful challenge, should the victim be at an absolute, irreparable disadvantage in terms of senority status as compared to whites? Or, should the victim be awarded constructive seniority (also referred to as retroactive, fictional or super-seniority) from the date of his or her application for employment? Also, should relief be available to all persons in a class-action suit?

The Supreme Court in *Franks* ruled that awarding constructive seniority to *identifiable* victims of *post*-Act discrimination was imperative in order to fulfill one of the central purposes of Title VII, " 'to make persons whole for injuries suffered on account of unlawful employment discrimination' " (*Franks* 1976, 1264; citing *Albemarle Paper Co. v. Moody* 1975, 2372). The Court went on to say that "[a]dequate relief may well be denied in the absence of a seniority remedy slotting the victim in that position in the seniority system that would have been his had he been hired at the time of his application. It can hardly be questioned that ordinarily such relief will be necessary to achieve the 'make-whole' purposes of the Act" (*Franks* 1976, 1264-65).

Constructive seniority is obviously an important remedy, but it must be kept in mind that, based on the *Franks* decision, it is awarded only to identifiable victims of post-Act discrimination. Thus, members of a class-action suit, unless actual victims, will not be awarded constructive seniority. This being the case, it would seem that the number of beneficiaries of retroactive seniority is very small. It should further be noted that the Court did not address the possibility of relief for *pre*-Act discriminatees, an issue that would later be decided in the landmark *International Brotherhood of Teamsters v. United States* (1977).

While the legality of departmental and job seniority systems was clear at least between 1968 and 1977, the legality of plantwide systems was less certain. It seems axiomatic that plant seniority provisions will also be harmful and will perpetuate the effects of past discrimination if women and minorities were initially barred completely from jobs. The effects of plant seniority were acknowledged by the district court in *Watkins v. Steelworkers, Local 2369* (1974), one of the first cases involving the bona fides of plantwide seniority systems. The conflict arose in a context involving layoffs based on a "last hired, first fired" principle. If women and minorities are the "last hired" as a result of previous discrimination, they will be hit hardest by layoffs based on this seniority principle.

The district court in *Watkins* (1974, 1226) found such a system illegal under Title VII stating that "employment preferences cannot be allocated on the basis of length of service or seniority, where blacks were, by virtue of prior discrimination, prevented from acquiring relevant seniority." The court went on to say that "[t]he Company's history of racial discrimination in hiring makes it impossible now for blacks . . . to have sufficient seniority to withstand layoff. In this situation, the selection of employees for layoff on the basis of seniority unlawfully perpetuates the effects of past discrimination" (*Watkins* 1974, 1226).

The court did not award constructive seniority in *Watkins,* but rather ordered the company to recall enough black employees so that the percentage of blacks in the employer's work force would be equal to the percentage of blacks that were present at the time the last new employee was hired. The court reasoned that this type of remedy was necessary to ensure the employment of blacks in the company.

In a decision that only obscured the legality of plant seniority, the Fifth Circuit Court of Appeals reversed the lower court's ruling in *Watkins.* The appellate court found that this particular plantwide seniority system did not perpetuate the effects of past discrimination because none of the plaintiffs in this case were *actual* victims of past hiring discrimination. As such, the court said that the plaintiffs could not benefit from the relief ordered by the district court. It is important to note that the appeals court did not find plantwide seniority systems in general bona fide and, hence, legal within the meaning of Section 703(h). The court set forth little guidance, however, as to what constitutes a bona fide plant seniority system.

Other cases provide more explicit, yet convoluted, interpretations of the applicability of Section 703(h) to the use of the plantwide seniority. In *Waters v. Wisconsin Steel Works* (1974), for example, the Seventh Circuit Court of Appeals found plantwide seniority systems as bona fide under Title VII on the grounds that other courts (beginning with *Quarles*) had often required plantwide seniority as a specific remedy for discriminatory departmental seniority systems. The logic of the appeals court in *Waters*, however, seems somewhat flawed.

In *Watkins* (1974, 1226) the district court clearly addressed this issue stating that:

Plant seniority was held to be a racially neutral standard in [departmental seniority] cases, not because it is *per se* valid, but because blacks had not been excluded from the plant (as distinct from certain departments or jobs) and thus had been able to earn plant seniority.

The *Waters* court completely overlooked this seemingly common sense factor. The decision ultimately proved detrimental to victims of hiring discrimination seeking relief from the use of plant seniority.

Perhaps the most harmful decision regarding plant seniority systems came with the Third Circuit's ruling in *Jersey Central Power & Light Co. v. I.B.E.W.* (1975). The appellate court in this case ruled that whether a plantwide seniority system perpetuates past discrimination is irrelevant in assessing the bona fides of seniority systems. The court said:

We believe that Congress intended to bar proof of the "perpetuating" effect of a plant-wide seniority system as it regarded such systems as "bona fide." . . . It is not fatal that the seniority system continues the effect of past employment discrimination. We believe this result was recognized and left undisturbed by Congress in its enactment of Section 703 (h) and (j) (*Jersey Central* 1975, 706-707).

There are several noteworthy aspects of the court's ruling in *Jersey Central*. First, the court completely ignored the Equal Employment Opportunity Commission's (EEOC's) interpretation that seniority systems which perpetuate past discrimination into the present are unlawful under Title VII. (It is very common for courts to defer to the interpretation of the administrative agency responsible for particular statutes.) Second, the court, in setting forth criteria for ascertaining the bona fides of seniority systems, ignored the U. S. Supreme Court's landmark *Griggs v. Duke Power Co.* (1971) ruling. The Third Circuit's criteria in *Jersey Central* included whether the seniority system was facially neutral, and whether it *intended* to discriminate.

In *Griggs* (1971, 854), the Supreme Court held that "good intent or absence of discriminatory intent does not redeem employment procedures or testing mechanisms that operate as 'built-in headwinds' for minority groups and are unrelated to measuring job capability." The Court went on to say that "Congress directed the thrust of the Act to the *consequences* of employment practices, not simply the motivation" (*Griggs* 1971, 854). The Third Circuit's decision in *Jersey Central* failed to acknowledge the Supreme Court's conclusion in *Griggs*.

In addition, by setting forth these criteria, the *Jersey Central* court drew a distinction between an appropriate test for the bona fides of a departmental as compared to plant seniority system. The former, as discussed above, considered whether the seniority system perpetuated into the present the effects of past discrimination. Fine (1975, 91) has noted that "[t]he *Jersey Central* opinion is singularly unenlightening regarding the logic or the desirability of such a distinction and totally devoid of any statutory, legislative, or judicial basis for imposing it." The *Jersey Central* decision was a serious blow to the category of discrimination which focuses on adverse or disparate impact as it applies to seniority systems. In addition, the decision represents the first time a court disregarded discrimination in the form of perpetuating the effects of past discrimination.

In sum, it appears that at least prior to the *Waters* and *Jersey Central* decisions, courts sought to strike a balance between the use of seniority, whether departmental or plantwide, and female and minority employment. The courts seemed to recognize the historical importance of seniority but they also recognized the importance of equal employment opportunities for women and minorities. As such, the use of seniority was not ruled out entirely, but courts suggested that its unconditional use could no longer be permitted in light of these other values which have social as well as economic significance.

Attempts to balance these seemingly disparate interests were severely thwarted by *Waters* and, in particular, *Jersey Central*, which emphasized the intent rather than effects of seniority systems. Echoing *Jersey Central*, the balance was virtually destroyed in 1977 with the U.S. Supreme Court's landmark ruling, *International Brotherhood of Teamsters v. United States*. This decision dramatically altered the bona fides of *all* types of seniority systems.

In *Teamsters*, racial minorities charged that the collectively bargained seniority system was discriminatory. For calculating "benefits" (such as pensions, vacations, and so on), seniority was defined as the total length of service with the organization, which takes into account different jobs held in different bargaining units.

"Competitive status" seniority, however, which is used in bidding for jobs and determining layoffs and recalls from layoff, was calculated on the basis of length of service in a particular bargaining unit. The upshot is, if an employee seeks to transfer from one bargaining unit to another unit with more desirable, higher-paying jobs, the employee loses her/his accumulated competitive seniority. In *Teamsters*, racial minorities were predominantly found in bargaining units with jobs such as city bus drivers, as compared to units with higher-paying jobs such as line (i.e., long-distance) drivers. The seniority system discouraged racial minorities from competing for these more desirable jobs.

The district court in *Teamsters* found that the collectively bargained seniority system was discriminatory because it "impede[d] the free transfer of minority groups into and within the company" (*U.S. v. T.I.M.E.-D.C., Inc.* 1974, 694). The Fifth Circuit Court of Appeals upheld the district court's conclusion here. The U.S. Supreme Court, however, reversed. The Court held that a bona fide departmental seniority system is lawful under Section 703(h) even if it perpetuates into the persent the effects of pre-Act discrimination. The Court said that "Congress did not intend to make it illegal for employees with vested seniority rights to continue to exercise those rights, even at the expense of pre-Act discriminatees"(*Teamsters* 1977, 1864).

Even though the Court explicitly referred to the present effects of *pre*-Act discrimination, it appears that the pivotal issue in the legality of seniority systems according to the *Teamsters* Court was not whether the discrimination preceded or followed the Act but rather whether the seniority system was "bona fide."[19] The Court stated that "Section 703(h) on its face immunizes all *bona fide* seniority systems, and does not distinguish between the perpetuation of pre- and post-Act discrimination" (*Teamsters* 1977, 1861, at note 30, emphasis in original). This conclusion was consistent with the Court's decision in another case, *United Air Lines v. Evans* (1977), ruled on the same day as *Teamsters*. (This issue was also clarified with a later Court ruling, *American Tobacco Co. v. Patterson*, 1982.[20])

In determining what constitutes "bona fide," the *Teamsters* Court set forth standards that are still applied today on a case-by-case basis. These standards consider:

1) whether the seniority system operates to discourage all employees equally from transferring between seniority units;
2) whether the seniority units are in the same or separate bargaining units (if the latter, whether the structure is rational and in conformance with industry practice);
3) whether the seniority system had its genesis in racial discrimination; and
4) whether the system was negotiated and has been maintained free from any illegal purpose (*James v. Stockham Valves and Fittings Co.* 1977, 352).[21]

In applying these standards, the *Teamsters* Court ruled that the seniority system was bona fide and, hence, legal under Section 703(h). Then, the union's and employer's conduct in maintaining the system did not violate Title VII.

Perhaps the most far-reaching standard in determining the bona fides of seniority was and continues to be the *intent* of the seniority system. If the intent is discriminatory, it will not be bona fide, thereby leading to a finding that the seniority system is illegal under Title VII (*Lorance v. AT&T* 1989). Hence, the parties involved may be liable for any relief awarded by the courts. If there is no intent to discriminate, however, its use will be upheld, despite its *effects*.

Unlike the *Jersey Central* court, the *Teamsters* Court addressed the "intent versus effect" issue in light of *Griggs v. Duke Power Co.* (1971). In *Griggs*, as noted earlier, the Supreme Court ruled that practices and policies that are neutral on their face and in *intent*, but discriminate in *effect*, are in violation of Title VII. The Court in *Teamsters* (1977, 1861) said the "[o]ne kind of practice 'fair in form, but discriminatory in operation' is that which perpetuates the effects of prior discrimination." Citing *Griggs*, it went on to say that "[u]nder the Act, practices, procedures, or tests neutral on their face, and even neutral in terms of intent, cannot be maintained if they operate to 'freeze' the status quo of prior discriminatory employment practices" (*Teamsters* 1977, 1861-62). Notwithstanding, the Court concluded that "[w]ere it not for Section 703(h), the seniority system in this case would seem to fall under the *Griggs* rationale" (*Teamsters* 1977, 1862).

The Court's ruling in *Teamsters* has proven to be a serious setback to the dismantling of barriers that hinder the employment progress of women and minorities. The irony is that Title VII was aimed at dismantling such barriers. The Court's decision was particularly astonishing because it challenged the legal definitions of discrimination under Title VII (at least with respect to seniority systems) employed in a long line of cases beginning with *Quarles*. As discussed earlier, the *Quarles* court found the seniority system discriminatory because of its disparate *effects* on black employees. Even more surprising in the *Teamsters* ruling, the Court rejected its own definition of discrimination set forth in *Griggs*.

The Court rationalized its use of an "intent test" by relying on the statements submitted by Senators Clark and Case. But, it is interesting that nothing in these statements suggests that Congress was concerned with intent. In fact, Congress was extremely vague regarding what constitutes a bona fide seniority system (Schell 1984).

The upshot of relying on intent is that the ability of women and minorities to achieve equality and equity is severely limited; indeed, these groups remain the perpetual victims of discrimination. This seems contrary to the *overall* purpose of Title VII, as Justice Marshall, in his dissenting opinion in *Teamsters* recognized.

Justice Marshall first criticized the majority's blatant disregard for past judicial, administrative as well as scholarly opinion in strong support of the interpretation that Section 703(h) does not protect seniority systems that perpetuate the effects of past discrimination. He then proceeded to challenge the majority's reliance on Section 703(h) on substantive as well as procedural grounds.

Marshall referred to that portion of Section 703(h) which states that different privileges of employment are legal when emanating from a seniority system, "*provided that such differences are not the result of an intention to discrimination because of race, color, religion, sex or national origin*" (*Teamsters* 1977, 1878, emphasis in original). Marshall goes on to say that the differences in employment benefits are "precisely the result of prior, intentional discrimination in assigning jobs. . . . Thus, if the proviso is read literally, the instant case falls squarely within it, thereby rendering Section 703(h) inapplicable" (*Teamsters* 1977, 1878). In finding Section 703(h) applicable, argued Marshall, the Court majority, in effect, reconstructed the language of the proviso, which was unwarranted by the legislative history of the Act.

Marshall also criticized the majority's reliance on the Clark-Case memorandum. He argued that the statements were submitted several weeks before Section 703(h) was introduced and, as such, provide no guidance on the meaning of this Section. According to Marshall, the Court erred in relying on such statement.

A final noteworthy aspect of Justice Marshall's dissent relates to the 1972 amendments to Title VII. Marshall argued that in amending Title VII, "Congress made very clear that it approved of the lower court decisions invalidating seniority systems that perpetuate discrimination" (*Teamsters* 1977, 1883). The majority's dismissal of such amendments, as Marshall points out, contravenes Supreme Court precedents as well as principles.

The Court's ruling in *Teamsters* has resulted in immense discourse and debate regarding a proper balance between the interests of protected class members as prescribed by Title VII and seniority rights. As will be seen in the following section, the participation of the lower courts in this debate has been quite interesting, particularly in those cases where the lower courts have rejected the application of *Teamsters*. Despite the interpretations of the lower courts, the Supreme Court in 1984, and again in 1989,[22] reaffirmed the applicability of *Teamsters* to a broad range of circumstances. This has had serious implications especially for public sector work forces under affirmative action consent decrees or court orders.

Affirmative Action, Layoffs and Seniority in the Public Sector

The tension between seniority and affirmative action became particularly apparent in the public sector in the early to mid-1970s when women and minorities began to make some (albeit limited) progress in public sector work forces. The progress has generally been tied to enforcement of Title VII, which was extended to public employment with the 1972 Equal Employment Opportunity Act. Consent decrees and court orders to increase the numbers of women and minorities were very common in state and local government work forces.

The employment gains women and minorities began to make were thwarted, however, by a number of factors including overt attempts by employers and unions to keep them out. For example, departmental seniority systems (as will be further addressed in Chapter 5) were commonly employed to hinder the employment progress of women in such professions as police and corrections. Even more devastating, fiscal crises portended massive reductions-in-force (rifs), generally decided on the basis of seniority, which threatened to wipe away years of progress made in the hiring and promoting of women and minorities.

Three notable cases involve Toledo, Boston and Memphis, which during the early 1970s and 1980s, entered into consent decrees to increase the percentage of blacks and Hispanics in police and firefighting positions at various levels (Roberts 1985). As a result of ensuing fiscal problems, each city was forced to reduce its work force. The reductions were scheduled to be made on the basis of last-in first-out (LIFO) seniority systems, which were collectively bargained and/or mandated by state law. In each case, the city, union and nonminority employees argued that the LIFO systems must be granted greater weight than the consent decrees. In each case, however, the district courts modified the initial consent decrees and issued injunctions to prevent the layoffs of minorities. The appellate courts in each case upheld the lower court rulings.

The courts rationalized the modifications to the consent decrees on several grounds. In *Boston Chapter, NAACP v Beecher and Boston Firefighters Union and Boston Police Patrolmen's Association* (1982, 977), for example, the First Circuit Court of Appeals ruled that

[t]he fact of past discrimination agreed to in [the decrees] constitutes a "compelling need" for a minority-conscious remedy. The proper test is one of reasonableness.... The orders of the district court meet the test of reasonableness. They were necessary to prevent the departments from regressing to the state of precipitous racial imbalance that prevailed at the commencement of this litigation more than ten years ago.

The court went on to conclude that

[w]hile seniority was the normal way to decide who must go first, there is nothing magical about seniority, and here common sense suggests that it should be tempered by other entirely rational considerations so that the racial equity achieved at considerable effort in the past decade not be erased. . . . If the evil of racial discrimination is to be fought openly, we must not allow ourselves to be caught in a semantic web of aphorisms such as "reverse discrimination" that in the final analysis serve only to perpetuate the discrimination of the past (*Boston* 1982, 978).

In a similar ruling involving the integration of minorities into Toledo's fire department, the Sixth Circuit's *Brown v. Neeb and Fire Fighters Local Union* (1981, 559)[23] affirmed the lower court's ruling, concluding that "enjoining the layoff of minorities [was a] necessary action to implement the consent decree." The court said that "permitting the city to lay off the recently-hired minority firefighters would make a mockery of the consent decree. By its very terms, compliance with the decree is measured by black and Hispanic *employment* in the fire division" (*Brown v. Neeb* 1981, 558, emphasis in original).

In the Memphis case, *Stotts v. Memphis Fire Department and Firefighters Local Union* (1982), the Sixth Circuit Court of Appeals also upheld the lower court's modification of the consent decree primarily on the grounds that changed circumstances (i.e., the economic crisis) warranted such an alteration. The court said that "[a] trial court has broad discretion in administering consent decrees. . . . While acting within its equity jurisdiction, a trial court has continuing jurisdiction to modify a consent decree upon a showing that 'changed circumstances' have transformed the original decree into an instrument of wrong" (*Stotts* 1982, 562-63). The court further noted that the layoff of minorities as a result of the seniority system would "wrench" the affirmative action relief that the city agreed to in the consent decrees.

Then, each of the appellate courts upheld the district courts' modifications to the affirmative action consent decrees, despite the existence of a LIFO seniority system. At this point the question arises, Did these courts consider the Supreme Court's decision in *Teamsters* and other related cases with respect to the bona fides of seniority systems? The courts in each case did, in fact, refer to the *Teamsters* decision, but found the Supreme Court's ruling inapplicable in light of prevailing circumstances. In *Brown v. Neeb*, for example, the court rejected the union's argument that enjoining the seniority-based layoffs was contrary to the *Teamsters* ruling.

The court stated that

we do not think that *Teamsters* can bar relief sought to remedy constitutional violations under Section 1983, or under a consent decree. While a bona-fide seniority system may not itself violate the law, such a system cannot be allowed to obstruct remedies designed to overcome past discrimination . . . To the extent that the seniority system is an obstacle to the city of Toledo's duty to eliminate past discrimination, the district court can set it aside (*Brown v. Neeb* 1981, 564).

Similarly, the *Boston* court ruled that the *Teamsters* as well as *American Tobacco Co.* (1982) decisions did not apply to the issues at stake in Boston's police and fire departments. The First Circuit, relying on the Supreme Court's decision in *Franks,* said that "Section 703 (h) does not bar appropriate relief if an illegal discriminatory practice occurring after the effective date of the Act is proved" (*Boston* 1982, 974). The court went on to say that the U.S. Supreme Court's prior decisions do not preclude "a court from ordering relief to remedy discrimination that exists apart from the adoption or application of a bona fide seniority system. The original consent decrees . . . were directed at such independent violations" (*Boston* 1982, 974).

The district court in *Stotts v. Memphis* went even further to conclude that the seniority system employed by the fire department was not bona fide under Title VII because of its discriminatory effects. The appellate court ruled that the lower court erred in its finding here, but, nonetheless, upheld the district court's injunction to prevent the layoff of minority firefighters on the ground that a "consent decree can alter existing seniority provisions [even] over the objections of an adversely affected union" (*Stotts* 1982, 564). To support its ruling, the court advanced three theories.

The "settlement theory," said the court, permits alterations to existing seniority provisions in order to settle (e.g., through a consent decree) employment discrimination. Thus, although the appellate court vacated the district court's determination that the seniority system was not bona fide, by relying on this theory, the court appeared to be saying that whether the seniority system is bona fide or not it could be altered to settle employment discrimination under Title VII.

The second theory, known as "preferred means," propounds that "a consent decree, the preferred means of resolving an employment discrimination suit, does not decrease the power of a court to order relief which implicates the policies of Title VII and 42 U.S.C. Sections 1981 and 1983" (*Stotts* 1982, 566). As such, the appellate court ruled that the district court possessed the authority to override the union's seniority system.

Finally, the third theory allows an employer to "temporarily override the provision of a collective bargaining agreement pursuant to a valid affirmative action plan" (*Stotts* 1982, 566). This was, indeed, the situation faced by the Memphis fire department and, so, the appellate court again affirmed the lower court's decision to override the union's collective bargaining provisions.

Then, the *Stotts* court went a step further than the *Boston* and *Brown* courts. All three courts ruled that court-ordered relief to redress past discriminations cannot be outweighed by collectively bargained (or state-mandated) seniority systems which threaten to destroy the relief already granted. The *Stotts* court, however, suggested that this holds true, despite the bona fides of the seniority system.

Another noteworthy aspect of the *Stotts* case is that the so-called collective bargaining contract between the city and union was actually a "memorandum of understanding." In fact, the plaintiffs argued that such an agreement is unenforceable under Tennessee law. Although the appellate court did not rule on this issue, the plaintiffs may have been correct since the state of Tennessee mandates collective bargaining only for teachers (Shafritz, Hyde and Rosenbloom 1986; Kearney 1984). Moreover, the Tennessee Supreme Court ruled in *Fulenwider v. Firefighters Assn. Local Union 1784* (1982) that the memorandum of understanding confers no enforceable rights because of the limits on collective bargaining as prescribed by state law. This leads to two related concerns.

One, in light of the three theories presented by the appellate court in *Stotts*, "collective bargaining" provisions were not necessarily overriden because, technically, these provisions are not recognized by state law. Moreover, even though the city unilaterally adopted the seniority system proposed in this memorandum, the city could have unilaterally modified the system. That is, when collective bargaining is not authorized by state law, executive order or judicial mandate, the public employer can *legally* modify personnel policies without union involvement. If a public employer is genuinely committed to redressing employment discrimination, seniority provisions could be explicitly modified so as not to counteract the effects of affirmative action consent decrees

On the other hand, of course, it could be argued, given that *Stotts* was decided based on "union-negotiated" seniority provisions, that the courts tacitly acknowledged the powers of this firefighting union, even in the absence of express statutory collective bargaining authority. Then, as discussed in Chapter 1, perhaps unions operating in the public sector— particularly in the uniformed services—possess greater power than is expected. In effect, even in those government sectors where collective bargaining is not mandated by law, we overlook the ability of unions to hinder the employment opportunities of women and minorities in public sector work forces. Ultimately, formulas for alleviating discrimination erroneously omit unions.

Only one of the three cases, *Stotts v. Memphis*, reached the Supreme

Court. (The official title of the Supreme Court case is *Firefighters Local Union No. 1784 v. Stotts, Memphis v. Stotts*, 1984, hereafter referred to as *Memphis v. Stotts.*) It is interesting to note at the outset that the Court refused to render the case moot, despite the fact that all of the laid-off white employees had been recalled by the time the Court ruled on the case. It appears that the Court wished to reassert its position on the use of seniority in employment decisions, notwithstanding its effects on affirmative action efforts.

In reversing the lower court's decision, the Supreme Court first reaffirmed its position in *Teamsters,* stating that the seniority system did not intend to discriminate against racial minorities and, therefore, was bona fide. The *Memphis v. Stotts* Court (1984, 2587) said that "Section 703(h) . . . permits the routine application of a seniority system absent proof of an intention to discriminate." The Court then stated that the appeals court was correct in vacating the district court's finding that the seniority system was not bona fide. But, the Court said that the appellate court erred in upholding the lower court's injunction. A primary criticism of the Court was that by modifying the consent decree, the plaintiffs were inappropriately awarded competitive seniority.

The Supreme Court referred to its holdings in *Franks* and *Teamsters,* where it ruled that individual plaintiffs who can demonstrate that they are actual victims of past discrimination (e.g., in the form of hiring), can be awarded competitive seniority and be "given their rightful place on the seniority roster" (*Memphis v. Stotts* 1984, 2588). The Court further clarified, however, that even if an individual proves that she or he is a victim of past discrimination, that individual is not entitled to "bump" white males from their jobs.

The *Memphis v. Stotts* Court held that in the present instance, none of the minorities were *actual* victims of past discrimination. It thus concluded that the relief ordered by the district court exceeded what could have been awarded if the case, rather than being settled by consent decree, actually went to trial and the plaintiffs proved the existence of a pattern or practice of discrimination.

The Court's conclusions of law are remarkable, given the circumstances surrounding this case. The dissenting opinion, in fact, focused on these circumstances and, in so doing, pointed to several "errors" made by the Court majority. First and foremost, the dissenting Justices argued that this case should not have been ruled on by the Court because the issue was moot, that is, the actual controversy was no longer alive.

The Court majority reasoned that the case was not moot because there were continuing effects from the preliminary injunction, that is, the injunction could be invoked in the event of future layoffs. The dissenting Justices, however, argued that any lingering effects could have been erased by vacating the appellate court's ruling "which is this Court's long-standing practice with cases that become moot" (*Memphis v. Stotts* 1984, 2595).

The dissenting Justices then turned to the Court's ruling that the plaintiffs were inappropriately awarded competitive seniority. They stated that the Court majority arrived at this conclusion not by reviewing the goals of the consent decree and whether the proposed layoffs warranted the lower court's modification of that decree. Rather, the Court majority instead turned to Title VII. The dissent did not state whether turning to Title VII was correct or not, but did state that the majority's conclusion with respect to appropriate remedies was clearly wrong.

Referring to *Teamsters,* the dissent first stated that individual plaintiffs of a Title VII class-action suit are entitled to individual relief if they can demonstrate that they are actual victims of discrimination. The dissent further stated, however, that race-conscious class relief can also be appropriate in Title VII class-action suits, as Courts of Appeal have unanimously held. The dissent stated that "[t]he purpose of such relief is not to make whole any particular individual, but rather to remedy the present class-wide effects of past discrimination or to prevent similar discrimination in the future" (*Memphis v. Stotts* 1984, 2606). The dissenting Justices also said that the relief can take many forms, including the use of percentages as contained in the consent decree at issue in this case.

The dissent also argued that the plaintiffs in this case did not request competitive seniority, nor, contrary to what the majority stated, did the district court award such a remedy. The district court merely required racial balance in certain job categories in the city's fire department. This requirement did not preclude the city from laying off individual minorities, provided that the balance was maintained. It should also be noted that the city could have avoided layoffs entirely if it accepted the union's proposal of reducing the work time of *all* employees in the fire department.

The dissent further said that it was "improper and unfair" for the majority to rule that the plaintiffs were not victims of past discrimination since they did not have the opportunity to demonstrate whether they were victims at a trial. Indeed, the purpose of the consent decree was to *avoid* litigation. As such, the Court majority's ruling was based purely on speculation of what would have happened had the case gone to trial. This was a serious flaw.

The ultimate effect of the majority's ruling in *Memphis v. Stotts* was to strengthen the use of seniority in employment decisions but also to weaken affirmative action efforts, at least those aimed at the retention of protected class members during periods of layoff. It is obvious that the Court majority in *Memphis v. Stotts* just as in *Teamsters* was simply unwilling to balance the interests of affirmative action against the use of seniority in employment decisions.

In a related, more recent case, *Wygant v. Jackson Board of Education* (1986), the Supreme Court again voiced its support for the last-in first-out seniority principle in layoff decisions.[24] In *Wygant*, the Court was asked to rule on the constitutionality of a collectively bargained layoff provision that required the use of seniority but also required racial balance on the teaching faculty in the school district. Specifically, the contract stipulated that, in the event of layoffs, the most senior teachers would be retained, "except that at no time will there be a greater percentage of minority personnel laid off than the current percentage of minority personnel employed at the time of the layoff" *(Wygant* 1986, 1845).

When it became necessary, layoffs were made in accordance with the collective bargaining provision. Consequently, minorities with less seniority were retained and white teachers with greater seniority were laid off. The displaced white teachers challenged the constitutionality of the collective bargaining provision.[25] The federal district court ruled that such racial preferences as embodied in the labor contract were permitted under the Equal Protection Clause of the Fourteenth Amendment particularly since the preferences were aimed at remedying past societal discrimination by providing "role models" for minority students. The Court of Appeals for the Sixth Circuit upheld the lower court's ruling.

On appeal, the U.S. Supreme Court reversed on the grounds that the use of racial classifications in the layoff plan was not justified by a "compelling state interest." In the plurality opinion of the Court, Justice Powell first stated that "[t]his Court never has upheld that societal discrimination alone is sufficient to justify a racial classification. Rather, the Court has insisted upon some showing of prior discrimination by the governmental unit involved before allowing limited use of racial classifications in order to remedy such discrimination" (*Wygant* 1986, 1847). Then, there would have been a compelling state interest to employ the use of racial preferences had the school board been seeking to rectify its own prior discrimination.

Powell went on to say, however, that even if the Board's purpose was to remedy its own past discrimination, the means selected (the layoff plan) to achieve that goal were not "sufficiently narrowly tailored" (i.e., the layoff plan was not the least restrictive way to achieve the goal). Powell wrote that "[o]ther, less intrusive means of accomplishing similar purposes—such as the adoption of hiring goals—are available" (*Wygant* 1986, 1852).

In effect, as Powell reasoned, affirmative action is appropriate in some situations but not others. The appropriateness depends upon the impact of affirmative action on "innocent" persons. Powell argued that affirmative action is appropriate in hiring, since the burden to be borne by "innocent parties" is diffused among society. In contrast, when affirmative action is employed during layoffs, the "entire burden of achieving racial equality [is placed on] particular individuals, often resulting in serious disruption of their lives. That burden is too instrusive" (*Wygant* 1986, 1851-52).

This is a critical aspect of the *Wygant* decision and was echoed in the more recent rulings of the U.S. Supreme Court in *Sheet Metal Workers v. EEOC* (1986), *Firefighters v. Cleveland* (1986), *U.S. v. Paradise* (1987), and *Johnson v. Transportation Agency* (1987). Briefly, the rulings in these cases taken together suggest that the use of affirmative action in hiring and promotions, whether it involves voluntarily developed goals or court-ordered quotas, is legal under Title VII and constitutional under the equal protection clause if it is intended to remedy past employment discrimination or racial and gender imbalances in the work force.[26] Moreover, the decisions suggest that the plaintiffs need not demonstrate that they were actual victims of the past discrimination to benefit from the race- or gender-conscious remedies. The rulings further indicate, however, that use of affirmative action will not be upheld in layoff decisions.

In sum, beginning with the *Teamsters* ruling in 1977, seniority systems that do not intend to discriminate against women and minorities will be found legal under Title VII. This ruling was reaffirmed in 1984 with the Supreme Court's decision in *Memphis v. Stotts,* where the Court upheld the use of seniority in layoffs despite its effect on protected class members. In 1986, the Supreme Court in *Wygant* again expressed its support for the use of seniority in layoffs, which has served as a final blow to affirmative action efforts aimed at retention of women and minorities during periods of layoff.[27] Other recent Supreme Court rulings, however, suggest that affirmative action efforts are entirely legitimate.

In essence, a majority of Supreme Court Justices is unwilling to balance affirmative action against seniority rights. The upshot is that women and minorities will systematically be the "underclass" in the workplace. Although hiring gains may be made, at least at the entry level, layoffs based on seniority can easily wipe away those gains. As illustrated in this chapter, the role of unions here is clear. With the exception of the teachers' union in *Wygant,* union support for seniority is unrelenting. The union's position in *Wygant* is particularly interesting and suggests that some teachers' unions may be willing to compromise their position on seniority for the sake of affirmative action. Future research should examine this issue in order to better understand the motivations of teachers' unions to shift their support away from seniority.

Conclusions

As discussed in the first part of this chapter, unions have certain legal obligations to refrain from discrimination against women and minorities. A duty of fair representation (DFR) is imposed on unions based on judicial interpretation of various statutes and unions can also be liable for their discriminatory practices.

However, the legal obligations of unions seem to vary. For example, if the union and employer develop hiring criteria which have an adverse impact on women and minorities, the union and employer may be jointly liable for their actions under Title VII. But, a union and employer will not be found liable if they develop a seniority system that adversely affects women and minorities. Unions may be jointly liable with the employer under Title VII only if the seniority system *intends* to discriminate against protected class members.

Thus, the legal obligations of unions seem to be contingent upon how the courts define discrimination, that is, in terms of adverse impact or intent. This distinction is important especially where seniority systems are concerned, yet it is perplexing because it suggests that unions have legal obligations to promote equal employment opportunities for women and minorities in some situations but not others. Unions have a legal obligation under Title VII, for example, to protect women and minorities from promotion decisions that adversely affect them. On the other hand, as unions develop and implement seniority systems, they have no obligation to protect the employment interests of women and minorities. This disparity seems extraordinary and, given the U.S. Supreme Court's recent decisions on affirmative action and seniority, is unlikely to change in the near future.[28]

Notes

1. These obligations can sometimes be explicit for public sector unions, as will be discussed later in the text.

2. It should be noted that these doctrines are not mutually exclusive. That is, the duty of fair representation (DFR) does not preclude a finding of union liability for damages. See, for example, *Bowen v. U.S. Postal Service* (1983).

3. See, for example, Schlei and Grossman (1983) for a discussion of when Section 301 of the LMRA is applicable and when the various sections of the NLRA are applicable.

4. There is an exception to the NLRA that permits an employee to present a grievance directly to the employer providing that the employer's adjustment or response to the grievance does not interfere with the collective bargaining agreement, and providing that the union is given the opportunity to at least be present when the employer addresses the grievance. This exception, however, does not diminish a union's obligation to fairly represent all members of the bargaining unit (*Local 12, United Rubber Workers v. NLRB*, 1966).

5. Remedies under Section 1981 include compensatory and punitive damages.

6. In fact, many states, in response to the number of growing cases, have amended existing labor statutes to impose an express DFR requirement on labor unions. For a discussion, see Bradburn (1980).

7. In the private sector, at least before 1962, a union's breach of its DFR was never found to be an unfair labor practice by the NLRB. Since then, however, the

NLRB has in many instances found DFR breaches to be unfair labor practices (Sovern 1966).

8. When administrative procedures are available, they need not be exhausted in DFR claims in the private sector (and perhaps public, depending upon the jurisdiction) if the union has denied employees access to that administrative process. See, for example, Bradburn (1980).

9. See, for example, *Moore v. City of San Jose* (1980).

10. See, for example, *Golden v. Local 55, Firefighters* (1980) and *Ford v. University of Montana* (1979).

11. It is worth nothing that there may be some procedural and tactical differences between cases brought under Title VII as compare to Section 1981. For example, a suit based on Section 1981 entitles the plaintiff to a jury trial but filing suit under Title VII alone does not. In addition, compensatory and punitive damages are not available under Title VII but are recoverable under Section 1981 even if the claim is made under both Section 1981 and Title VII (Schlei and Grossman 1983). This being the case, the choice of statute— Title VII or Section 1981—may be a strategic one.

12. Labor relations in the U.S. Postal Service are technically overseen by the Postal Reorganization Act of 1970. See Rosenbloom and Shafritz (1985).

13. It is important to note, however, that the U.S. Supreme Court, in *Karahalios v. National Federation of Federal Employees* (1989), has ruled that federal employees cannot sue their unions for a DFR breach in a federal court under the CSRA. Rather, due to the statutory scheme of the CSRA, they must bring the case before the Federal Labor Relations Authority (FLRA). Also see, Wood (1988).

14. In *Brown v. General Services Administration* (1976), the U.S. Supreme Court held that Section 717 of Title VII provides an exclusive remedy for federal employees, thereby precluding use of Section 1981 against federal *employers*. However, the case did not involve unions and, so, there are unresolved questions regarding the applicability of the exclusivity of remedy principle to unions representing federal government employees. This is addressed in the text.

15. The 1981 claim is a charge only of racial discrimination, not gender-based. As Schlei and Grossman (1983) point out, courts have overwhelmingly held that Section 1981 does not apply to discrimination based on gender.

16. The U.S. Supreme Court in *Bowen v. U.S. Postal Service* (1983) also found that postal employees have a cause of action against their union under the Labor Management Relations Act. This case is not discussed in the text because it does not involve race or sex discrimination.

17. See Schlei and Grossman (1983), for example, for a discussion of union liability under Section 1981.

18. Craft union referral systems (i.e., hiring halls) that give preference to senior workers were also struck down as discriminatory. For a discussion, see Fine (1975).

19. It should be noted, however, that the issue of pre- versus post-Act discrimination is important in developing a remedy for past employment discrimination (e.g., in hiring). Building on *Franks*, the *Teamsters* Court ruled that constructive seniority could be awarded to the victims of discrimination occurring *after* but not before the Act. The Court further held that such a remedy is available only to identifiable victims of that discrimination.

20. In *American Tobacco Co. v. Patterson* (1982), the U.S. Supreme Court expanded and resolved some unanswered questions in *Teamsters*. In *American Tobacco*, the Court explicitly stated that a seniority system that does not intend to discriminate is protected under Section 703(h), despite whether it was adopted before or after the effective date of Title VII. In the same year the Court issued *Pullman-Standard v. Swint* (1982), where the Court reaffirmed its decision in *American Tobacco*.

21. The Court's criteria were actually the basis for *James v. Stockham Valves and Fittings Co.* (1977). The *James* court, in essence, refined the standards set forth by the *Teamsters* Court. See *Teamsters* (1977) at 1865.

22. The 1984 case referred to here is *Memphis v. Stotts*, which will be discussed later in the text. The 1989 case is *Lorance v. AT&T*, where the U.S. Supreme Court not only reaffirmed *Teamsters*, but also ruled that challenges to a seniority system must be brought within 300 days of its adoption. See, in particular, Justice Marshall's dissent in *Lorance* at 4657.

23. It should be noted that this case was brought under Sections 1981 and 1983 of 42 U.S.C. as well as Title VII.

24. It should also be noted that the union here supported the use of affirmative action in layoffs. The motivation of the union's support is not clear from the legal record. One might assume that minorities represented a reasonable and perhaps vocal constituency. In any event, the union support is worth noting.

25. The plaintiffs also initially filed under Title VII, but these charges were dismissed on cross motions for summary judgment.

26. It is important to see each ruling, however, because approaches to law are different under the Constitution as compared to Title VII. For example, a "strict scrutiny" test must be met under the Constitution. See Nalbandian (1989) and the Supreme Court's recent ruling in *City of Richmond v. Croson Company* (1989).

27. In its 1989 *Lorance v. AT&T* decision, the U.S. Supreme Court again said that if a seniority system is bona fide, it is legal under Title VII, despite its adverse impact on women and minorities. This case, however, involved the demotion, not layoff, of women at an AT&T plant.

28. See, for example, *Lorance v. AT&T* (1989), *supra* note 27.

References

Aaron, Benjamin. "The Duty of Fair Representation: An Overview." In Jean T. McKelvey (ed.), *The Duty of Fair Representation*. Ithaca, New York: New York State School of Industrial and Labor Relations, Cornell University, 1977:8-24.

————."Unfair Labor Practices and the Right to Strike in the Public Sector: Has the National Labor Relations Act Been a Good Model?" *Stanford Law Review* 38 (1986), 4:1097-1122.

Albemarle Paper Co. v. Moody 95 S.Ct. 2362, 422 U.S. 405 (1975).

Allen v. Butz 390 F. Supp 836 (E.D. Pa. 1975).

Allen v. Seattle Police Officers' Guild 645 P.2d 1113 (Wash. App. 1982).

Allen v. Seattle Police Officers' Guild 670 P.2d 246 (Wash. 1983).

American Tobacco Co. v. Patterson 102 S.Ct. 1534, 456 U.S. 63 (1982).

Boston Chapter, NAACP v. Beecher and Boston Firefighters and Boston Police Patrolmen's Association 679 F.2d 965 (1st Cir. 1982).

Bowen v. U.S. Postal Service 103 S. Ct. 588, 459 U.S. 212 (1983).

Bradburn, Pamela G. "Protection of Employees: The Duty of Fair Representation." *Public Sector Labor Law* 1 (Gonzaga Special Report), 1980:145-158.

Brown v. General Services Administration 96 S.Ct. 1961, 425 U.S. 820 (1976).

Brown v. Neeb and Fire Fighters Local Union 92 644 F.2d 551 (6th Cir. 1981).

City of Richmond v. Croson Company 57 *Law Week* 4132, January 24, 1989.

Congressional Record, vol. 110, 1964.

Fine, Howard F. "Plant Seniority and Minority Employees: Title VII's Effect on Layoffs." *University of Colorado Law Review* 47 (1975), 1:73-113.

Firefighters Local No. 93 v. Cleveland 106 S.Ct. 3063, _U.S._ (1986).

Firefighters Local Union No. 1784 v. Stotts, Memphis v. Stotts 104 S.Ct. 2576, 467 U.S. 561 (1984).

Ford v. University of Montana 598 P.2d 604 (1979).

Fossum, John A. *Labor Relations: Development, Structure and Process.* Dallas, Texas: Business Publications, Inc., 1982.

Franks v. Bowman Transportation Co. 495 F.2d 398 (5th Cir. 1974), *rev'd and remanded,* 96 S.Ct. 1251, 424 U.S. 747 (1976).

Fulenwider v. Firefighters Assn. Local Union 1784 649 S.W. 2d 268 (1982).

Golden v. Local 55, Firefighters 633 F. 2d 817 (9th Cir. 1980).

Goodman v. Lukens Steel Co. 107 S.Ct. 2617, _U.S._ (1987).

Griggs v. Duke Power Co. 91 S. Ct. 849, 401 U.S. 424 (1971).

International Brotherhood of Teamsters v. United States 97 S.Ct. 1843, 431 U.S. 324 (1977).

James v. Stockham Valves & Fittings Co. 394 F. Supp. 434 (N.D. Ala. 1975), *rev'd and remanded,* 559 F.2d 310 (5th Cir. 1977), *cert. denied,* 98 S.Ct. 767, 434 U.S. 1034 (1978).

Jennings v. American Postal Workers Union 672 F.2d 712 (8th Cir. 1982).

Jersey Central Power & Light Co. v. I.B.E.W. 508 F.2d 687 (3d Cir. 1975).

Johnson v. Transportation Agency, Santa Clara County, California 107 S. Ct. 1442, _U.S._ (1987).

Karahalios v. National Federation of Federal Employees 57 *Law Week* 4311, March 7, 1989.

Kearney, Richard C. *Labor Relations in the Public Sector.* New York: Marcel Dekker, Inc., 1984.

Local 12 United Rubber Workers v. NLRB 368 F.2d 12 (5th Cir. 1966).

Lorance v. AT&T 57 *Law Week* 4654, June 13, 1989.

McKelvey, Jean T. (ed.). *The Changing Law of Fair Representation.* Ithaca, New York: New York State School of Industrial and Labor Relations, Cornell University, 1985.

Moore v. City of San Jose 615 F.2d 1265 (9th Cir. 1980).

Nalbandian, John. "The U.S. Supreme Court's 'Consensus' on Affirmative Action." *Public Administration Review* 49 (1989), 1:38-45.

Newbold v. U.S. Postal Service 614 F.2d 46 (5th Cir. 1980), *cert. denied,* 101 S.Ct. 225, 449 U.S. 878 (1980).

Newman, Harold R. "The Duty in the Public Sector." In Jean T. McKelvey (ed.), *The Changing Law of Fair Representation.* Ithaca, New York: New York State School of Industrial and Labor Relations, Cornell University, 1985:85–92.

Papermakers, Local 189 v. United States 416 F.2d 980 (5th Cir. 1969), *cert. denied,* 90 S.Ct. 926, 397 U.S. 919 (1970).

Pullman-Standard v. Swint 102 S.Ct. 1781, 456 U.S. 273 (1982).

Quarles v. Philip Morris, Inc. 279 F. Supp. 505 (E.D. Va. 1968).

Reynolds, Stacia E. "*Allen v. Seattle Police Officers' Guild:* Duty of Fair Representation Extended to Locally Certified Unions." *Willamette Law Review* 20 (1984), 3:593-598.

Riccucci, Norma M. and Carolyn Ban. "The Unfair Labor Practice Process as a Dispute-Resolution Technique in the Public Sector: The Case of New York State." *Review of Public Personnel Administration* 9 (1989), 2:51-67.

Roberts, Robert N. "The Public Law Litigation Model and *Memphis v. Stotts.*" *Public Administration Review* 45 (1985), 4:527-532.

Rosenbloom, David H. and Jay M. Shafritz. *Essentials of Labor Relations.* Reston, Virginia: Reston Publishing Co., Inc., 1985.

Schell, George K.H. "Bona Fide Seniority Systems." *UCLA Law Review* 31 (1984), 4:886-920.

Shafritz, Jay M., Albert C. Hyde and David H. Rosenbloom. *Personnel Management in Government.* New York: Marcel Dekker, Inc., 1986.

Schlei, Barbara L. and Paul Grossman. *Employment Discrimination Law.* Washington, D.C.: Bureau of National Affairs, 1983, American Bar Association, 2d ed.

Sheet Metal Workers Local 28 v. EEOC 106 S.Ct. 3019, _U.S._ (1986).

Simon, David Offen. "Union Liability Under Title VII for Employer Discrimination." *The Georgetown Law Journal* 68 (1980), 4:959-987.

Sovern, Michael I. *Legal Restraints on Racial Discrimination in Employment.* New York: The Twentieth Century Fund, 1966.

Steele v. Louisville & Nashville Railroad Co. 65 S.Ct. 226, 323 U.S. 192 (1944).

Stotts v. Memphis Fire Dept. 679 F.2d 541 (6th Cir. 1982).

United Air Lines v. Evans 97 S.Ct. 1885, 431 U.S. 553 (1977).

United States v. Paradise 107 S.Ct. 1053, _U.S._ (1987).

United States v. T.I.M.E.-D.C., Inc. 6 FEP Cases 690 (1974).

Vaca v. Sipes 87 S.Ct. 903, 386 U.S. 171 (1967).

Volz, William H. and Joseph T. Breitenbeck."Comparable Worth and the Union's Duty of Fair Representation." *Employee Relations Law Journal* 10 (1984), 1:30-47.

Wallace Corp. v. National Labor Relations Board 65 S.Ct. 238, 323 U.S. 248 (1944).

Waters v. Wisconsin Steel Works 502 F.2d 1309 (7th Cir. 1974).

Watkins v. Steelworkers, Local 2369 369 F. Supp. 1221 (E.D. La. 1974), 516 F.2d 41 (5th Cir. 1975).

Willenborg, Eileen."Comparable Worth and Potential Union Liability for Wage Discrimination." *Women's Rights Law Reporter* 8 (1984), 1/2:133-150.

Wood, Stephen L. "Federal Employees, Federal Unions, and Federal Courts: The Duty of Fair Representation in the Federal Sector." *Chicago-Kent Law Review* 64 (1988), 1:271-334.

Wygant v. Jackson Board of Education 106 S.Ct. 1842, _U.S._ (1986).

4

WOMEN, MINORITIES, AND JOINT LABOR-MANAGEMENT COOPERATION

Joint labor-management cooperation is virtually becoming a staple of public sector labor relations, particularly as the general citizenry demands greater efficiency in the delivery of government services. It exists at every level of government and for a variety of purposes. Some committees are formed to specifically address productivity, while others attempt to solve problems of poor morale, unsafe working conditions and even cutback management. Whatever the purpose, the most important characteristic of cooperative efforts is the desire of labor and management to address a common need or to tackle a mutual problem for the ultimate benefit of both.

Perhaps the earliest and most well-known cooperative effort in the public sector was undertaken during the early days of the Tennessee Valley Authority (TVA), the government corporation formed in the 1930s for flood control and to generate electric power. The TVA and the Tennessee Valley Trades and Labor Council, representing craft workers, formed a cooperative committee to address several issues including productivity, improvement in quality of work and services, promotion of education and training, safeguarding health and increasing morale (National Center for Productivity and Quality of Working Life 1976). Today, joint committees at the TVA representing craft workers as well as white-collar workers (e.g., engineers and scientists) address similar types of concerns.

One area of joint labor-management cooperation that has not been explored in the public sector is equal employment opportunity/affirmative action (EEO/AA).[1] This chapter provides a preliminary examination of such cooperative efforts. Specifically, it is asked, Is EEO/AA a substantive focus of labor-management cooperation in the public sector? Should those unions that have made some effort to improve the employment status of women and minorities (e.g., in the area of comparable worth) rely on joint efforts to promote EEO/AA? Could cooperation over EEO/AA be useful even in those segments of public sector work forces where unions and management have a history of discrimination against women and minorities? For example, should we expect joint apprenticeship commit-tees (JACs), another type of labor-management cooperation, to promote EEO/AA given their negative attitudes and behaviors toward women and minorities? These issues will be addressed in the following sections, with particular emphasis given to the role of JACs in female's and minorities' attempts to gain entry into apprenticeship programs.

Joint Labor-Management EEO/AA Committees

We know very little about the pervasiveness of joint labor-management committees in the area of EEO/AA. Moreover, it would be extremely difficult to determine in any definitive sense the extent to which they exist in the public sector, because for one thing, committees may not be labeled "EEO" or "EEO/AA," yet they may either directly or indirectly address the issues. Nonetheless, it would be beneficial to examine the usefulness of EEO/AA committees in general and also the workings of at least a sample of such committees in order to get an idea of their feasibility as well as their effectiveness.

How Desirable and Useful Is Cooperation over EEO/AA?

Joint labor-management cooperation in any area may be desirable to unions whose scope of bargaining is limited by statutory or case law. In fact, this may be one of the overall advantages of cooperation in the public as compared to private sector. Many private sector unions have long argued that labor-management cooperation can usurp the bargaining process and can result in the co-optation of unions. This argument certainly has some merit particularly if management seeks to place critical issues such as wages and terms and conditions of employment in a cooperative rather than adversarial setting. But, if we consider the fact that many public sector unions cannot legally bargain over these issues, cooperation provides unions with some access to them. In this sense, a union's scope of bargaining would be widened.

Addressing EEO/AA cooperatively may actually expand the scope of bargaining of both public and private sector unions, since, with the exception of some professions (e.g., the skilled crafts), EEO/AA policy is devised unilaterally by the employer.[2] As such, cooperation provides unions with an opportunity to participate in the development and sometimes implementation of an issue that they would otherwise not have access to. For unions that support EEO/AA, for whatever reason, the benefits of cooperation seem obvious. There may also be benefits to cooperation even when unions are apathetic, but not resistant, to EEO/AA.

As the population of women and minorities in certain government departments and agencies grows, unions, even if not genuinely interested in EEO/AA, can demonstrate their commitment to these groups by becoming involved in joint programs. This can have a positive effect on a union's relationship with its constituents, which can ultimately bolster union membership and, hence, strength.

For unions that oppose EEO/AA, cooperation may simply be unrealistic. Cooperation over EEO/AA works only when it is perceived as being integrative as compared to distributive. The latter refers to situations where labor and management are in conflict over a certain issue and a win to one party represents a loss to the other. Integrative bargaining is marked by mutual gains or a win-win situation for labor and management. The parties see an issue or problem as a common concern and, hence, work together toward its solution (Walton and McKersie 1965).

EEO/AA would be viewed as distributive if, for example, management favored a strong affirmative action program but a union saw that as a threat to its goal of advancing the interests of its white male constituency. This is often the case in the protective services, for example, where management, usually under threat of a lawsuit, is willing to advance affirmative action goals. EEO/AA under such circumstances becomes a source of conflict and, hence, threatening to the union. The upshot is that the union would be unwilling to cooperate over this issue. It seems that some unions may never see EEO/AA as an integrative issue, no matter how the benefits are presented and, therefore, will vehemently oppose any effort, cooperative or not, in this area.

Then, addressing EEO/AA cooperatively, rather than adversarially, may be useful in *some* situations even if EEO/AA is not viewed as a priority by one of the parties. In situations where either one or both parties are willing to circumvent EEO/AA policies, however, and unions in particular have the power to do so, it would be unreasonable to expect the parties to cooperate over EEO/AA. This issue will receive more attention later when joint apprenticeship committees (JACs) are discussed.

A Cursory Review of Some Joint EEO/AA Committees

Collective bargaining contracts in the public sector at every level of government may call for some form of joint EEO/AA committee. For example, in 1979, some 30 percent of over 3,000 federal labor contracts called for the formation of "EEO Committees" (Sulzner 1982). As of 1988, some 34 percent of approximately 2,261 federal agreements provided for the creation of such committees (LAIRS 1988). It should be stressed at the outset, however, that unless money is appropriated to support committee staff and activities, the existence of such contract clauses does not guarantee that the parties are actually working, jointly or otherwise, toward the achievement of affirmative action and equal employment opportunity. In general, contract clauses are not always a good indication of union behavior.

A good example of this can be seen in "antidiscrimination" clauses, which most public and private sector unions have negotiated at least since passage of the Civil Rights Act. These clauses typically pledge union support for EEO, that is, the elimination of discrimination on the basis of race, color, religion, sex and national origin. Needless to say, many unions have continued to discriminate against women and minorities, despite the presence of such clauses in their labor contracts. The existence of antidiscrimination clauses in many cases has served as a defense mechanism or gesture of good faith in the event a union was accused of discrimination. And, so, they cannot be relied upon as a reflection of the attitudes and behaviors of unions toward women and minorities.

The same can be said for contract clauses establishing joint EEO/AA committees. It should also be noted that such contract clauses become particularly questionable when we consider contractual provisions on seniority. That is, even those unions that have bargained for EEO/AA committees will continue to strongly promote the use of seniority in employment decisions, thereby counteracting EEO/AA efforts. This is not to say, of course, that these unions oppose EEO (and perhaps AA), but rather that they are unwilling to shift their priorities. With these caveats, examples of contract language calling for EEO/AA committees and the variance in committee structure and operation are presented.[3]

As noted earlier, many labor-management committees are created not solely for EEO/AA, but will address this issue as one function. For example, a Joint Cooperative Improvement Committee of a National Federation of Federal Employees (NFFE) local and the Farmers Home Administration (FHA) was established to address improvements in working conditions and personnel practices. Some of the functions of the Committee include reducing absenteeism, promoting employee productivity and morale, improving supervisor-employee communications, as well as promoting EEO.

Other contracts will call for cooperation in the area of at least EEO, but will not actually establish a committee to oversee the cooperative efforts. For example, a contract between a local of the NFFE and the General Services Administration (GSA) reads:

The Employer and the Union agree to cooperate in providing equal employment opportunity for all persons. . . . The Parties agree that the Employer's Affirmative Action program will be administered in accordance with law, rules, and government-wide regulations. The Union agrees to become a positive force in this endeavor and to work with the Employer in the exploration and implementation of ideas and programs by which equal employment opportunity will be achieved.

Interestingly, some contracts call for committees but they set either ambiguous meeting schedules or never establish a schedule at all. For example, the EEO Advisory Committee between the National Treasury Employees Union (NTEU) and the Financial Management Service of the Treasury Department states that the committee "shall meet bimonthly each calendar year." However, "[i]f there is no agenda [for the meeting], the Chairperson shall generally cancel the meeting."

A contract between an American Federation of Government Employees (AFGE) local and the Altus Air Force Base, Altus, Oklahoma is even less specific. It states that the Equal Employment Opportunity Advisory Committee "will meet upon call of the Chair*man*" [emphasis added].

While many joint committees address only EEO, some will address AA as well. There is variance, however, in the extent to which the committees actually address concrete issues of affirmative action such as goals and timetables. For example, the Federal Energy Regulatory Commission (FERC) and a local of the AFGE have established an EEO Committee that does not set goals and timetables but at least "reviews the goals established by the FERC Affirmative Action Plan and their effectiveness."

Thus far, only joint cooperation at the federal level has been discussed but joint labor-management EEO/AA committees are also contractually called for at the state and local levels of government. A contract between the State of Minnesota and the Minnesota Association of Professional Employees, for example, provides for a joint Affirmative Action Committee which "meet[s] as determined by the parties to discuss issues of mutual concern."

Contracts between New York State and two major employee unions, the Civil Service Employees Association (CSEA) and the Public Employees Federation (PEF), call for joint Affirmative Action Advisory Committees "which shall develop appropriate recommendations on matters of mutual interest in the areas of equal employment and affirmative action." Importantly, these committees tend to be agency-specific rather than statewide. Unlike statewide committees in New York State such as the Committee on Work Environment and Productivity (CWEP), agency-specific committees carry no dollar appropriations.

As noted earlier, cooperation can sometimes expand the scope of bargaining for public sector labor unions. It has been very common for some unions legally prohibited from negotiating over wages to work cooperatively with employers in developing wage systems that are based on comparable worth. This is the case with the Maine State Employees Association (MSEA) which, as will be seen in Chapter 6, is forbidden by law to bargain over such issues as job classification. In an effort to address comparable worth, a common concern to both parties, the MSEA and the state of Maine formed a labor-management committee. This committee is responsible for progress in the area of comparable worth, an area that might not have been addressed without a cooperative endeavor.

A unique form (indeed, "model") of cooperation over EEO/AA is occurring in an educational sector of New York State. The state along with the United University Professions (UUP), which represents university professors and professionals throughout the State University of New York (SUNY) system, have established a joint Affirmative Action Committee responsible for developing ways to recruit, promote and retain women, minorities, disabled persons and Vietnam-era veterans.

The Committee was first negotiated for in the 1985-1988 contract in response to a mutually agreed-upon need to step up affirmative action efforts. Over $550,000 was appropriated for Committee staff and activities. A major portion of that was allocated to the most ambitious project of the Committee thus far, the Dr. Nuala McGann Drescher Affirmative Action Leave Program, which provides those faculty and professional staff who are protected class members with either a one semester or a full year leave of absence at full pay.

The program is specifically aimed at retention of these persons. The rationale for a leave program comes from the tendency to overtax protected class persons with various service commitments. Because these groups constitute a relatively small percentage of the University's population, they are spread thin by requests to serve on (often as tokens) various university, departmental or college committees. Such work is important in tenure decisions, but "service" is only one criterion. A more important criterion is "research," which women and minorities are called away from when they are asked to serve on, or involuntarily placed on, committees. (Even when asked to serve on a committee, the untenured female or minority faculty member usually has no choice but to accept since the requests come from one's superiors or tenured colleagues, the persons that ultimately make tenure decisions.)

It might be questioned at this point, what the union's motives were in agreeing to establish a joint Affirmative Action Committee, given that women and minorities comprise a relatively small percentage of UUP's bargaining unit (about 28 percent).[4] Notwithstanding this low percentage, there was in fact an element of pragmatism in the union's willingness to establish the affirmative action committee.

The union was responding to the demands of women and minorities, whose population at this point in time was actually growing at the four-year colleges of the SUNY system. By strongly articulating their demands, these groups mobilized themselves into a notable power base. Many union leaders recognized the viability of this power base and, therefore, were willing to push for affirmative action in the form of a joint committee. Thus, despite the overall low percentage of women and minority faculty, their presence as a strong, active and *vocal* constituency encouraged the union to respond to their needs.

There were many union leaders who opposed and continue to oppose not the Committee itself, but the programs of the Committee, especially the affirmative action leave program. Moreover, there has been some resistance to the leave program by some white male faculty members who feel slighted.

The union has not publicly responded to such opposition. Importantly, however, the union does, through other joint programs, make money available to senior faculty members, who tend to be white males. This may represent one response to the opposition. On the other hand, perhaps the opposition, at least publicly stated, from university faculty may not be that great. This may relate to a unique aspect of labor relations at SUNY. That is, this set of university professors may find it politically imprudent to publicly protest programs that benefit women and minorities. As such, white male faculty are unwilling to pressure the union into opposing the affirmative action leave program or related activities and, so, it is unlikely that the union will withdraw its support for affirmative action.

A recent polling of the bargaining unit indicates overwhelming support, at least from women, minorities and liberal factions among the university faculty and professional staff, for the continuation of the joint Affirmative Action Committee and its programs. The state and UUP negotiated a new contract in 1988 and, in response to these articulated demands, both parties asked for additional monies to support the Committee. A little over $1 million was allocated to the Committee for the next three years. In addition, the union also won about $1 million to support activities that would benefit and appease white male professors and professionals.[5] The union's desire to respond to the needs of its female and minority constituents will inevitably be strategically balanced against the union's ability to represent its white male constituents.

These are just a few examples of cooperative efforts in the public sector. It seems that those unions interested in appealing to their female and minority constituents would make a greater effort to establish joint ventures with employers, particularly if their scope of bargaining is narrow (e.g., federal sector unions). Such an appeal would demonstrate that the union is actively pursuing EEO and AA, which would ultimately impress upon incumbent women and minorities.

Thus far, cooperative efforts designed specifically for EEO/AA have been addressed. Of greater significance, however, is how other forms of cooperation will not only deliberately thwart affirmative action measures but also result in overt or covert discrimination against women and minorities. The cooperative efforts referred to here are apprenticeship programs that are run either jointly by labor and management or unilaterally by unions. There is, in fact, a long history of discrimination by at least private sector unions against women and minorities seeking entry into the skilled crafts via apprenticeship training. As such, an examination of cooperative EEO/AA efforts must look at the practices of unions in the area of apprenticeships.

Joint Apprenticeship Programs/Committees

One of the more unique forms of labor-management cooperation can be seen in the area of apprenticeships. It is unusual insofar as the benefits produced by the cooperation are extremely tangible (i.e., actual jobs), which is also a reflection of the power possessed by the groups that run apprenticeship programs. As will be seen in the following sections, apprenticeship programs have been in existence in the private sector for some time but they are relatively new to the public sector scene for a variety of reasons.

It should be noted that apprenticeship programs are in some instances conducted unilaterally by employers, but in other cases are administered by JACs representing both labor and management. This holds true for the public and private sectors. A unique aspect of JACs in the private sector, however, is that unions generally have unilateral control on a de facto basis. Union control is most vigorously exerted over entry into apprenticeships. Overall, unions do not seem to have this sort of absolute control in the public sector. As will be seen later, this is an important point in the examination of barriers to women and minorities in apprenticeship programs.

It may be useful to begin with some general information about the history and operation of apprenticeship programs. In addition, an overview of apprenticeships in the private sector and the role of unions will be discussed to provide a backdrop for an examination of the operation and practices of apprenticeship programs and JACs in the public sector.

Historical Overview of Apprenticeships

Apprenticeship is a system of training for the well-paying, skilled crafts or trades. It combines anywhere from one to six years on-the-job training under the supervision of an experienced craft or journey worker with classroom study so that the "apprentice" can acquire the skill and knowledge associated with or needed for a particular craft (Joint Report 1976).

The tradition of apprenticeship was first transferred to America from England around 1619. Interestingly, it involved the indenturing of both boys and girls from almshouses of London to farm owners in America (Abbott 1938). The use of apprenticeships in this fashion made it virtually indistinguishable from the indentured servant system (New York State Commission Against Discrimination 1960), which, while important to America's economy, represented a system of employment for the lower classes.

This system that evolved in America did not really resemble apprenticeships in England, which were very prestigious and difficult to acquire. Since the Middle Ages, apprenticeship in England had been strictly regulated by customs and law. The responsibility for enforcement rested in artisan groups or guilds, which controlled standards, quality of work, and entry into the apprenticeship. Unlike in early America, this tightly run and closely monitored system resulted in a closed labor market with high craft wages (Rorabaugh 1986).

Guilds, the precursor to trade unions, were not very successful in organizing in America, and those that did organize were virtually powerless. Rural America, with its unique economy (largely agricultural) and not yet fully developed legal system, simply could not and would not support the existence of artisan groups.[6] This greatly altered the system of apprenticeships in America. As Rorabaugh (1986, 4-5) notes:

Since the American colonies had no guilds, the interlocking regulatory system that prevailed in England really did not exist in the colonies. In America anyone could call himself a master artisan, and any such artisan could take an apprentice. If he took an apprentice, and if the apprentice was legally bound, then English law governed the terms. But there was no guild to guarantee that the apprentice was trained in the trade.

As the American economy shifted, apprenticeship further evolved. For one thing, it became more closely guarded by fathers and master artisans (i.e., employers) who passed skilled crafts on to their sons and apprentices. Rorabaugh (1986, 33) notes that "[s]ecret family recipes, passed from generation to generation orally, enabled a family to gain a reputation and to retain an exclusive control of production that was better than any patent." In addition, as guilds (or unions) became more powerful, systematically, around the late 1800s, early 1900s, greater control was exerted over standards, in particular over entry into apprenticeships. As such, apprenticeship in America was on its way to becoming a closed, lucrative system of employment.

By its very definition, any closed system excludes certain persons or groups. The most obvious and socially acceptable groups to be excluded from apprenticeships were women and minorities. It is interesting to note, however, that in the early days, women were sometimes allowed to break tradition and enter either apprenticeship programs or the actual trade when master artisans stood to benefit financially. For example, employers brought women into such trades as shoemaking, cigar making and silk weaving in an effort to break or bust unions, thereby lowering craft wages. This ultimately enabled employers to invest in machinery that curtailed the need for skilled labor altogether and, at the same time, further cut labor costs (Cowan 1979; Levine 1979; Baker 1964).

Slaves were also exploited in a similar vein. In fact, in the South, slavery produced its own form of artisanship, where slaves were taught crafts by their owners so that craft work could be done on the owner's property. This eliminated slave owners' dependence on expensive outside labor (Rowan and Rubin 1972; Spero and Harris 1968). Rorabaugh (1986, 177) notes that the "[owner] encouraged artisanship among his slaves because it increased their productivity, and hence his wealth, and because it made the slave more valuable."

Today, apprenticeship programs are an extremely exclusive system of employment for white men. As noted earlier, the exclusivity became more pronounced as trade unions began to gain more control over apprenticeships. Women and minorities continue to be underrepresented in or excluded from apprenticeship programs and, consequently, the crafts or industries all together.

Table 4.1 presents the percentage of female and minority apprentices in the U.S. for 1978, 1979 and 1987. It is important to note that 1979 is the last year for which the Equal Employment Opportunity Commission (EEOC) provides data in summary form on female and minority apprentices. The official reason for this is lack of funding. The 1987 data, which is not as comprehensive, comes from the Bureau of Apprenticeship and Training (BAT), the agency within the Department of Labor that is authorized by the National Apprenticeship (Fitzgerald) Act of 1937 to oversee apprenticeship programs registered with the Labor Department.

As the data show, women in particular are not well represented in apprenticeship programs, where in 1987, they constituted only 6.2 percent of the total apprenticeships in this country. This is extremely low when compared to the percentage of women in the working-age population. Moreover, the rate of admission was extremely low for 1978 and 1979. Only 3.7 percent of the female applicants in 1978 and 6.4 percent in 1979 were actually admitted to apprenticeship programs.

On the whole, the data look slightly better for minority males,[7] especially when compared to minorities in the working-age population; but a closer look at the record shows a different picture. For example, the admittance rate of minority males into apprenticeships was only 11.3 percent in 1978 and increased to 14.2 percent in 1979; but, importantly,

Table 4.1 Female and Minority Apprentices in the United States, 1978, 1979, 1987

	1978*		1979*		1987**	
	Women %	Male Minorities %	Women %	Male Minorities %	Women %	Minorities %
Applicants	40,839 (9.9)	86,820 (21.1)	37,205 (10.1)	71,068 (19.3)	---	---
Dropouts	979 (4.8)	5,005 (24.3)	1,601 (7.2)	5,317 (23.8)	---	---
Graduates	539 (1.8)	4,837 (16.0)	783 (2.8)	4,768 (17.0)	---	---
Apprentices	5,506 (3.7)	27,989 (18.7)	8,878 (5.0)	31,221 (17.7)	14,321 (6.2)	45,429 (19.6)
Rate of Admission	3.7	11.3	6.4	14.2	---	---
Percent in Population***	41.7	12.3	42.1	12.4	44.2****	13.4****

*SOURCE: EEOC Reports. *Minorities and Women in Apprenticeship Programs and Referral Unions.* 1978, 1979.

**SOURCE: U.S. Department of Labor, Bureau of Apprenticeship and Training, December 1987. Includes only those programs registered with the BAT and does not include data from California, Washington, D.C., Puerto Rico, Hawaii, Rhode Island and Virgin islands. These data are not separated by race and sex, so there is some overlap in the categories (i.e., "women" includes women of color; "minorities" includes women of color).

***SOURCE: *Statistical Abstract of the U.S.,* 1987, Bureau of the Census. This includes all persons in labor force. These data are not separated by race and sex, so there is overlap in the categories.

****1985 data.

there was a drop in minority male applicants from 1978 to 1979, accompanied by an increase in dropouts and a decrease in graduates from apprenticeship programs (see raw numbers). This suggests that minority males may not have been recruited as heavily in 1979, and less effort may have been given to the retention of minorities once admitted to apprenticeships.

It is also important to emphasize that the data in Table 4.1 represent aggregate figures for the entire United States. As such, they fail to reveal that minority males are disproportionately represented in less-skilled (hence, less prestigious) traditionally nonwhite crafts. For example, minority males represented as high as 47.9 percent of the cement mason apprentices in 1979 and as low as 7.5 percent of the stone worker apprentices for the same year.

The same disparities hold true for women, who comprised as high as 17.5 percent of the baker apprentices and as low as 0.6 percent of the autobody repair apprentices in 1979. Thus, a closer look at the picture seems to indicate that women and minorities are more apt to be found in apprenticeship programs that may be deemed traditionally female and minority. As will be discussed later, without more comprehensive and reliable data on female and minority apprentices, the ability to monitor their progress and address the problem of underrepresentation is severely hindered.

The obstacles that women and minorities face as they seek entry into apprenticeship programs can be attributed in part to the practices and policies of unions. What follows is a discussion of some of the general barriers that have prevented female and minority accession to apprenticeship programs. A separate section on the exclusionary practices and policies of unions is then presented, given the direct or indirect power that unions possess in operating apprenticeship programs.

General Barriers That Women and Minorities Face in Entering Apprenticeships

Despite legislation at the federal level[8] as well as state level[9] mandating equality of opportunity and, in some cases, affirmative action, women and minorities have experienced many obstacles to entry into apprenticeships. For example, perhaps one of the main criteria for gaining entry into an apprenticeship program is to have a relative, friend or neighbor in the craft to support the application (Rust-Tierney 1984; Marshall and Briggs 1968; Kursh 1965). In simple terms, apprenticeships are characterized by a form of nepotism, which hinders the ability of women and minorities to gain access to apprenticeships.

Apprenticeship openings are not usually made public. Rather, they are communicated by word-of-mouth and craft workers convey openings in this fashion to family and friends. In effect, women and minorities are deprived of the information regarding vacancies and, hence, are unable to bid for them. They simply do not have access to the network which leads to apprenticeship opportunities and ultimately marketable, well-paying skilled craft jobs. The system, in this sense, becomes one based on "inbreeding," where white males sponsor and endorse other white males.

If women and minorities do become aware of openings (usually through government-sponsored programs or community groups), they often face other obstacles. For example, apprenticeship openings are sometimes restricted to particular job units or job titles (e.g., semi-skilled) which tend to be dominated by white males. Thus, women and minorities may be aware of the openings but are not eligible to apply because they do not meet certain entrance criteria.

Another obstacle that women and minorities face is rooted in socialization. For women, this refers to sex-role stereotyping, where they are not socialized to consider apprenticeships as a career option (Rust-Tierney 1984; Briggs 1974). Moreover, unlike young boys, they are not trained in early childhood to develop the skills needed to enter apprenticeship programs. For example, young women are not encouraged to become familiar with such "male" chores as fixing cars, painting, building, and so forth. This places women at a disadvantage since entering an apprenticeship program often requires minimal knowledge of certain tools and their functions in a particular trade. In this sense, young women are ultimately deprived the opportunity to develop the "pre-apprenticeship" skills needed for entry.

Socialization is also a hindrance for racial minorities. It is manifested more as a product of institutionalized segregation and discrimination. More clearly, the exclusion of minorities is so institutionalized in our society that the hopes and aspirations of minorities, in particular young minorities, to enter apprenticeships can only be dampened. In effect, although the circumstances are different, minorities, like women, are not socialized to consider apprenticeships as a career option. Marshall and Briggs (1968, 16-17) succinctly make the point that the "aspirations of [black] youngsters were conditioned by the realities of the situation they faced, and the occasional [black] who attempted to crack the [apprenticeship] system faced such overwhelming odds that few of them tried it, and few of their parents or [school] counselors encouraged them to do so."

These factors as well as others[10] work against women and minorities seeking apprenticeships. But perhaps the most salient obstacle has been and continues to be the practices and policies of labor unions. In fact, union policies are often the source of some of the factors discussed above (e.g., the promotion of nepotism). As such, the obstacles that unions present deserve special attention.

Unions as a Barrier to Women and Minorities

It seems widely recognized that unions are the primary barrier blocking the entrance of women and minorities into apprenticeships (Rust-Tierney 1984; Jackson and Fossum 1976; Rowan and Rubin 1972; Marshall and Briggs 1968).[11] Unions at least in the private sector exercise a good deal of control over entry standards either through JACs or acting on their own.[12] No matter how an individual learns of an apprenticeship opening, it is generally unions that develop selection criteria and tests or that are responsible for nominating individuals to apprenticeship programs (Kursh 1965). Experience tells us that unions do not nominate or select women or minorities, and the entrance tests they devise tend to adversely affect them.

The typical scenario is this: in order to secure a job in a particular craft, one must be a union member;[13] in order to become a union member, one must successfully complete an apprenticeship; in order to secure an apprenticeship, one must apply to the union or a JAC, which will very likely be controlled by the union. The upshot is that if the union excludes certain groups from apprenticeships, it effectively excludes them from the craft altogether.

It should be noted that apprentices may also be selected from existing employee rosters. When this is the case, however, the rosters are typically based on union-negotiated contract clauses that give preference to senior workers, who tend to be white males. In addition, for many trades, management may be represented on the JAC that controls apprenticeship entry but will often defer to, or acquiesce to, union practices.[14] In effect, "the union choice of an apprentice may be accepted by management without reference to formal procedures" (New York State Commission Against Discrimination 1960, 89).

The wide latitude explicitly or implicitly granted to unions in the operation and administration of apprenticeship programs has severely hindered the employment opportunities of women and minorities. As Dubinsky (1973, 29) points out, "[t]he power of the union to issue certification of union journey[person] status and make job referrals gives the leadership great power and autonomy [which works against] local groups or individuals outside the union who seek training, certification, and employment."

As implied in the discussion of Table 4.1, the discriminatory practices of unions seem to vary from craft to craft. For example, at one extreme is the United Steelworkers of America, which has demonstrated some support for blacks in apprenticeship training. The 1979 landmark case, *United Steelworkers v. Weber*, illustrates this support.

In the early 1970s, the United Steelworkers and Kaiser Aluminum and Chemical Corporation recognized a racial imbalance in the corporation's craft work force. In an effort to reduce that imbalance, the union and Kaiser bargained for an affirmative action plan to cover fifteen Kaiser plants. The plan called for an apprenticeship or on-the-job training (OJT) program to prepare unskilled production workers—both white and black—for craft jobs. Fifty percent of the apprenticeships or trainee positions were reserved for blacks.

In its first year of operation, the plan was challenged by a white production worker, Brian Weber, whose bid for an apprenticeship at the Gramercy plant was rejected. When Weber learned that he was passed over by less senior black workers, he sued claiming that he had been discriminated against on the basis of his race in violation of Title VII of the Civil Rights Act of 1964. The U.S. Supreme Court ultimately ruled against Weber on the grounds that voluntary, race-conscious affirmative action programs developed by private parties are needed to eliminate past discriminatory employment practices and, as such, are legal under Title VII.

The pertinent part of the case is that this particular union was willing, for whatever reasons, to redress discriminatory practices in Kaiser's craft work force. This response, however, appears atypical. In particular, at the other extreme are sheet metal workers' unions which have one of the worst records of discrimination. Rowan and Rubin (1972, 15) point out that "the sheet metal workers probably rank first on the present discriminatory scale. Although there are variations locally, few organizations have stood so steadfastly throughout the country against increased opportunities for minorities."

Other craft unions may not overtly exclude protected class members but they will promote other practices indicating that women and minorities are not welcomed. For example, the trowel crafts—bricklaying, plastering, and cement finishing—have admitted blacks for years, but have placed them in segregated, inferior locals. The white locals tend to control the distribution of available work and have generally given the less desirable work assignments to blacks (Rowan and Rubin 1972). So, for example, minorities may constitute a relatively high percentage of cement mason apprenticeships, but the high representation would be deceptive if minorities were placed in segregated locals.

A discussion of the 1986 landmark U.S. Supreme Court decision *Sheet Metal Workers Int'l Assoc. Local 28 and Joint Apprenticeship Committee v. EEOC* might be useful here because it illustrates the pervasiveness and insidiousness of union/JAC discrimination against racial minorities. The formal case against the union local and JAC dates back to 1964 when the New York State Commission for Human Rights found that the union local and the JAC were illegally excluding blacks from apprenticeship programs. Among other things, the Commission found that the " 'admission to apprenticeship is conducted largely on a nepot[is]tic basis involving sponsorship by incumbent union members' " (*Sheet Metal Workers* 1986, 3025).

The Commission's findings were affirmed by the New York State Supreme Court, which directed the union and the JAC to cease and desist their discriminatory practices and develop more objective standards for apprenticeship selection. Despite additional legal challenges, the union and JAC refused to integrate racial minorities into apprenticeship programs and union membership.

This legal battle took an important turn in 1975 when a federal district court determined that the union and JAC "violated both Title VII and New York law by discriminating against nonwhite workers in recruitment, selection, training, and admission to the union" (*Sheet Metal Workers* 1986, 3026). Given the union's continued egregious discriminatory behaviors and repeated bad faith efforts to correct them, the court ordered a remedial membership goal of 29 percent to be reached by 1981. (The goal was based on the percentage of minorities in New York City's labor pool.)

In the court's examination of union/JAC treatment of racial minorities, several discriminatory practices in the administration of apprenticeship programs were discovered. Some of the practices included, for example, a high school diploma requirement and the use of an entrance exam, both of which adversely affected minorities and were not job related. Moreover, the court found that to ensure the exclusion of minorities, the union and JAC subsidized a special training program for friends and relatives that would assist them in passing the entrance exam.

The practices go beyond discrimination in apprenticeships, but are worth discussing because they point to the measures this white union was willing to take to exclude racial minorities from skilled craft jobs. For example, when the sheet metal workers' union was unable to furnish local contractors with the workers it needed, rather than allowing skilled minorities in the area access to membership in the union, the local recalled pensioners (i.e., retirees). In so doing, the union issued literally hundreds of temporary work permits to *nonmembers* in an effort to prevent minorities from entering the union and, hence, the craft jobs within the industry. What is particularly intriguing here is that the union was willing to induct nonmembers to fulfill contractors' employment demands, yet the union continually insists upon a closed shop arrangement, where only union *members* can secure jobs.

In a related effort, the union sought to meet employment needs by requesting temporary workers from sheet metal workers' locals all across the country, as well as from construction unions such as carpenters, plumbers and iron workers, rather than procure workers from a nearby sheet metal workers' local that was comprised of minorities. Once again, minorities were denied employment opportunities by the union local.

The court also found that Local 28 was in the practice of selectively organizing those nonunion shops that were primarily white. And, if those shops had some minorities, they were refused admission to the union and ultimately denied access to the lucrative jobs controlled by the local. In addition, the union refused to organize sheet metal workers in a nearby blowpipe industry because the workers were predominantly minority group members.

The case reached the U.S. Supreme Court on an appeal from the union and JAC, which refused to comply with the court-ordered membership goal on the grounds that it violated the rights of whites under Title VII. The union and JAC further argued that affirmative action can provide relief for only the actual victims of discrimination. The Court majority rejected the union's arguments and said that Title VII

does not prohibit a court from ordering, in appropriate circumstances, affirmative race-conscious relief as a remedy for past discrimination. Specifically, we hold that such relief may be appropriate where an employer or a labor union has engaged in persistent or egregious discrimination, or where necessary to dissipate the lingering effects of pervasive discrimination . . . [Title VII] does not say that a court may order relief only for the actual victims of past discrimination (*Sheet Metal Workers* 1986, 3034-35).[15]

There are several points that can be highlighted from this case. First and foremost relates to the absolute control certain craft unions can exercise over entry into apprenticeships and, hence, the craft. Even if a JAC is present, where presumably employer representatives participate in policy setting, unions will develop ways to usurp control and use their power to exclude minorities (as well as women) from the craft. Second, even if the union is willing to enforce its own apprenticeship standards (e.g., entrance test), it can and will ensure that friends and family of incumbent union members will meet those standards by providing them with pre-apprenticeship skills or training. These sorts of practices will continue to adversely affect women and minorities and deprive them of employment opportunities in the well-paying crafts.

Thus far, only the entry barriers set up by unions have been discussed. But unions, often through their rank-and-file, will continue discriminatory practices against women and minorities once such groups are able to gain access to the apprenticeship system. (This access often occurs with the help of government-sponsored outreach programs or the courts.) Sexist and racist remarks, for example, are an integral part of the apprenticeship culture; they are so ingrained that the incumbent craft workers view such remarks as harmless and *friendly* banter (Silver 1986). But these as well as other customs result in serious problems for women and minorities.

The apprenticeship system requires that apprentices work closely with and under the direct supervision of craft workers. It is unreasonable to expect female and minority apprentices to successfully complete an apprenticeship if, day after day, they must withstand resentment and belligerence from the very persons they must depend upon to succeed. Rust-Tierney (1984, 231) points out that "[h]azing and sexual harassment by co-workers and supervisors is a major problem for women. At a conference of over 300 tradeswomen from the Midwestern states, hazing and harassment were . . . often cited as the reason many women did not complete their apprenticeship programs."

In addition to the overt harassment, women are often forced out of apprenticeships by the "patronizing and condescending orientation" of men (Silver 1986, 117). This stems from male craft workers' views that women are inexperienced, physically helpless, and in constant need of assistance from male craft workers. Interestingly, while women are patronized and harassed for supposedly being physically *incapable* of performing craft work, minority males are harassed because they are perceived as being physically *able* to perform this type of work. It would seem that the issue of who is suitable for craft work does not necessarily revolve around the experience and physical capabilities of apprentices, but rather race and sex.

Union involvement here can take many forms. Perhaps the most obvious is a union's refusal or failure to act and respond to the grievances of women and minorities. Support and protection from unions is critical in the apprenticeship system. Without it, women and minorities will either become so discouraged that they drop out of the apprenticeship program or they turn to outside bodies such as the courts for assistance. This latter alternative may be viable, but it could also fuel resistance from craft workers and their unions, the very groups that women and minorities must rely upon to successfully complete the apprenticeship.

In sum, unions represent a serious obstacle to women and minorities as they seek entry into, as well as retention in, apprenticeship programs. It should be stressed, however, that while this is well documented in the private sector, the practices and behaviors of unions in public sector apprenticeship programs are less well known. This may be due in part to the underutilization and, hence, limited knowledge of apprenticeship programs in the public sector, as will be seen in the following section.

Public Sector Apprenticeship Training

Apprenticeship programs until recently have not been very popular in the public sector. One of the primary reasons for this relates to the legacy of merit in the employment selection process. Since at least 1883 with the passage of the Pendleton Act, the use of "paper and pencil" merit exams has been highly valued in determining who is qualified for public sector employment. Given this tradition, apprenticeships have been viewed as a threat to merit because, although written entrance exams are sometimes required, the true measure of qualifications comes during the apprenticeship and, in particular, upon graduation.

Perhaps another reason that apprenticeship training has not been very popular in the public sector is that government is often more interested in training workers only for specialized tasks—required for some particular government operation—rather than developing well-rounded craft workers. As Marshall and Briggs (1968, 5) point out, "[government] employers are more interested in flexibility of [human resources] utilization across several craft lines."

A related and deeper concern involves retention of apprenticeship graduates. An apprenticeship program that is either registered or at least eligible for registration by the federal Bureau of Apprenticeship and Training (BAT) or a State Apprenticeship Council (SAC)[16] will not only afford a sense of prestige and status to graduates but will also offer immense mobility. As Marshall and Briggs (1968, 8) note,

[t]he graduate of a registered apprentice program knows that his [or her] training is a passport to jobs all over the country; his [or her] certificate of completion attests to the acquisition of certain minimum standards. The [apprentice] who successfully completes his [or her] apprenticeship therefore acquires a certain status in [the] trade and possesses a certain identification with others who have had similar experiences.

In this sense, the government employer would be enhancing the marketability of its apprenticeship graduates to ultimately create competition for itself. That is, the government sector in general has had a hard time competing for labor with private sector employers because of the difference in wage structures. While government employers can offer greater job security and stability, they will generally pay lower wages. Therefore, upon completion of apprenticeship training, the skilled craft worker may decide to leave government service for a better-paying job in the private sector. This may ultimately discourage some public sector employers from considering and actually developing apprenticeship programs.

Despite some of these disincentives, many government employers have been embracing the idea of apprenticeship training. This may be due in part to shifting attitudes of personnelists and human resources management specialists, who perceive that apprenticeship training poses no threat to merit but rather can augment it. In addition, they are acknowledging that apprenticeship programs are a viable, cost-effective way to produce qualified skilled craft workers. As such, apprenticeship programs, although still relatively small in most sectors, are slowly emerging at every level of government.

Table 4.2 presents aggregate data on the number and size (in terms of apprentices) of apprenticeship programs in the public sector. As the data show, state, local and federal programs represent only 3.4 percent of all programs in the United States and military programs constitute only 0.1 percent. Looking at the total number of apprentices shows a different picture at least for uniformed military programs, where 21.5 percent of the apprentices in this country are found. Only 7.2 percent of the apprentices are in state, local and federal programs.[17]

It would seem, then, that the largest programs in the public sector are at the federal level within the various military departments, that is, Navy, Army and Marines. In the tradition of encouraging persons to enter the military service by providing lucrative educational benefits, these departments run apprenticeship programs for crafts ranging from carpentry to firefighting. The programs lead to certification by the Department of Labor as journey person, which virtually assures a craft job in civilian life.

In general, the programs operate as those in the private sector. "Soldier-apprentices" complete a certain amount of hours of classroom study and on-the-job training (OJT) under the supervision of experienced

Table 4.2 Number and Size of Public Sector Apprenticeship Programs Registered with the BAT* or SACs** as of December 31, 1987***

	No. of Programs %	Total Apprentices %
State, Local and Federal Programs	1,069	16,690
	(3.4)	(7.2)
Military Programs (uniformed personnel)	17	49,613
	(.1)	(21.5)
All Programs (public and private)	29,776	230,615

SOURCE: Bureau of Apprenticeship and Training, U.S. Department of Labor, Washington, D.C., 1987.

*Bureau of Apprenticeship and Training
**State Apprenticeship Councils
***Excludes California, District of Columbia, Puerto Rico, Hawaii, Rhode Island and Virgin Islands. These are SAC states that have not yet agreed to submit apprenticeship data to the BAT.

journey persons, who themselves are either officers or enlisted persons. The OJT portion of the apprenticeship program for firefighting, for example, requires soldier apprentices to complete training in such areas as forcible entry (e.g., demonstrating use of forcible entry tools), rescue techniques, and ladder use. Classroom study consists of instruction in such courses as "Fire Truck Operation," "Fire Prevention Technician" and "Fire Protection Systems." Importantly, these programs are run unilaterally by the military; unions are not involved in any aspect of their operation.

Although on a much smaller scale, federal agencies other than the military also sponsor apprenticeship programs. For example, various federal prisons run apprenticeship programs for correctional officers. Also, the General Services Administration (GSA) provides apprenticeship training for some craft titles. Apprenticeship training is important in the GSA, which maintains a cadre of craft workers who are supplied to federal agencies as needed. (In addition, the GSA contracts out to the private sector to meet skilled craft needs that it cannot meet on its own.)

Several state and local governments have also instituted apprenticeship programs in recent years. Although not evident from Table 4.2, there is no one set way that the programs operate but there are some similarities. For example, one feature that seems to be common to many programs is that the apprenticeships cover only certain job titles in certain agencies. Many states including California, Washington, Maryland and Tennessee, for instance, sponsor apprenticeship training for firefighters, police and/or correctional officers.[18] Apprenticeship training may be important for these job titles, but they are virtually public-sector specific.

Other states may be even more specific in defining apprenticeship coverage. For example, Wisconsin runs an apprenticeship program for Electrical Highway Technicians in the Department of Transportation. Perhaps these restrictions address the concerns noted earlier regarding government's interest in limiting the scope of apprenticeship programs to ultimately ensure the retention of apprenticeship graduates.

Some states, to further ensure retention, require apprenticeship graduates to work for the state for a specific period of time. For example, the State of Delaware has launched an apprenticeship program for secretaries in the Department of Labor in an effort to address a serious labor shortage for this job title.[19] To ensure that the graduating secretaries do not immediately leave state service for better-paying jobs in the private sector, the state requires graduates to remain in state service for a minimum of 18 months. Those who leave before this time are required to reimburse the state for apprenticeship training costs.

Union participation in the operation of public sector apprenticeship programs seems to vary by program. Table 4.3 provides aggregate data on union involvement. In only 5.3 percent of the group programs and in 26.3

Table 4.3 Joint and Nonjoint Apprenticeship Programs in the Public Sector, Registered with the BAT or SACs as of December 31, 1987

	Group of Employers		Single Employer	
	Joint	Nonjoint	Joint	Nonjoint
	(Percentages)		(Percentages)	
State, Local and Federal Programs	57	12	281	719
	(5.3)	(1.1)	(26.3)	(67.3)
Military Programs	0	0	0	17
				(100)
All Programs (public and private)	4,161	615	2,973	22,027
	(14.0)	(2.1)	(10.0)	(74.0)

SOURCE: Bureau of Apprenticeship and Training, U.S. Department of Labor, Washington, D.C., 1987. (Excludes California, District of Columbia, Puerto Rico, Hawaii, Rhode Island and Virgin Islands.)

percent of the single-employer programs are unions involved through JACs. By comparison, almost 70 percent of the programs are run unilaterally by management. A similar pattern seems apparent in the private sector, but these data do not reflect that the majority of apprentices in the private sector are found in programs run jointly with unions. That is, the joint programs are much larger than the nonjoint programs, which in most cases will offer a very small number of apprenticeships. This is not the case in the public sector where, other than the military, which runs its uniformed apprenticeship programs without union participation, the number of apprentices in joint and nonjoint programs is about the same.

Although not evident from the aggregate data, there is also variation by department or agency within the state, city or federal government. For example, in the State of Washington, apprenticeship programs in fire departments are run jointly by JACs. Apprenticeship programs in sheriff departments, however, are run unilaterally by management. This seems to suggest that the state has a greater desire to retain unilateral control over policing functions in the state as compared to other vital protective services. Also not evident from Table 4.3, some states that permit collective bargaining in the public sector (e.g., Massachusetts) require unions to waive their rights to participation in the operation of apprenticeship programs for state employees.

In some states, union participation in apprenticeship programs is mandated by law. For example, California statute requires that an apprenticeship program for a job title covered by an existing collective bargaining agreement will be operated by a JAC. Moreover, JACs in California tend to afford unions a good deal of control over entry standards. For instance, when written exams are deemed appropriate for certain job titles, unions are allowed to participate in test development and evaluation. For some programs (e.g., stationary engineer), unions make apprentice selections along with management.

In other states where JACs operate apprenticeships, unions may have some control over the programs, but on a conditional basis. For example, public employee unions in New York State participate in the hiring, evaluation and advancement of apprentices, but management retains ultimate control over these processes.

In the federal government, other than the military where uniformed apprenticeship programs are run unilaterally by management, union participation in general is very limited.[20] This is not surprising, given the overall legal restrictions placed on unions operating in the nonpostal, federal sector (Rosenbloom and Shafritz 1985; Kearney 1984).

This cursory discussion of union involvement in JACs is imperative when looking at female and minority participation and representation in public sector apprenticeship programs. For one thing, it suggests that there is variance across states in the ability of unions to set up *formal* barriers to prevent female and minority access. This is not to say, of course, that informal barriers are not set up by unions, or that the absence of union involvement in apprenticeship programs will ensure fair representation of women and minorities.

The following section describes female and minority representation in various public sector apprenticeship programs that are operated by JACs. The discussion and data presented should not be interpreted as an attempt to empirically link union involvement with female and minority representation. It may be too soon to develop such linkages, given that apprenticeship training is relatively new to most public sector work forces. We can certainly make some inferences about union involvement, however, particularly in apprenticeship programs for police, firefighting and corrections, given the past and current practices of unions in the protective services towards women as well as minorities.

Table 4.4 Women and Minorities in Public Sector Apprenticeship Programs Registered with the BAT or SACs as of December 31, 1987

	Total Apprentices	Women (%)	Minorities (%)
Public Sector Programs (Includes Military)	66,303	4,276 (6.4)	20,916 (31.5)
Private Sector Programs	164,312	9,955 (6.0)	24,513 (14.9)
All Programs (public and private)	230,615	14,231 (6.2)	45,429 (19.6)

SOURCE: Bureau of Apprenticeship and Training, U.S. Department of Labor, Washington, D.C., 1987. These data are not separated by race and sex, so there is some overlap in the categories. (Excludes California, District of Columbia, Puerto Rico, Hawaii, Rhode Island and Virgin Islands.)

Female and Minority Representation in Public Sector Apprenticeship Programs: A Preliminary Look at Potential Union Involvement

Table 4.4 provides data on female and minority representation in public and private sector apprenticeship programs. As the data show, the percentage of women in apprenticeship programs, whether public or private, is quite low. The percentage of minorities in public sector programs, however, is much higher than the percentage of minorities in private sector programs. Racial minorities represented 31.5 percent of the public sector apprentices and only 14.9 percent of the private sector apprentices. Perhaps this reflects a greater commitment on the part of government employers to promote the employment opportunities of at least minorities.

On the other hand, these data are in aggregate form and, therefore, do not point to the growing number of racial minorities in, for example, city transit apprenticeship programs and craft positions (Hill 1985). As Gould

Table 4.5 Distribution of Women and Minorities to Joint and Nonjoint Public Sector Apprenticeship Programs Registered with the BAT or SACs as of December 31, 1987

| | Joint | | Nonjoint | |
	Women (%)	Minorities (%)	Women (%)	Minorities (%)
Public Sector Programs (Includes Military)	442 (10.3)	1,950 (9.3)	3,834 (89.7)	18,966 (90.7)
Private Sector Programs	6,337 (63.6)	17,954 (73.2)	3,618 (36.4)	6,559 (26.8)
All Programs	6,779 (47.6)	19,904 (43.8)	7,452 (52.4)	25,525 (56.2)

SOURCE: Bureau of Apprenticeship and Training, U.S. Department of Labor, Washington, D.C., 1987. These data are not separated by race and sex, so there is some overlap in the categories. (Excludes California, District of Columbia, Puerto Rico, Hawaii, Rhode Island and Virgin Islands.)

(1977, 419) points out, blacks in particular have made substantial gains in the urban transit industry, not because of employers' affirmative action efforts but rather because "whites increasingly do not seek transit employment in large numbers—principally because of the urban crime problem." In any event, racial minorities are receiving training for craft jobs in the urban transit industry.

Table 4.5 presents aggregate statistics on the distribution of women and minorities to joint and nonjoint apprenticeship programs. In the public sector, both women and minorities are disproportionately represented in programs that are run unilaterally by government. Only 10.3 percent of the women and 9.3 percent of the minorities are participating in apprenticeship programs run jointly by unions.

Interestingly, women and minorities have greater representation in private sector programs that are run jointly as opposed to nonjointly. This almost seems inconsistent with the evidence presented earlier which suggests that unions in the private sector restrict apprenticeship opportunities of women and minorities. There may in fact be several explanations for the greater representation of women and minorities in JAC-operated programs in the private sector. First, the data in Table 4.5 are in aggregate form. They do not reflect important differences between craft and industrial apprenticeships and, more importantly, inequities among apprenticeships within these two categories.

The industrial unions involved in apprenticeship programs may, in fact, depend upon female and minority participation. For example, women are disproportionately found in "service" apprenticeships such as bakers, cooks and chefs. These traditionally female professions have attracted certain unions such as Service Employees International Union (SEIU). As such, high numbers of women may be found in JAC-operated apprenticeship programs, but these programs are less prestigious and lower paying. In this sense, the employment opportunities of women are restricted, but not necessarily by unions.

For minorities, the issue is not simply the distinction between craft and industrial apprenticeships but rather institutionalized segregation within the craft or industry. For example, it was noted earlier that minorities constitute a high proportion of the cement mason and bricklaying apprenticeships in this country. Unions have admitted minorities into these apprenticeships for years but have tended to place them in segregated locals. So, there may, in fact, be a higher percentage of minorities in jointly run programs, but they are still being discriminated against by unions as well as employers in job opportunities. This is not reflected in Table 4.5.

The point here is that women and minorities may not be found in high numbers in JAC-operated programs for apprenticeships that are traditionally white male and more prestigious. The question of whether the programs are jointly run is critical, then, but perhaps we should first ask whether the apprenticeships are traditionally white male.

In the public sector, aside from the urban transit industry as noted earlier, most of the apprenticeship programs appear to be emerging in traditionally white male professions such as firefighting, police, corrections and other "crafts." This being the case, it is not surprising that a relatively low percentage of women and minorities are found in jointly run programs. As described in other chapters, "craft" unions such as police and fire have not been receptive to women or minorities.

Tables 4.6 and 4.7 illustrate the representation of women and minorities in jointly operated firefighting apprenticeship programs in the localities of two states. As the data show, women in both California and Washington are not well represented in these apprenticeships. Male minorities, however, appear to be doing poorly in Washington, but not in California. Of course, it should be noted that these data, too, are in aggregate form and, as such, they do not point to disparities across the state of California. For example, male minorities may have greater representation in apprenticeship programs in urban areas, which, compared to rural areas, are more populated with minorities. In any event, the point is that if unions or union locals resist the entry of women and minorities into the profession of firefighting, they will resist their entry in apprenticeships.

In other states, apprenticeship programs are also emerging in traditionally white male professions. In New York State, for example, the job titles

Table 4.6 Apprentices in Jointly Run Firefighting Programs, California, 1982, 1986

	1982 (%)	1986 (%)	Percent Change
Women	2	60	
	(.6)	(7.8)	96.7
Male Minorities	66	214	
	(21.0)	(27.6)	69.2
White Males	246	500	
	(78.3)	(64.6)	50.1
Total	314	774	59.4

SOURCE: California Department of Industrial Relations, Division of Apprenticeship Standards, 1982, 1986.

Table 4.7 Apprentices in Jointly Run Firefighting Programs, Washington, December 1987

Total	Women	Male Minorities
54	0	0

SOURCE: Washington Department of Labor and Industries, Apprenticeship and Training Section, 1987.

targeted for apprenticeship tend to be dominated by white males. Such titles include electrician and stationary engineer. In addition, the JAC-devised criteria for entrance into an apprenticeship tend to be biased against women and in some cases minorities. For example, selection of apprentices is based in part on whether one currently works for the state. Particular emphasis is then given to the bargaining unit one is currently in. One unit, operational services, is weighted heavily; this unit is dominated by males. Other selection criteria include math and science training in high school, college or vocational school training, and work experience that is directly related to the trade. These criteria work against women as well as minorities since these groups tend to have less formal training in math and science and less apprentice-related experience. In this sense, JAC-operated programs in traditionally white male professions set up subtle barriers that keep women and minorities out. The data in Table 4.8 point to the underrepresentation of women and minorities in one of New York State's jointly operated apprenticeship programs.

It appears that Delaware, as noted earlier, is the only state that has developed an apprenticeship program for a traditionally female pro-fession—secretary. (At this point, unions are not involved in the program.) Interestingly, the BAT and SACs do not recognize the job title, secretary, as apprenticable. It evidently is not seen as a "skilled craft," worthy of status and recognition as plumbers and carpenters are. An intriguing aspect of this apprenticeship program is that it was developed out of a high demand for and low supply of secretarial labor. These are primary characteristics of the well-paying, skilled crafts. It seems that professions dominated by women may be undervalued, despite supply and demand factors.

In sum, women and minorities are not well represented in jointly operated apprenticeship programs in the public sector. Unions may present some barriers to these groups, but further research is certainly needed to demonstrate this. Nonetheless, given the past as well as current treatment of certain public sector unions toward women and minorities, we can infer from these descriptive statistics that they are not particularly welcomed in jointly run apprenticeship programs such as police, fire-fighting and corrections.

Conclusions and Policy Recommendations

Two opposing views of the utility of joint labor-management committees in the area of EEO/AA have been presented in this chapter. As discussed, joint labor-management committees can be an extremely viable tool for promoting EEO/AA when both parties are genuinely supportive of EEO/AA. Even if one or both parties do not see EEO/AA as a priority, joint

Table 4.8 New York State Stationary Engineer Apprentices in Office of General Services, 1981, 1982

| | 1981 | | | | 1982 | | |
	White Male (%)	Female (%)	Minority Male (%)		White Male (%)	Female (%)	Minority Male (%)
Total Selected	20 (80)	3 (12)	2 (8)		16 (80)	2 (10)	2 (10)
Total Retained	17 (85)	1 (5)	2 (10)		9 (75)	0 --	3* (25)

* One minority male apprentice was added later in the program.

committees can be effective. Unions in particular can demonstrate a commitment to women and minorities, which can have a favorable impact on union membership and power. This is especially true when money is appropriated to the joint EEO/AA committee and tangible benefits can be derived from joint efforts. This is evident in the UUP/NYS Affirmative Action Program, as discussed in this chapter.

When one or both parties oppose EEO/AA, however, labor-management cooperation can only perpetuate the exclusion of women and minorities from certain segments of the labor force. Perhaps the best illustration of this can be seen in the work of joint apprenticeship committees (JACs), which have not been receptive to the presence of women and minorities in apprenticeship training programs and, hence, skilled craft jobs.

Then, efforts should be made to foster labor-management cooperation over EEO/AA in some segments of both public and private sector work forces, but not others. In such areas were JACs operate, it is necessary to monitor the cooperation to prevent further abuses against women and minorities. A foremost problem that needs to be addressed is the inaccessibility, indeed lack, of data on female and minority apprentices. There needs to be a better system of data collection and dissemination on the social characteristics of apprentices in this country. The problem of the lack of female and minority progress in apprenticeship programs, whether JAC-operated or not, cannot be effectively monitored and addressed without adequate, accurate and accessible data. EEOC data in particular, which is very comprehensive and accessible when available, must be kept up-to-date.

In addition, there needs to be greater enforcement of EEO laws and regulations. The EEOC, for example, especially under the Reagan Administration, has not vigorously pursued Title VII violations by JACs for discriminating against women and minorities. The BAT is also empowered to enforce EEO regulations issued in 1963 by the Department of Labor. The BAT can, for example, deregister programs that violate these regulations. Yet, the BAT rarely imposes sanctions against unions or employers for EEO violations (Rust-Tierney 1984). State Apprenticeship Councils (SACs) are also authorized to enforce state EEO regulations, but seldom do.

Greater enforcement by the U.S. Labor Department's Office of Federal Contract Compliance Programs (OFCCP) is also necessary. The OFCCP is empowered to administer and enforce Executive Order 11246 as amended by 11375 (amended to prohibit sex discrimination), which requires federal contractors and subcontractors to promote EEO and, in some cases, affirmative action.

The OFCCP has the power to debar contractors that violate the Executive Order. However, it has been observed that the OFCCP has not vigorously exercised this authority. The provisions of 11246 apply to almost 75,000 private companies employing over 23 million workers. Yet, under the Carter Administration only thirteen federal contractors lost their contracts for 11246 violations and only two were debarred under the Reagan Administration (Press and McDaniel 1985).

The important point to be made here is that if greater sanctions were imposed on federal contractors and subcontractors, greater pressures could in turn be placed on JACS to promote affirmative action, since contractors generally turn to JACs to fill their employment needs. It should be noted, however, that although greater enforcement effort is imperative, it may, as noted earlier, fuel resistance from craft unions. In simple terms, it may do little to change the attitudes of unions toward women and minorities. Perhaps key to addressing negative attitudes is education. Setting up "sensitivity training" programs, for example, may, over time, help to break down negative stereotypes about women and minorities.

Education must go beyond the adult population, however, to encompass young children as well. The way in which young women and minorities are trained and socialized affects the way they think about careers and career opportunities. Young women and minorities need to be made aware of the opportunities in the skilled crafts and, through vocational and high school counseling, need guidance in terms of the tools and skills required to gain entry into apprenticeship programs.

The BAT and SACs could also expand the scope of apprenticable crafts. As discussed earlier, the job titles which are deemed apprenticable are largely male-dominated. But, as is the case in the state of Delaware, job titles dominated by women are sometimes in short supply and high demand, making them very amenable and suitable for apprenticeship training. Of course, this might perpetuate the segregation of job titles, but it would also assure that women are being paid adequately for work that is valued and highly demanded by an employer.

As many have argued, the work of community groups needs to be strengthened and expanded. Such groups as the Urban League have been extremely effective in providing outreach services as well as pre-apprenticeship training skills. Programs aimed specifically at outreach services are in particular need of expansion. As Rust-Tierney (1984) has testified before a congressional oversight hearing on the National Apprenticeship Training Act, despite the importance of outreach services, there is only one remaining outreach program for women in this country—PREP, Inc., which is based in Cincinnati, and operates in six major cities. Other federally funded outreach programs are now defunct due to federal cutbacks. Without such government-funded programs, women and minorities will be totally cut off from apprenticeship openings and, ultimately, the skilled crafts.

Certain economic incentives may perhaps encourage employers to develop pre-apprenticeship programs specifically for women and minorities. For example, tax credits could offset the high costs of apprenticeship training programs, thereby encouraging employers to develop and implement such programs (Bell 1984). Of course, if recalcitrant unions were present, the success of such programs, despite existing incentives, might be greatly impaired.

Apprenticeship training is becoming increasingly popular in the public sector. To enhance the potential effectiveness of apprenticeship programs, policy makers can rely on the private sector experience for insight. In particular, if policy makers are genuinely committed to the equal employment of women and minorities, union involvement in developing and implementing apprenticeship programs must be carefully controlled for and monitored. The ability of unions to hinder females' and minorities' attempts to gain access to public sector apprenticeship programs should not be underestimated by government officials.

Notes

1. Importantly, EEO and AA are not one and the same thing. In this chapter, they are viewed as extensions of one another, but use of "EEO/AA" terminology does not imply that they are the same.

2. Indeed, EEO and, in some cases, AA, are mandated by statutory and case law, which further precludes their negotiability.

3. These efforts have been learned of through a review of the literature and contacts with state and federal government officials.

4. These data are for women and minorities in nonlibrarian faculty positions. Data are not yet available for professional titles.

5. This allocation is for faculty travel awards, professional study leaves and librarian study leaves. It is not possible to determine at this point how much money will actually be alloted to those programs which tend to benefit white males.

6. This represents, and is tied to the seminal concerns for the strong antiunion sentiment in the United States. See Rosenbloom and Shafritz (1985), for example, who discuss the social and legal impediments to artisan groups seeking to exert control over their crafts.

7. Racial minorities began the battle to enter the crafts years before women and, so, this may account for the greater progress. This in no way suggests that the battle is over, however, and that minorities are no longer victims of discrimination.

8. Civil Rights Act of 1964, as amended. In addition, Executive Order 11246, as amended by 11375 requires federal contractors and subcontractors to refrain from discriminating against employees because of race, color, religion, sex or national origin. In some cases, it requires them to take affirmative steps to ensure that persons are employed without regard to such factors. Also, Title 29, Part 30, Code of Federal Regulations, issued by the Department of Labor in 1963, prohibits discriminatory practices in apprenticeship programs registered with the Bureau

of Apprenticeship and Training (BAT). The BAT is authorized to enforce these regulations.

9. Fair Employment Practices legislation would apply here. In addition, apprenticeship programs registered with a State Apprenticeship Council (SAC) are subject to equal employment opportunity standards and laws adopted by the SAC, Labor Department or other pertinent body operating in the state.

10. For a discussion of other factors see, for example, U.S. Commission on Civil Rights (1976), in particular pp. 76–94, and Briggs (1974).

11. It should be stressed that these practices pertain primarily to private sector unions. There is a certain gray area, however, that makes the public-private sector distinction a difficult one. For example, when a government employer contracts out for skilled craft workers, it feeds off of the private sector labor market. If union discrimination is a characteristic of this labor market, the government employer may be an indirect party to it (see, for example, *Gaynor v. Rockefeller* 1965).

12. It should be noted that guidelines are set by the national union, the federal Bureau of Apprenticeship and Training (BAT) and, when present, State Apprenticeship Councils (SACs). But local JACs exercise enormous control by managing the day-to-day activities, including final selection of apprentices.

13. This is what is known as a "closed shop," which has been outlawed since 1947 with the Taft-Hartley Act, but continues to operate on a de facto basis in several crafts and industries.

14. Of course, this is not to say that management would be unwilling to discriminate against women and minorities if it had greater or unilateral control. Indeed, many contractors are former craft workers; hence, they share characteristics with majority group members and may be very willing to limit females' and minorities' access to apprenticeship programs and craft jobs.

15. The Court majority also ruled that the equal protection component of the Due Process Clause of the Fifth Amendment was not violated by the membership goal (see *Sheet Metal Workers* 1986, 3052-53).

16. SACs are the state equivalent to the BAT. They are responsible for administering apprenticeship programs in SAC states.

17. Civilian apprentices in military installations are included in the category "federal programs."

18. Alaska is in the process of developing a joint apprenticeship program for certain titles in the Marine Highway Department.

19. Although this training for secretaries is officially referred to as an internship program, it operates just as an apprenticeship for any skilled craft, combining on-the-job training with classroom training.

20. Interview with Mr. Bing Downey, Bureau of Apprenticeship and Training, April 26, 1988.

References

Abbott, Grace. *The Child and The State*. Vol. 1, Legal Status in the Family Apprenticeship and Child Labor. Chicago: University of Chicago Press, 1938.

Baker, Elizabeth F. *Technology and Woman's Work*. New York: Columbia University Press, 1964.

Bell, John. Statement. *Oversight Hearings on the National Apprenticeship Training Act*. Hearings before the Subcommittee on Employment Opportunities, November 15, 17, 1983. Washington, D.C.: Government Printing Office, 1984:232-240.

Briggs, Norma. *Women in Apprenticeship—Why Not?* Washington, D.C.: U.S. Department of Labor, Research Monograph No. 33, 1974.

Cowan, Ruth S. "From Virginia Dare to Virginia Slims: Women and Technology in American Life." In Martha M. Trescott (ed.), *Dynamos and Virgins Revisited: Women and Technological Change in History*. Metuchen, New Jersey: The Scarecrow Press, Inc., 1979:30-44.

Dubinsky, Irwin. *Reform in Trade Union Discrimination in the Construction Industry*. New York: Praeger, 1973.

Gaynor v. Rockefeller 256 N.Y.S. 2d 584 (1965).

Gould, William B. *Black Workers in White Unions*. Ithaca, New York: Cornell University Press, 1977.

Hill, Herbert. *Black Labor and the American Legal System*. Madison, Wisconsin: University of Wisconsin Press, 1985.

Jackson, John H. and John A. Fossum. "Attitudes of Apprenticeship Committee Members Toward Affirmative Action Programs: A Preliminary Examination." *Labor Law Journal* 27 (1976), 2:84-88.

Joint Report. *Registered Apprenticeship Training in New York State*. Albany, New York: New York State Department of Labor, September 1976.

Kearney, Richard C. *Labor Relations in the Public Sector*. New York: Marcel Dekker, Inc., 1984.

Kursh, Harry. *Apprenticeships in America*. New York: W.W. Norton & Co., 1965, 2d ed.

LAIRS (Labor Agreement Information Retrieval System). Washington, D.C.: U.S. Office of Personnel Management, January 1988.

Levine, Susan. "Ladies and Looms: The Social Impact of Machine Power in the American Carpet Industry." In Martha M.Trescott (ed.), *Dynamos and Virgins Revisited: Women and Technological Change in History*. Metuchen, New Jersey: The Scarecrow Press, Inc., 1979:67-76.

Marshall, F. Ray and Vernon M. Briggs. *Equal Apprenticeship Opportunities*. Washington, D.C.: National Manpower Policy Task Force, November 1968.

National Center for Productivity and Quality of Working Life. *Recent Initiatives in Labor-Management Cooperation*. Washington, D.C.: Government Printing Office, February 1976.

New York State Commission Against Discrimination. *Apprentices, Skilled Craftsmen and the Negro: An Analysis*. New York: Commission Against Discrimination, 1960.

Press, Aric and Ann McDaniel. "The New Rights War." *Newsweek* 106 (30 December 1985), 27:66-68.

Rorabaugh, W. J. *The Craft Apprentice*. New York: Oxford University Press, 1986.

Rosenbloom, David H. and Jay M. Shafritz. *Essentials of Labor Relations*. Reston, Virginia: Reston Publishing Co., 1985.

Rowan, Richard L. and Lester Rubin. *Opening the Skilled Construction Trades to Blacks*. Report No. 7. Philadelphia: Industrial Research Unit, The Wharton School, University of Pennsylvania, 1972.

Rust-Tierney, Diann. Statement. *Oversight Hearings on the National Apprenticeship Training Act.* Hearings before the Subcommittee on Employment Opportunities, November 15, 17, 1983. Washington, D.C.: Government Printing Office, 1984:197-231.

Sheet Metal Workers Int'l Assoc. Local 28 and Joint Apprenticeship Committee v. EEOC 106 S.Ct. 3019, _U.S_ (1986).

Silver, Marc. L. *Under Construction.* Albany, New York: State University of New York Press, 1986.

Spero, Sterling Denhard and Abram L. Harris. *The Black Worker.* New York: Atheneum, 1968.

Sulzner, George T. "The Impact of Labor-Management Cooperation Committees on Personnel Policies and Practices at Twenty Federal Bargaining Units." *Journal of Collective Negotiations in the Public Sector* 11 (1982), 1:37-45.

U.S. Commission on Civil Rights. *The Challenge Ahead: Equal Opportunity in Referral Unions.* Washington, D.C.: Government Printing Office, 1976.

United Steelworkers v. Weber 99 S.Ct. 2721, 443 U.S. 193 (1979).

Walton, Richard E. and Robert B. McKersie. *A Behavioral Theory of Labor Negotiations.* New York: McGraw-Hill, 1965.

5

WOMEN IN UNIFORMED SERVICE JOBS: THE ROLE OF UNIONS

Women and minorities have historically been underrepresented in what are collectively known as the uniformed services, that is, fire, police, corrections and sanitation (Riccucci 1987; Weisheit 1987; Colker 1986; Bowersox 1981; Cayer and Sigelman 1980). Although the reasons for this underrepresentation may be different for women as compared to male minorities,[1] the outcome has been the same—complete exclusion or extreme underrepresentation of these protected class groups in uniformed service jobs.

After Title VII was extended to the public sector in 1972 with passage of the Equal Employment Opportunity Act, government employers as well as unions found it increasingly difficult to *overtly* discriminate against protected class groups. Consequently, during the post-1972 period, various subtle barriers were often devised which continued to exclude women and minorities from certain uniformed service jobs or, if they had already gained entry, kept them in low-status or low-paying positions such as clerical or dispatching. For example, employers, sometimes at the urging of unions, instituted minimum height and weight requirements and written examinations which had no relationship to job performance (Colker 1986). These selection devices adversely affected women in some cases[2] and minorities in others.[3]

Chapter 3 demonstrated that many of the early successful legal challenges to overt and covert discriminatory employment practices were made by male racial minorities. Ironically, however, the elimination of some of these discriminatory practices led to the development of other selection devices such as physical agility exams which continue to have a disproportionately harsh impact on women.[4] Colker (1986, 766) succinctly makes the point that

[m]any police and fire departments have considered rank-order physical abilities tests the easiest and best solution to the historical problem of employment discrimination against black, Asian, and Hispanic men, because these examinations produce no disparate impact on the basis of race or national origin. Yet, that solution is unacceptable and often unlawful because it imposes a high price on women of all races and national origins.

This is not to say, of course, that minority males have overcome all the discriminatory obstacles that were either intentionally or unintentionally used by government employers and uniformed service unions. Indeed, they continue to face barriers to entry,[5] promotion,[6] and retention.[7] In addition, minority males continue to be objects of racial harassment and hostility on the job. A 1985 federal district court ruling, *Snell v. Suffolk County*, points to some of the abuses to which minority correctional officers have been subjected by white correctional officers. The court noted, for example, that minorities

have repeatedly been mimicked in derogatory ways . . . . [I]n [one instance,] White correction officers dressed a[n] Hispanic inmate in a straw hat, sheet, and a sign that read "Spic." The White officers referred to the inmate as "Ramos' son." Officer Ramos complained . . . [but was] accused . . . of trying to "make waves" (*Snell* 1985, 525).

The court also directed attention to racist materials "which were posted on official bulletin boards at the jail" (*Snell* 1985, 525). The court pointed to, for example, "a cartoon depicting a Klu Klux Klan member who after shooting a Black person remarks to a ranger 'Whatcha mean, "Out of Season"?' " Other racially demeaning materials included a

highly offensive depiction of a large-breasted Black woman in some form of native garb . . . a national geographic magazine-type photograph of a naked Black woman with the words "Yo Mama" and a bone added above her head . . . a Black person, this time accompanied by the words "Official Runnin' Nigger Target" and what appear to be bullet holes . . . a questionnaire that begins "photo not necessary since you all look alike" and asks such questions as "[how many] years [spent] in local prisons?" and "[give] approximate estimate of income [from] theft, welfare . . . false insurance claims" (*Snell* 1985, 525).

As suggested in Chapter 3, these racially motivated, discriminatory actions and behaviors continue to pose serious legal questions and deserve further study.

This chapter tends to place heavy emphasis on union involvement in the use of physical agility exams as a selection tool for uniformed service jobs and the effects of such exams on women. Also considered are other union practices that deter female employment and discourage promotion, transfer, and retention in the uniformed services. Again, however, although the primary focus is on women, it in no way suggests that minority males have conquered the battle against discrimination in the uniformed services.

Female Employment in the Uniformed Services

As noted at the beginning of this chapter, women are relatively underrepresented in uniformed service jobs. As Table 5.1 illustrates, they have made some progress in these jobs over the past ten years but, overall, they constitute an extremely small proportion of the uniformed services. There are substantial numbers of women in those agencies but they are overwhelmingly in clerical positions. For instance, in 1980, over 85 percent of the clerical jobs in police departments were held by women. In addition, during that same year, women comprised over 75 percent of the clerical staff in fire departments, 90 percent in corrections and about 76 percent in sanitation (EEOC 1982).

Prior to 1972, uniformed service jobs across the country were often explicitly closed to women. That is, women were not even allowed to *apply* for employment in the uniformed services except for clerical jobs (Colker 1986). The years following 1972 posed a serious challenge to those wishing to keep women out of the uniformed services. By law, these departments could no longer overtly discriminate against women. This meant that state and local laws and ordinances or civil service rules had to be modified so that women could at least apply for jobs in the uniformed services. Police and corrections had even a greater impetus to make these changes, since funding from the Law Enforcement Assistance Administration (LEAA) could be suspended if these agencies engaged in employment discrimination.

Even so, subtle barriers were constructed that perpetuated the effects of prior discrimination and delayed full implementation of equal employment opportunity. As noted earlier, minimum height and weight requirements were often introduced, as were stringent, rank-ordered physical agility exams (Colker 1986; Feinman 1986). Today, most employers no longer use artificial barriers such as minimum height and weight requirements, since they were found unlawful under Title VII by the U.S. Supreme Court's *Dothard v. Rawlinson* (1977) ruling.[8] Other barriers persist, however, including physical agility exams. They adversely affect women but, in large part, they are seldom challenged.

Table 5.1 Female Representation in Uniformed Services, 1975, 1980, 1985

	1975*	1980**	1985***
Police	3.7	6.1	9.2
Fire	.1	.4	.9
Corrections	10.2	13.4	15.4
Sanitation	.5	1.7	2.4
Percent in working-age population****	40.0	42.5	44.2

Figures represent women in uniformed, nonclerical jobs (e.g., police patrol officers, firefighters, correctional officers and sanitation workers), at local and, for police and corrections, state levels.

*SOURCE: *Minorities and Women in State and Local Government, 1975.* U.S. Statistical Summary, Volume 1. Equal Employment Opportunity Commission, 1977.

**SOURCE: *Job Patterns for Minorities & Women in State and Local Government, 1980.* Equal Employment Opportunity Commission, April 1982.

***SOURCE: "State and Local Government Information, Summary Report for 1985 EEO-4 Survey." Equal Employment Opportunity Commission, 1985.

****SOURCE: *Statistical Abstracts of the U.S., 1987.* U.S. Bureau of the Census. (This includes all persons in the labor force.)

What role have unions played in obstructing equal employment for women in nonclerical, uniformed service jobs? Various union attitudes and behaviors have deterred women at all stages of employment, from entry to retention, and even in promotion (Riccucci 1988). For example, unions have supported the use of minimum height and weight requirements set well above the average height and weight of females, ultimately excluding women from uniformed service jobs (*White v. Nassau County Police* 1977).

They have supported the use of seniority systems set up before women were legally protected in the workplace as a primary constraint to such employment decisions as promotions, assignments and layoffs. The effect has been to freeze prior discriminatory patterns in place. Unions also continue to support the use of stringent agility exams for entrance into the uniformed services.

Traditional role prejudices, which hold that women are not physically or psychologically capable of performing dangerous, stressful or physically demanding duties, either have been perpetuated by unions or have not been challenged by union leaders. A troublesome example is the reaction by William Ryan, former president of the International Association of Fire Fighters (IAFF), Local 280, facing the prospect of female entry into the Syracuse, New York, Fire Department: "I'm a male chauvinist and I know a lot about firefighting. Women can't do the job—not unless they're Amazons" *(Syracuse Post Standard* 20 March 1980, 1).

Too often traditional role expectations have been accepted as empirical realities and labeled "merit" requirements for a job. It then becomes an argument for the maintenance of high work standards to reject women based upon examinations that are not truly job related. To the degree that unions are participating in the development of those standards, they are perpetuating discrimination. One example here revolves around the complex issue of physical strength standards or requirements for uniformed service jobs.

There is much disagreement over the importance of physical strength as a component of such jobs as police officer, firefighter, correctional officer and sanitation worker. Certainly, physical strength is important for such jobs, but the question has been posed, How important? It has been argued that firefighters exams, for example, inappropriately place too much emphasis on physical strength. These critics have argued that endurance and stamina are more important to the job of firefighting and, hence, should be weighted more heavily in physical agility tests (*Berkman* 1982, 212).

Similar arguments have been advanced for the occupation of police or patrol officer. Indeed, many have characterized police work as being largely sedentary, requiring a very small amount of anaerobic and aerobic fitness (Charles 1982). Hence, as Horne (1980a, 84) points out, "[n]ot as much strength and agility is needed as the media and many police officers would have us believe."

Another source of disagreement involves how to measure physical strength. For many years, minimum height and weight requirements were employed to measure strength. Such requirements, however, have not been useful or accurate indicators of performance. Campion (1983, 529), for example, points out that "these standards are usually set arbitrarily, and their relationship to job performance is not demonstrated." As such, courts will rarely permit the use of minimum height and weight standards.[9]

More recently, hiring authorities have favored and, hence, employed "physical fitness" exams (Campion 1983). Such exams consist of chin-ups, broad jumps, flexed-arm hangs, hand grip exercises, push-ups and sit-ups. Interestingly, there have been many efforts to validate such exams (Considine, et al. 1976; Hubbard, Hunt and Krause 1975; Guyor 1974), but the results have generally indicated that exam performance does not necessarily predict future job performance (Considine, et al. 1976). Recent judicial decisions, including *Berkman v. New York*, which will be discussed later, have acknowledged this.

Another critical issue regarding physical strength requirements is the lack of knowledge about *how much* physical strength is needed for uniformed service jobs. Some degree of strength is obviously needed but, despite the immense body of knowledge in the areas of work physiology, industrial psychology and anthropometry (Campion 1983), little research has been done to measure the actual amount of physical strength needed to perform protective service jobs.[10] Charles (1982, 196), for example, points out that "little scientific effort has been directed toward assessing either the physical demand of policing or the degree of fitness needed by officers to perform these tasks."

In effect, the physical performance measures incorporated in merit exams are not totally accurate and indeed may be based on subjective assessments of strength requirements. Ultimately, when applicants are tested for physical strength, they are not necessarily tested for the physical strength requirements of the job. Charles (1982, 196) points out that

[t]he results of this lack of quantitative data on the physical requirements of policing has allowed qualitative judgments which are tainted by the male police officer's preoccupation with the dangerous aspects of policing . . . to skew the police perception of the physical aspects of this profession. In addition, since most male police officers identify with the traditional role ascribed to women in our society, such as that women are physically weak, it is not surprising that male officers, as a whole feel that women would make poor patrol officers and even worse patrol partners.

Importantly, then, there is no guarantee that "merit" exams will lead to the selection of qualified or the "most qualified" persons for the job. The U.S. Supreme Court recognized this in its 1987 *Johnson v. Transportation Agency* decision, where it ruled that determining who is meritorious or qualified for a job is very subjective. Quoting from a brief submitted by the American Society for Personnel Administration, the Court said that "[i]t is a standard tenet of personnel administration that there is rarely a single, 'best qualified' person for a job . . . final determinations as to which candidate is 'best qualified' are at best subjective" (*Johnson* 1987, 1457).

The experiences of women seeking jobs in the uniformed services indicate that unions cannot be relied upon to challenge the use of physical agility exams but, indeed, continue to insist upon their use. Also, as will be seen shortly, unions' position on this issue may be a subterfuge for their desire to keep women out of the various uniformed services. In some cases (e.g., police and corrections) women have been able to break through entry barriers, yet they continue to face opposition from unions in their bids for promotion, transfer and even retention.

Fire

As noted earlier in this chapter, women comprise not even one-tenth of a percent of the uniformed firefighters in this country. A comparison of the various uniformed services indicates that the occupation of firefighting may be the most protected male bastion and, hence, the most resistant to the entry of women. It is, indeed, an occupation built on " '*sons* joining fathers' " (Chertos and Phillips 1986, 5; emphasis added).

Historically, the job of firefighting, both volunteer and professional, has been closed to women. The few exceptions to this rule are worth noting, since they indicate the degree to which women were utilized or valued. For example, one of the earliest known cases of female employment in fire departments is that of a black slave known only as "Molly." She was a member of the volunteer company, Oceanus No. 11 in New York City in the 1780s. There is very little known about the work she performed for the fire company (Dunshee 1952). We can only infer based on slavery's repressive and oppressive treatment of blacks that she was inducted involuntarily and was exploited. Indeed, the only recorded instance of her participation in the actual fighting of fires was on one occasion when Molly, during a severe snowstorm, was harnessed as a horse would be with the fire engine, "pulling away for dear life" (Dunshee 1952, 53).

Women have served in one other known capacity. During the early days of firefighting, when technology was yet unsophisticated, women were allowed to volunteer their services to "bucket lines." Here, two lines were formed; one to pass full buckets of water to the fire, the other line to pass empty buckets back to the water source. Men comprised the first line, women and children the second. It appears that women were utilized only out of sheer desperation for human resources power and, as is the case today, there was a sexual division of labor. Furthermore, as technology improved, women were no longer needed, nor wanted.

Today, women are severely underutilized in fire departments. With few exceptions, it appears that women are not wanted in fire houses and so they are not recruited. When women do apply, they face intransigent employers, unions and employees, who appear to disguise their opposition by insisting upon the use of stringent physical agility exams, which tend to adversely affect women and are rarely job related. Most interesting, the continued and widespread use of such exams goes largely unchallenged. As such, "few fire departments are under court order to hire women" (Colker 1986, 802).

Perhaps the most expansive body of lawsuits has emanated from females' attempts to gain entry into New York City's Fire Department, one of the largest in the country. Their efforts were met with extreme resistance from the Uniformed Firefighters Association (UFA), the ramifications of which have been severe. The legal battle began in 1978 when women, for the first time, applied to the city for jobs as firefighters. Women were absolutely barred from taking the exam prior to at least 1972. Although the female applicants performed extremely well on the written exam (389 out of 410 earned passing scores), not one passed the agility exam, which, at the admission of a city official, " 'was the most arduous test [the city has] ever given for anything' . . . [and was] 'substantially different' from the last physical test, administered in 1971" (Maitland 1978, 3).

Brenda Berkman, one of the women who failed the test, filed a class-action suit against the city charging that the test unfairly discriminated against women (*Berkman v. New York City* 1982). The UFA, appearing as intervenor in the case, strongly defended the use of the exam. Nicholas Mancuso, president of the union, argued that the "exam assessed the qualities necessary for what he called a 'physically demanding job, a hazardous job and a dirty job' " (Fried 1982, 10). He went on to say that " 'It's not that we're opposed to females coming on the job . . . but we don't want a reduction in standards for entrance to the job' " (Fried 1982, 10). Mancuso insisted that the " 'U.F.A.'s interest is to insure that only those individuals who are physically able to perform the job are appointed to the position of firefighter' " (Kennedy 1982, 3).

Despite these claims, other explanations for the union's behavior emerged. For example, a *New York Times* editorial suggested that the issue of "merit" became a subterfuge for the union's desire to keep women out of the fire department. The *Times* inferred from the union's resistance that "Mancuso is upset mostly by the thought of women invading the male preserve of the stationhouse" (*New York Times* 29 August 1982, 18).

The federal district court judge rejected the union's and city's defense of the agility exam. The court ruled that the test had an adverse impact on women and also that it was invalid. The court said:

The proposition that the physical portion of [the exam] is content valid must be rejected. Defendants themselves and their outside consultants did not consider it to be such until the validity of their test was attacked. In all events "the abilities that the test attempts to measure are . . . [not] the most observable abilities of significance to the particular job in question" (*Berkman* 1982, 206).

The court ordered that a new test be devised and forty-five positions reserved for women. In addition, the court advised that in selecting firefighters, speed and strength should not be the overriding predictors of performance. It said that "what must be identified are not those who are strongest or fastest but, instead, those who, with the benefit of training in pacing or because of their native capacities of endurance, can perform the punishing tasks of firefighting as they are actually required to be performed" (*Berkman* 1982, 212).

The UFA would not concede to the court's decision. First, it appealed, albeit unsuccessfully, the district court's ruling. In addition, it attempted to block women's entry by seeking an injunction to prevent the new exam from being administered. The UFA was unsuccessful here, too, and so the revised exam was administered. Of the seventy-one women taking the new exam, fifty-one passed and forty-two accepted positions as probationary firefighters. Even though these women were able to demonstrate their abilities, the union as well as fire department officials continued to deter the integration of women into the department.

For example, once the women passed the exam, they were next required to train successfully for six weeks at the Fire Academy. This is standard procedure for all new hires. The prospect of women in firefighting, however, brought a new training program, which represented another obstacle to the women. Unlike in the past, the new hires were placed in ladder companies, where they worked independently rather than in teams. The advantage of working in teams is that the process of socialization into the organization is smoother, because new hires are allowed to "learn the ropes" (i.e., the formal and informal rules and procedures) from their peers. Working independently in the fire academy tends to set employees up for failure. Under other circumstances, a union would vigorously seek to prevent an employer from changing its personnel procedures in this fashion. In this case, however, the union did nothing.

The training program in the fire academy, then, became a deterrent to the women. In fact, two women were dismissed from the academy upon completion of the training on the grounds that they did not perform successfully and, hence, were not qualified for firefighting. One woman was Berkman; the other Zaida Gonzalez, who, along with Berkman, had taken the lead in complaining about the harassment of probationary female firefighters. The women went to court to seek reinstatement and, once again, the union offered no support (*Berkman* 1983). The women claimed that their dismissals were discriminatory, based on their gender. They argued that the dismissals stemmed from arbitrary evaluations as well as discriminatory treatment on the job (e.g., extensive sexual harassment) which prevented them from improving their skills and performing well.

The district court ruled that female firefighters had been discriminated against and subjected to various forms of sexual harassment and ridicule. The court found, for example, that the women were physically harassed:

the tires of one woman's car were slashed; women were deliberately intruded upon in washrooms; crude and obscene graffiti were regularly posted on bulletin boards; physical properties were often stolen or defaced (e.g., the women often found their boots glued to a firehouse floor or filled with urine); and, in one case, a woman's air hose had been removed from her air tank, ultimately placing her life in danger. Given such working conditions, we would expect a union to step in and protect the aggrieved and harassed employees. The UFA, however, refused to support or protect the women.

It was also found that women were completely ostrasized by their male colleagues. They were not spoken to and were excluded from meals and recreational activities. The court recognized the severity of this sort of treatment in a profession that requires not only communal living but a high degree of trust. The court said that "[i]n the face of the unique forms of cooperative effort, joint social activity, and communal life developed in the City's firehouses in response to the unusual demands of the job, the Department did next to nothing to foresee and prevent retaliation and sexual harassment which was one obviously foreseeable response . . . [caused] by women joining the fire force" (*Berkman* 1983, 231). Again, the all-male union would not assist or protect the women, even though the female firefighters had joined the UFA. The only group of workers in support of the women were minority firefighters and their leaders, who themselves had been victims of such discrimination.

The court ordered that the women be reinstated with back pay. The problems for Berkman, Gonzalez and other incumbent women, however, have not been resolved. The men continue to ostracize, abuse and humiliate them (Daley 1986). Moreover, the women are still combating the problems that have resulted from their deployment one to a company upon completion of training. This is not the norm for probationary firefighters. The women said that this "policy sent a clear signal to the men that women were a liability. In addition, it [has] isolated them from one another and from any comfort they might have received from talking together" (Daley 1986, 6).

The department has taken some steps to alleviate these problems, but the outcome has not been satisfactory. For example, the department developed a "sensitivity" program for the men and said that it would hire a consultant to assist in addressing the problems. Only a small percentage of men actually went through the sensitivity training, however, and, as of this writing, a consultant is yet to be hired. Berkman has commented that " '[w]hen you look at the record on this, it doesn't look like they're too serious, does it?' " (Daley 1986, 6).

The most recent battle to integrate women into New York City's Fire Department involves the use of a revised physical agility exam. This exam is similar to the one passed by the Berkman contingent, but it is preventing additional women from gaining entry into the department. This revised test was legally challenged due to its adverse impact on women but, because it was found "valid" by a concurrent validation strategy, the exam will be used to select future firefighters (*Berkman* 1987).[11] The UFA, which strongly defended the newly revised test in the lawsuit, praised the court's decision (Lubasch 1987). Mancuso sees the continued use of the exam as " 'a victory for the New York City Fire Department and for the people of our great city' " (May 1987, 1, 7).

It seems, then, that females already in or seeking entry to New York City's Fire Department may not make much progress in the coming years. Also, despite the claims of the union president, many of the barriers can be attributed to the UFA and its constituency. The union is simply unwilling to support the employment of women as firefighters.

Women have gained entry into fire departments in other large cities, but not without a struggle with employers and/or unions.[12] One very interesting case involves the political forces which led to a woman's entry, for the first time, into Chicago's fire department. Lauren Howard and the largest contingent of minorities were brought in as strikebreakers, in an effort to break a 23-day strike in 1980 by the Chicago Firefighters Union over the right to collectively bargain (Zusy 1987, Bureau of National Affairs 1982).

The practice of using women as well as minorities to break strikes is not new. It was employed successfully in the 1800s and early 1900s in such industries as silk, cigar making and steel. Today, the strategy is even more divisive and costly, because employers will sometimes retain the women and minorities after the strike. This was the case in Chicago's Fire Department, which, in addition to retaining the woman and minorities, rehired all the strikers. According to Holland, president of the firefighters' union, the use of a woman and minorities in this fashion has caused serious problems not only for labor relations but for race and gender relations. He said that the strikers will " 'never, ever forgive' the strikebreakers" (Bureau of National Affairs 1982, 32).

Following this incident, Holland said that he did not foresee the hiring of additional female firefighters in Chicago. He said that " '[t]he general duties of a firefighter are simply too strenuous' [for women]" (Bureau of National Affairs 1982, 33). Notwithstanding the union's position, the city, in the 1986–87 year, hired an additional thirty-six women to serve as firefighters and it is in the process of reevaluating its testing system to ensure greater access by females (Zusy 1987).

As other cities across the country begin to consider hiring women as firefighters, unions will voice their opposition, which, as seen in the *Berkman* cases, can pose serious problems. For example, officials in Albany, New York, are attempting to recruit women into its fire department. Interestingly, some women believe that the city's "drive is motivated less by a desire for equality than 'to beat a court case' " (Jochnowitz 1987b, 6). As of the 1987 fiscal year, there were only ten minority males and no women among the department's 270 firefighters (Kelly 1987).

The Albany Permanent Professional Firefighters Association expressed its concerns over the city's efforts to recruit women. The president of the union has said that firefighters will "strenuously" object to the hiring of women as firefighters (Jochnowitz 1987a). (The union's objections are similar to those discussed earlier, for example, that women are physically unsuited for firefighting jobs.) Another concern he raised is that firehouses are not "unisex," in that there are no doors on bathrooms and showers. This complaint is often raised by unions and city officials seeking to bar women from the occupation of firefighting. Despite the union's opposition, one woman in July of 1988 was sworn in as Albany's first female firefighter.

A cursory review of women in volunteer fire departments is in order, despite the fact that unions are absent from such employment scenes. For one thing, volunteer fire departments represent a high percentage of the firefighting forces in this country. In New York State alone, for example, there are about 1,780 volunteer fire companies as compared to the ninety or so paid fire departments (Schick and O'Hara 1987). A discussion of the practices in volunteer departments also raises interesting questions about the importance of "merit" in firefighting.

Unlike paid departments, volunteer departments seldom require job applicants to pass agility exams. Rather, membership is based on a vote of incumbent firefighters. There are a few exceptions, but, traditionally, women have not been voted in by the incumbent volunteers. In New York State, for instance, faring slightly better than the national picture, it is estimated that only 3 percent of the 140,000 or so volunteers are women (Grondahl 1986).

Volunteer companies' policies and regulations on membership are written into their bylaws and constitutions, which may not explicitly bar women from joining but may require "men to serve as volunteers" (Winerip 1983). Generally, this requirement is taken literally. For example, the chief of the volunteer fire department in Lee, Massachusetts, who adamantly opposes female membership, has said that " 'it's right in the bylaws ... Forty-five firemen. Fire*men*' " (Gordon 1986, 1; emphasis in original).

The membership practices of volunteer departments are not governed by Title VII. Rather, state legislation, generally in the form of human or civil rights laws, is perhaps the main source of regulation over the activities of volunteer departments. Hence, if a female wished to challenge the practices of volunteer departments as discriminatory, she would file a charge not with the EEOC but with the state division of human or civil rights. There have, in fact, been such challenges. For example, a hearing officer for the New Jersey Division on Civil Rights found that a woman had been discriminated against by the Basking Ridge Volunteer Fire Department when she was denied membership (*New York Times* 26 July 1977). The case ultimately resulted in an order issued by the civil rights division of the state's Department of Law and Public Safety that required the volunteer department to open its membership to women and to amend any policies and regulations that discriminate against them (Cook 1977).

Of course, as noted earlier, there are some volunteer departments that have voted women in (Schick 1987). Fire chiefs of such companies in New York and New Jersey have appeared supportive of their new volunteers. One chief said that " 'we're getting a *girl,* and I'm for it' " (Winerip 1983, 2; emphasis added). Another said that the incumbent men " 'accept them as fellow firefighters. The *girls* have proved themselves in their training' " (Haitch 1975, 61; emphasis added). And yet another has said that his new volunteer " 'is a fine young *lady*' " (Haitch 1975, 74; emphasis added).

It is interesting that one of the primary arguments against women joining paid departments is that they cannot pass the agility exam and, hence, are not qualified to perform the work. In volunteer departments, women are not required to pass an agility exam to gain membership, yet they are still excluded from firefighting. The disparities here lead to questions, first, regarding arguments by unions and employers that females are excluded not because they are women but because they cannot pass "merit" tests. It seems that women *are* excluded because of their gender if we consider the practices of volunteer departments, which do not base membership on "merit." It must further be questioned, Is "merit" more important in paid fire departments? Are citizens in volunteer districts at greater risk because "less qualified" firefighters comprise the force? What does this tell us about firefighters' "abilities" to fight fires in volunteer districts?

The battle for women in firefighting is not over. They will continue to face barriers that are set up and perpetuated by unions, their constituents, and employers. The barriers seem to stem largely from the so-called "masculine" culture of firefighting, which simply works against women. Women are sometimes able to break through the barriers with the help of the courts or threat of a lawsuit. On the other hand, the harassment, ostracism and continual pressure to demonstrate their "qualifications" tend to create a chilling effect, which discourages women from even considering the occupation of firefighting.

Female satellite groups such as the United Women Firefighters are critical here, because they seek to break down the barriers that hinder or discourage women from becoming firefighters. Their work is important symbolically, where they lend moral support and a sense of cohesiveness to females' movement in firefighting. Such groups also permit women to participate legitimately in the employment decisions which ultimately affect their status. That is, spokespersons for the group are able to go directly to high-ranking officials with problems rather than to immediate supervisors, who often share the views of rank-and-file about women in firehouses. The work of these satellite groups—as well as the courts and women such as Brenda Berkman—will be instrumental in females' access to uniformed firefighting jobs.

Police

Women have been employed in the occupation of policing since the mid-1800s, but their duties were historically limited to typing, answering phones, custodial work, youth programs, and searching female prisoners. Their role was one of nurturing, aptly captured by their official classification of "police matron" (Higgins 1951). By 1910, women in policing were officially classified as "policewomen,"[13] but their duties continued to differ from those of their male counterparts. Policewomen supervised and enforced dance hall, theater and skating rink laws, monitored billboard displays and located missing persons (Bell 1982).

As one might expect, the factors upon which prospective policewomen were judged were stereotypical or gender-biased. For example, in the early 1930s, women were required to have a good educational background and formal training in social work. By the 1940s, policewomen were required to be college graduates and not overly mannish, aggressive or callous. As recently as 1973, some municipalities advised policewomen not to wear makeup or suggestive clothing so as not to induce male colleagues into making sexual advances. Notwithstanding, policewomen were advised to always maintain their femininity (Bell 1982; Anderson 1973).

As many have pointed out, the work performed by females in police departments has remained the same. Their titles have become more comparable to males (e.g., police officers), but many female police officers do not perform patrol work; rather they continue to be assigned clerical or desk duties (Bell 1982; Melchionne 1974). Moreover, their bids for advancement or promotion have not been handled fairly. One reason for this has to do with resistance from unions and their male constituents.

Police unions such as the Fraternal Order of Police (FOP) and Patrolmen's Benevolent Association (PBA) have discriminated against women in hiring, promotions, assignments, transfers and layoffs,[14] mainly because they are threatened by the increased utilization—in particular, *equal* utilization—of female police (Horne 1980b). For one thing, unions believe that female police diminish the exclusiveness of police work. Economically, police unions benefit from maintaining an all-male environment because it gives them better control over the available pool of labor and, hence, wage rates. Socially, men simply may not want to associate with women as coequal working partners.

There is also something to be said for the desire to maintain the "maleness" of the work itself. Unions and their rank-and-file have a certain image of police work which reflects such male traits as physical prowess, emotional stability, and aggressiveness. When it is seen that women successfully perform the work, this masculine image becomes a mere myth.

Indeed, from society's standpoint, it seems to be coming to just that. There is a plethora of research demonstrating that women's performance as patrol officers is just as good as men's (Vega and Silverman 1982; Bloch and Anderson 1974). Moreover, despite the attitudes of unions and their male rank-and-file, the general public not only accepts female police, but finds them " 'more competent, pleasant and respectful' than men" (Burks 1977, 37). Nonetheless, the male rank-and-file continue to reject females as being suitable for police patrol work for reasons previously mentioned (Horne 1980b; Koenig 1979). As long as these attitudes prevail, police unions and associations will show little support for incumbent female police or women seeking to enter the police profession.

The case law here accurately describes the pervasiveness and ramifications of prevailing union behaviors toward women, including the use of "sophisticated pressure tactics and political leverage" to maintain an all-male police force (Horne 1980b, 201). This is not to say, of course, that the culpability lies solely with unions. Indeed, police officials have also been very resistant to women seeking patrol officer positions (Potts 1983; Bureau of National Affairs 1982). The resistance stems from their mutual belief that women are not physically or psychologically suited to perform the work.

This was succinctly expressed by Police Commissioner O'Neill of Philadelphia, who, in his legal defense of discriminatory hiring policies, provided the following responses when a federal district court asked why women cannot perform patrol work.

A. Because God, in His wisdom, made them different.
Q. From what respect?
A. Physically and psychologically.
Q. Physically, what differences . . . render females incapable of performing street work?
A. In general, they are physically weaker than males . . . I believe they would be inclined to let their emotions all too frequently overrule their good judgment . . . . I don't mean to embarrass either of the ladies, but there are periods in their life they are psychologically unbalanced because of physical problems that are occurring within them and I say that as a father of two females and the husband of one female and the son of one female (*Brace v. O'Neill* 1978, 853).

The point here is that discriminatory practices, not only in police but in other uniformed services as well, are sometimes attributable to both unions and employers. The further point should be made, however, that some police departments, initially resistant to letting women serve in uniformed nonclerical jobs, have pursued—for legal and financial reasons—affirmative action goals aimed at hiring and promoting women into such jobs. But, long after police officials have conceded, police unions often continue to resist.

For example, in *United States v. Miami* (1980), the FOP and the Miami PBA sought to vacate an affirmative action consent decree entered into by the City of Miami and the federal government. The decree was agreed to by the city after the U.S. government charged the city and police unions with discrimination against women as well as minorities in employment opportunities and conditions of employment. The unions, in particular the FOP, sought to dissolve the decree on procedural and substantive grounds.

Procedurally, the FOP argued that the trial court lacked the power to approve the decree without the consent of the FOP. The contention was that because the FOP's rights would be affected by the decree, it was necessary for the union to be a party to it. The Fifth Circuit Court of Appeals found this argument "meritless," stating that the FOP's rights and legitimate interests had in no way been abridged. The court said that "the consent decree [did] not violate the contractual relationship between the City and the FOP." (*Miami* 1980, 1329).

On substantive grounds, the FOP argued that the use of hiring and promotional goals in the consent decree violated Title VII and the Fourteenth Amendment to the Constitution. The appellate court, recognizing the union's disingenious attempt to nullify the consent decree, stated that "[a]t this point in the history of the fight against discrimination, it cannot be seriously argued that there is any insurmountable barrier to the use of goals and quotas. . . . To the contrary, affirmative relief is *required* to ensure that the effects of past discrimination are negated" (*Miami* 1980, 1335-36). The court concluded that the hiring and promotional goals established by the consent decree were not "unconstitutional, illegal or against public policy" (*Miami* 1980, 1337).

Another substantive challenge involved the FOP's claims that the consent decree illegally awarded constructive or retroactive seniority to women and minorities. The court rejected the FOP's arguments here, too, because the "consent decree [did] not award any retroactive seniority at all" (*Miami* 1980, 1340). Referring to the decree, the court pointed out that seniority is based on the total years of service with the city, and that "[t]his approach to seniority has nothing fictional or retroactive about it, as each employee is given seniority credit for the time . . . employed by the City" (*Miami* 1980, 1340).

The circumstances surrounding *United States v. Philadelphia* (1980) are very similar. In this case, the FOP *claimed* that it was taking a "neutral stance" to a consent decree entered into by the city and the United States to increase the recruitment, hiring and promotion of women in the police department. Yet, the FOP proposed that the consent decree be modified in a way that would favor the promotion of male police officers at the expense of women. The FOP suggested that if any male officer possessed " 'demonstrably superior qualifications' as compared to any female officer the promotion should go to the male officer" (*Philadelphia* 1980, 1201). In effect, the FOP's proposal ran counter to the relief outlined in the consent decree and, as the court concluded in rejecting the FOP's position, "would create more problems than it would solve" *(Philadelphia* 1980, 1201).

These are classic illustrations of police unions' opposition to affirmative action consent decrees aimed at hiring and promoting women.[15] The effect of such opposition, as suggested, is to close women out of desirable jobs in police departments. Although a city may be willing to redress its discriminatory practices against women, police unions may oppose changes to the status quo (i.e., a predominately male police force).

This is not to say, however, that police unions have never signed consent decrees. They have been party to affirmative action decrees and orders, but their involvement does not necessarily stem from support for affirmative action. Rather, they see no other alternative but to sign the decrees since such decrees generally follow a charge of discrimination by either the victims or the government. By signing, then, they avoid long and costly litigation, an actual finding of discrimination on the merits of the case, and an admission of guilt to unlawful discrimination (*United States v. Cincinnati*, 1985).

There are other practices of police unions, some subtle, others not, that lead to the conclusion that women are not welcomed in uniformed, nonclerical jobs. For example, unions have often required police officers to serve in patrol positions as a condition for promotion yet, at least prior to 1972, women were generally forbidden to serve as "patrolmen" (*Shortt* 1978; *Schenectady* 1975). Police unions have also supported the use of minimum height and weight requirements and agility exams that have absolutely barred women from patrol officer work (*White v. Nassau County Police* 1977). In addition, police unions have not always fairly represented their female constituents in grievance procedures. Other practices include the support for seniority in employment decisions as well as the arbitrary use of criteria, including seniority.

The legality of seniority systems in general was discussed in Chapter 3. It might be useful here to discuss seniority systems as employed specifically by police unions in order to make inferences about their behaviors toward women in the police profession.[16] For example, police unions have supported not only plantwide seniority systems but also departmental seniority systems, where seniority is determined by the amount of time worked in a particular department or job. For police work, the effect of such systems is clear.

After Title VII was extended to public sector employers in 1972, women seeking certain positions in police departments (e.g., patrol officer) could no longer be overtly discriminated against. That is, they could not be explicitly denied patrol work or openly segregated into children's and women's bureaus. In an effort to keep women in inferior police jobs, it was not uncommon for unions and employers to develop job or departmental seniority systems, which based promotion, transfers, demotions, and layoffs upon time in rank and/or division.

Let's say, for example, that female officers at date of hire by the department were assigned only to a women's bureau and were allowed advancement only in this bureau. If, during the post-Title VII period, a female from the women's bureau was seeking a promotion to sergeant in a more desirable bureau or division, such as investigations, but promotions were based on seniority in that particular bureau, men with less seniority in the investigations division would have a competitive edge over women with greater seniority in terms of total service.

Even females *hired* into desirable jobs such as patrol officer would be adversely affected by job seniority systems if unions and employers discriminated in promotions. For example, let's assume that females were hired for patrol work in 1972 but, due to contractually negotiated discriminatory policies, were not promoted to positions of sergeant or lieutenant until 1976. Let's further assume that several males were hired in 1974 and promoted in 1975. If layoffs or demotions were to be made on the basis of time in rank, the more senior females, in terms of total length of service, would be demoted or laid off before the less senior males.

This was the case in *Schaefer v. Tannian* (1975), where the U.S. district court found that past discriminatory practices in the police department denied women the opportunity to acquire the seniority needed to withstand layoffs and demotions. The court first found that the hiring and assignment practices discriminated against women. Such practices included separate eligibility lists for male and female applicants, as well as a requirement that females be at least twenty-one years of age with two years of college while males be at least eighteen with a high school degree or its equivalent. In addition, written exams for entrance were administered once a year to women, but once a week to men and, finally, until 1970, women were hired only into the Women and Children's Section.

The court also found that women had been explicitly discriminated against in promotions, thereby preventing them from accumulating time in rank. When the city of Detroit faced a budgetary crisis in the early 1970s, layoffs, and more pertinent to the discussion here, demotions were scheduled to be made. Such decisions would be based on the seniority provisions contained in the collective bargaining agreement between the city and the Detroit Police Lieutenants' and Sergeants' Association (DPLSA). Because this agreement called for a departmental seniority system, scheduled demotions would result in the demotion of women with greater seniority in terms of total length of service than men.

As the *Schaefer* (1975, 1142) court noted:

this result stems directly from the past discrimination . . . when men and women were divided into separate lines of progression in which the women's chances for promotion were substantially less than the men's chances. When the two lines were merged, the women, by virtue of the past discrimination, had already been denied the one qualification which would have enabled them to withstand the planned demotions—time in rank.

The court ruled that this job seniority system was not bona fide and, hence, illegal under Title VII.

Unions have historically been devoted to seniority, steadfastly refusing to compromise on its use in employment decisions. Yet, interestingly, some police unions have been willing to sacrifice its use when it leads to benefits for women at the expense of men. For instance, in *Schenectady v. State Division of Human Rights* (1975), a "policewoman" was blatantly passed over for an assignment as a patrol officer by a less senior male, notwithstanding the labor contract with the Schenectady Patrolmen's Benevolent Association requiring police officer vacancies to be filled on the basis of seniority.

The reliance on seniority has been abused in other ways as well. For example, in *United States v. Cincinnati* (1985), female police officers with the same seniority as males were not protected by their senior status during a period of layoffs. Due to a fiscal crisis faced by the city of Cincinnati, employees from several departments, including police, were scheduled to be laid off. Layoffs of police officers were to be made in accordance with the labor contract negotiated with the Fraternal Order of Police (FOP). Officers scheduled for layoff included seven white females, four black females and three black males. All were hired the same day as about forty white male officers who were not scheduled for layoff.

To justify the layoffs of women and minorities with the same date of hire as white males, a "composite score" was devised by the FOP and the city. This score incorporated, in part, an officer's performance on the entrance "merit" exam and interview. The union argued that this type of seniority system was bona fide and that the inclusion a nonseniority criterion such as composite scores did not detract from its soundness. Moreover, the FOP claimed that this nonseniority component was essential to the seniority system, and, hence, protected by Section 703(h) of Title VII.

The Sixth Circuit Court of Appeals rejected the FOP's claims. It recognized unions' and employers' need for freedom in creating seniority systems, but stated that this freedom "must not be allowed to sweep within the ambit of Section 703(h) employment rules that depart fundamentally from commonly accepted notions concerning the acceptable contours of a seniority system, simply because those rules are dubbed 'seniority' provisions" (*Cincinnati* 1985, 168).

The appellate court ruled that the use of composite scores was not a necessary part of, but rather an appendage to, the seniority system. It went on to say that because the "the 'seniority' aspect of such a scheme . . . might be covered by Section 703(h) does not mean that the [non-seniority] requirements would also be covered" (*Cincinnati* 1985, 168). The court concluded that the composite scores were illegal.

There are other instances where police unions have encouraged the arbitrary use of criteria in employment to the detriment of women. One case, *Shortt v. Arlington* (1978), points to such behavior and further demonstrates an intent to discriminate against women. It was customary at one time in the Arlington County Police Department to assign probationary police officers patrol duties. Female probationary officers, however, were assigned other duties such as youth investigator work, because their physical "stature and attributes" made them "unsuitable for patrol work." Such female officers were also compensated at a lower rate of pay than male probationary officers because they performed different work than their male counterparts. Union officials and male police officers did not object to these practices.

One female probationary officer, Linda Shortt, after successful completion of her probationary period in the Criminal Investigations Division as a youth investigator, and in accordance with the contractually negotiated promotional policy, qualified for and received a promotion. The promotion of Shortt led to a series of complaints from the male officers claiming that Shortt had not performed a year of patrol duty. Although not stipulated in the labor contract, the male officers believed patrol duty should have been a prerequisite for promotion. In an effort to appease the male officers, the union returned to the bargaining table and modified the promotional criteria to include the following stipulation: "[A]ll personnel (*females in particular*) must serve at least one year as a patrol officer before consideration for promotion" (*Shortt* 1978, 781; emphasis added by the court). Linda Shortt as well as other female officers, pursuant to this agreement, were demoted.

The Fourth Circuit Court of Appeals found these actions to constitute intentional sex discrimination in violation of Title VII. The court ruled that

[i]t is obvious from the very wording . . . that the adoption of the retroactive patrol duty requirement for promotion was merely a pretext . . . for demoting the plaintiff and the other female officers in her group. This memorandum of demotion . . . is directed at "females in particular." It was not a requirement based

upon any conclusion that patrol duty was an experience necessary for promotion (*Shortt* 1978, 781).

It seems reasonably clear that criteria which are supposedly incontrovertible can be and have been changed when those in power wish to do so. The effects of the changes almost invariably hurt women as well as minorities.

In addition to thwarting the employment opportunities of women in police departments, police unions have been lukewarm to female participation in the union itself. Historically, women were generally excluded from police associations or unions because the bylaws of these organizations limited membership to persons serving in patrol positions. Since women were excluded from police patrol assignments, they were, in effect, excluded from union membership. Even social membership in these organizations was off-limits to women. Social members enjoyed all the privileges as regular members with the exception of a vote or voice at meetings and elections. The bylaws of the Policemen's Organization, Erie Club of Buffalo, New York, for example, limited social membership to: "All male members in the Department of a higher rank than patrolmen who have received such rank through competitive examination and are members of the organization maintained by their own rank" (*By-Laws* 1933–34, 9).

To cope with the ostracism of unions, women generally established their own satellite agencies. For example, to promote the interests of the early women in police, the International Association of Policewomen was created. From its inception in 1915 to its demise in 1932, the Association worked to encourage police agencies to hire women. Although the Association supported the traditional "social work" role of women in policing, they nonetheless recognized, as is the case today, that women needed to form their own association or organization in order to enhance the opportunities of female police, and perhaps counter the resistance from all-male unions.

The Association was revived and renamed in 1956. The present day International Association of Women Police continues to promote the legitimacy and representation of women in policing (Horne 1980b), functions that police unions cannot be relied upon to perform. Other female satellite groups have contributed to the advancement of female police as well. For example, the Policewomen's Endowment Association (PEA) in New York City has filed complaints in court as well as before the city's Commission on Human Rights challenging the hiring, promotional and assignment practices of the city *and* police unions.[17]

Officer Lillian Braxton, president of the PEA, sums up the problem concisely. She has said that " '[t]here are still those few dinosaurs who think women belong in the kitchen' " (Wilkerson 1985b, 6). The PEA continues to combat these attitudes and the accompanying behaviors. One of PEA's priorities today is the development and implementation of pregnancy policies to protect female police when they interrupt their careers to have children. It is interesting to note that such policies have fueled the resistance of unions and their male constituents to the utilization and representation of women in uniformed, nonclerical police positions. The need for such policies appears to be one more reason for keeping women out.

Corrections

The employment patterns of women in corrections appear to resemble women's employment experiences in other uniformed services, particularly police. Beginning in the nineteenth century, women were able to gain entry into the profession of corrections because a group of women reformers was able to convince lawmakers and the public that female offenders were suffering from temporary lapses of morality and piety, which led to their incarceration. According to the reformers, with the appropriate rehabilitation, females could restore their virtuosity and, ultimately, re-enter "womanhood." The women reformers believed that the key to this rehabilitation was separation from the male prison environment as well as training and guidance from women. What better group than women could lead female offenders, in particular "fallen" women (i.e., prostitutes), down the path to righteousness (Feinman 1986)?

Separate correctional facilities for female offenders and, hence, a place for women in the profession of corrections grew out of this reform movement. Because it was couched in a sex-typed context, it was not particularly repugnant to prison officials. As Feinman writes: "Men in the prison system permitted women to enter the system because they knew and remained in their place. By establishing a matriarchy in corrections, women did not compete with men" (Feinman 1986, 135).

It seems that prison officials' views of women in corrections changed in conjunction with a number of factors, including shifts in society's views of female offenders. The crimes committed by women could no longer be looked upon as less serious than crimes committed by men, nor could they be rationalized as "unlady-like." These views, of course, could not be divorced from women's struggle to gain status and recognition in political, social and economic spheres. Women began to assert their employment rights in corrections the same way that men did. This shattered the image of "womanhood." Women were no longer willing to "remain in their place," which posed a threat to the male establishment of corrections.

Prior to the 1960s, women were absolutely barred from working in male prisons as correctional officers—also known as prison guards. The practice of restricting women to only female prisons limits the correctional jobs for women, since most states have only one female facility and it is almost always located in a rural area. (Parenthetically, although women were barred from male institutions, it was common for male correctional officers to be assigned to female facilities.)

Women eventually won the right to work as correctional officers in male prisons beginning in the 1960s, but their duties were limited only to searching female visitors; they were not allowed to supervise male inmates. It was not until the extension of Title VII to public sector employers in 1972 that women had the legal right to work in male prisons performing duties comparable to male correctional officers.

Despite this legal mandate, there was a good deal of resistance to the employment of female correctional officers in male facilities. The resistance manifested in many ways including the use of physical agility exams and height and weight requirements of the sort discussed earlier. When women were able to break through these barriers, they faced rigid state policies that restricted female correctional officers to low security-risk facilities. Also, within the male prisons, prison officials assigned female officers to only designated "safe" units and jobs (e.g., observing inmate visits) supposedly in response to what inmates called a "need for privacy." (Many view the "privacy" argument as a guise for male inmates' resentment to being supervised by women because of inmates' belief that it demeans their masculinity. On the other hand, there may be some merit to prisoners' claims, since privacy is deeply valued in the U.S. culture. This issue goes beyond the scope of this study.) The upshot of such policies was to severely limit the employment opportunities of female incumbents as well as women seeking to become correctional officers.

The courts have been instrumental in defining the employment rights of female correctional officers. For example, the courts have in general not allowed inmates' right to privacy to outweigh equal employment opportunities for female correctional officers (*Gunther v. Iowa* 1980; Reisner 1978). In addition, and having widespread applicability, the U.S. Supreme Court in *Dothard v. Rawlinson* (1977) struck down the use of height and weight requirements at correctional facilities in Alabama. The Court said that while physical ability may be needed for the job of correctional officer to maintain prison security, there needs to be a direct linkage between height and weight and the strength needed to perform the job. In other words, the Court said that a better measure of physical strength is needed because height and weight do not measure the necessary, job relevant factors (Potts 1983).

Another aspect of the *Dothard* ruling, however, has proven to be a blow to women seeking jobs as correctional officers in maximum-security prisons. The Court was called upon to review Alabama's policy of explicitly closing women out of the job of prison guard in maximum-security prisons. The Court majority upheld the state's practice on the grounds that a woman's ability to maintain order would be hindered by her "womanhood." The Court said that the essence of the job of correctional officer is to maintain order and a woman's gender precludes her from doing so. Interestingly, the Court substantiated its ruling here by discussing the threatening experiences of two women, neither of whom was a trained correctional officer—one was a clerical worker and the other a student on tour of the correctional facility.

The Court essentially upheld sex as a bona fide occupational qualification (BFOQ) for the position of correctional officer in prisons that pose a threat and danger to women (Horne 1985).[18] Title VII permits the use of sex as a BFOQ out of necessity by the "business" or organization. But, courts have generally interpreted the BFOQ exception to Title VII in narrow terms, rarely allowing an employer to restrict a job to members of one sex. The *Dothard* decision is significant, because it represents the first time the Supreme Court (or any federal appellate court) has upheld an employer's use of sex as a BFOQ (Jacobs 1981).

It is interesting to note that the district court in *Dothard* (*Mieth and Rawlinson v. Dothard*, 1976)[19] would not uphold sex as a BFOQ. It struck down the state's policy, claiming that insufficient evidence was produced to demonstrate that women were unqualified for the job. The district court also rejected the state's argument that maximum-security prisons are too dangerous for females (Jacobs 1981). In effect, the Supreme Court overturned the lower court ruling without evidence that women could not successfully perform the job of prison guard in Alabama's men's prisons.

Ultimately, the Court's ruling in *Dothard* is harmful because it reinforces negative stereotypes historically relied upon to segregate women in corrections. Women are portrayed as weak and dependent upon men for protection. Men are expected to provide protection in a paternalistic way (Bowersox 1981). Legal endorsement of such stereotypes hurts women's employment efforts in every sector. The district court in *Dothard* succinctly makes the point that "[l]abeling a job as 'strenuous' and then relying on the stereotyped characterization of women will not meet the burden of demonstrating a BFOQ.... There must be some objective, demonstrable evidence that women cannot perform the duties associated with the job" (*Mieth v. Dothard* 1976, 1180).

What has the role of unions been in the employment of female correctional officers? In short, it has been similar to that of other uniformed service unions. There has been a general resistance on the part of unions and their male constituents to the presence of female correctional officers in male prisons, especially in supervising male inmates. The arguments generally revolve around security issues where unions claim that women are physically and emotionally unsuited to the job. In addition, they will argue that the presence of women in male prisons will incite sexual aggressiveness among the inmates which could ultimately lead to assault and rape.[20] Finally, unions and their constituents feel that women will require the "protection" of male correctional officers, which poses threats to male officers (Zimmer 1982).

It is not surprising that there is no empirical proof to substantiate the beliefs of unions and male correctional officers. To the contrary, there has been some research demonstrating that women are able to perform the job of correctional officer just as well as men if provided with the opportunity to do so (Horne 1985; Flynn 1982). Nonetheless, the attitudes and accompanying behaviors of unions and male officers persist.

A review of the case law points to specific instances where unions have resisted efforts to hire and promote female correctional officers. For example, in *Local 526-M, SEIU v. Michigan* (1981), the union and several of its male employees filed suit against the state of Michigan charging that its affirmative action plan for women and minorities discriminated against white males in violation of the state constitution. The state appeals court ruled in favor of the state, which has ultimately assisted women in the correctional officer profession in Michigan.

In a similar case, *Minnick v. California Department of Corrections* (1981), two white males and their union, the California Correction Officers Association (CCOA), challenged the state's affirmative action plan on the grounds that it discriminated against white males in promotions.[21] The union's position is particularly interesting here. The CCOA argued that it "had been 'damaged' by the described employment practices because they frustrated its objectives as 'an organization actively opposed to racism and sexism, and working actively to increase the unity of all correctional officers' " (*Minnick* 1979, 263).

If the union was so committed to the elimination of sexism and racism in employment policies, this position would have been taken years ago when women and minorities were explicitly or implicitly excluded from the profession of correctional officer. It seems questionable, then, that the union would articulate this stance today. In addition, the sincerity of the union's position seems tenuous if juxtaposed against the goals of affirmative action programs.

The purpose of affirmative action is to address past discrimination against, as well as the underrepresentation of, protected class members in the work force (*Johnson v. Transportation Agency* 1987). In the case at hand, the state of California was seeking to rectify a gender and racial imbalance in its correctional officer classification. The importance of affirmative action programs in corrections cannot be overstated. Yet, if unions and their constituents continue to challenge them, the progress of women seeking jobs as correctional officers can be delayed (and also hindered in the event that a court rules for the union[22]). Genuine commitment on the part of unions to eliminate sexism and racism cannot ignore the history of discrimination against and underrepresentation of protected class members.

Unions have illustrated their lack of support for women in correctional officer positions in other ways as well. For instance, there have been cases where unions reversed their traditional stance on such issues as the use of sex as a BFOQ for assignment to correctional officer. Unions have been willing to do so when male correctional officers would benefit at the expense of females. For example, in *Commonwealth of Pennsylvania v. AFSCME* (1986), the union opposed the state's practice of prohibiting male correctional officers from bidding on certain assignments in its female facility. On face value, the union's opposition to sex as a BFOQ would seem favorable to women but, under the circumstances in this case, the opposition would specifically benefit male correctional officers and hinder the employment opportunities of females.

This facility is the only female prison in the state. At the time of the lawsuit, it housed 400 female and 140 male inmates. Sex was a BFOQ in certain assignments at the prison. For instance, one guideline specified: "Guards [would] not be assigned to work in open view of unclothed inmates of the opposite sex" (*Commonwealth* 1986, 1565). Given the large female-male inmate ratio at this female prison, the use of sex as a BFOQ, which normally adversely affects women, would, in fact, circumscribe the employment opportunities of males. Recognizing this, the union insisted that assignments be made on a gender-neutral basis.

The circumstances surrounding female officers' access to male facilities in New York State are somewhat similar to the Pennsylvania experience. The integration of female guards in New York State's male correctional facilities was extremely slow due to opposition from rank-and-file officers and their union, Council 82 of the American Federation of State, County and Municipal Employees (AFSCME). Among other things, the union supported the use of height and weight requirements as well as a physical agility exam, which had an exclusionary effect on women. Union leaders believed that "women did not belong in men's prisons and that their presence jeopardized the safety of male officers and the security of the institutions" (Zimmer 1982, 126).

As a result of political and legal pressures from female union members in the early 1970s, the union eventually supported an integration effort. The support was premised, however, on the requirement that female correctional officers be assigned only to "lobbies, visiting rooms and front gate areas and only if they supplemented existing staff" (Jacobs and Crotty 1978, 23).

By October of 1976, the union shifted its position and insisted that female correctional officers be allowed access to male facilities, working in the same capacity as male officers. The union's executive director said that "[w]e, Council 82, demand that a single, not separate, open competitive examination be given in the future for corrections officers. We further demand that the separate transfer list maintained by the Department of Correctional Services be abolished and be replaced by a single integrated transfer list" (Jacobs and Crotty 1978, 23). The department agreed to the union's proposals.

The reasons why the union shifted its position should be considered, however, because they illustrate that the union was not necessarily supportive of women but, rather, interested in expanding the opportunities of male officers and maintaining stable administrative arrangements. First, the union's new position would benefit male correctional officers seeking to work in female facilities (Jacobs 1981). Second, and unlike the police unions discussed earlier, the correctional officers' union was unwilling to compromise on the use of seniority in assignment and transfer decisions. To do so would undermine its power in the future. Then, if the union desired to preserve the integrity of its stance on seniority, and hence its continued use, it would need to support the use of seniority in female officers' bids on assignments to male prisons.

Pragmatically, the union's position would continue to work to the advantage of its male constituents because, systematically, due to the exclusion of women in the past, male correctional officers have more seniority than females. The continued use of seniority, then, would benefit a relatively small number of women, but many more men.

It seems axiomatic that the union's actions were not marked by altruism or equal opportunities for female correctional officers (Horne 1985; Zimmer 1982). This is further exemplified by the union's inertia in combating or preventing sexual harassment of female guards by male officers (Zimmer 1986). If the union was genuinely supportive of the integration effort, it would have anticipated the almost inevitable consequence of sexual harassment from male guards who resisted female entry. Mechanisms could have been established well in advance of the integration effort.

Women have made some inroads into corrections since the nineteenth century, but they are still underutilized in many capacities, particularly as correctional officers. And, unlike the other uniformed services, the use of sex as a BFOQ has been accepted by the U.S. Supreme Court in at least one case, which can only further hinder the employment opportunities of women in corrections. Unions have resisted female entry into the occupation of correctional officer and, so, they represent one more barrier to women seeking careers in this profession.

Sanitation

"You've Come a Long Way, Baby; Now You Can Pick Up the Trash," read the headline in a *Wall Street Journal* article (Johnson 1985) describing women's attempts to secure jobs as uniformed sanitation workers (a.k.a. garbage haulers or refuse workers). Perhaps the headline should have read:

"You've Come a Long Way; Now You Can Get *Paid* for Picking Up the Trash." This would have been more accurate, given that women have been hauling trash to the curb for a lifetime, but they are just now breaking into the paying occupation (Wilkerson 1985a).

Many have questioned why women would want the job of a sanitation worker since it appears so thankless and unglamorous. Of course, whether the work is glamorous or not is really insignificant. As with any job, the issue is that women be given equal opportunities or access to jobs that men have traditionally held. Women may seek such jobs for symbolic reasons, but more and more the reasons revolve around economics. Sanitation work is a good example of a traditionally male occupation which pays high wages and benefits relative to female-dominated jobs. In New York City, for example, the starting salary for sanitation workers is around $25,000. Those who earn bonuses and work overtime can earn up to $40,000 a year. In addition, sanitation workers in the city are entitled to five weeks of paid vacation per year, unlimited sick leave and excellent medical benefits (Carmody 1987; Wilkerson 1985b; *New York Times*, 27 July 1983).

The obstacles to women seeking jobs in this occupation will sound familiar by now. Prior to 1972, women were generally barred from taking sanitation worker exams. After 1972, they were permitted to take the exam, but were excluded from the occupation through other means including the use of tough physical agility exams. Because of these barriers, only about a half a dozen large cities today, including New York City, San Diego, Seattle, Cincinnati and Madison, Wisconsin, employ women in uniformed sanitation jobs. And, as Table 5.1 presented at the beginning of this chapter demonstrates, they are employed in relatively small numbers.

Sanitation workers' unions have generally resisted women's entry into the occupation. The resistance seems to stem from their belief that women lack the upper-body strength to haul trash. This is borne out, according to unions, by women's inability to pass "merit" tests. The union's involvement in women's struggle to gain entry into New York City's Sanitation Department is perhaps illustrative of unions' attitudes and behaviors toward female sanitation workers.

Women were first allowed to take New York City's sanitation workers' exam in 1974, but only one female out of sixty passed the physical agility test and she was never hired (Gross 1986). As later recognized by a state court, the 1974 test unfairly worked against women. It required applicants to scale an 8-foot wall and carry a 60-pound garbage can through an obstacle course, which simulated parked cars, parking meters and snow banks (*New York Times* 4 January 1974). Nearly ten years later, and under fear of mounting legal pressures, the city questioned, "how often does a sanitation worker have to scale an 8-foot wall . . . and run an obstacle course while carrying a garbage can?" (*New York Times* 30 August 1986).

In an effort to redress the "validity" problem as well as avoid the kinds of political and legal costs it incurred from excluding women from uniformed firefighting jobs, the city revised its sanitation workers' agility exam. Through a concurrent "time and motion" study, incumbent sanitation workers were tested to determine such things as the sequence of activities involved in refuse collection (e.g., distance walked from curb to garbage truck), the weights of bags hauled, and how bags and garbage cans were handled (e.g., lifted, carried, dragged). By testing incumbent workers, men ultimately set the standards for sanitation workers in the city.

At the beginning of this chapter, the issue of concurrent validity was addressed and it was noted that when physical strength is deemed an important attribute of the job, concurrent studies generally work against women. The circumstances surrounding the concurrent validation of the sanitation workers' exam in New York City prove instructive, however, because they raise questions regarding the overall level of physical strength needed for certain jobs.

The revised physical test for sanitation worker was administered between 1985 and 1986, and of the 1,822 women taking it, 1,357 earned perfect scores, 353 earned passing scores and 112 failed. The fact that women performed extremely well on this physical test, despite its being based on a concurrent study, leads to a number of questions regarding the physical strength actually needed to perform sanitation work. That is, perhaps the degree of physical strength needed is not as high as traditionally believed. If this is the case, and agility exams reflect the actual strength needed, women would not be excluded from uniformed sanitation jobs. But, if the tests inflate the amount of strength needed to perform the work, women will be excluded.

Based on their performance, women were certain to gain entry into the sanitation department. Before the city could hire its female sanitation workers, however, the Uniformed Sanitationmen's Association sought and won a temporary restraining order (*New York Times* 29 June 1986). The union's position seemed to suggest that it did not support women's entry into the department. This was recognized by the media as well as the courts (*Uniformed Sanitationmen's Association v. New York City* 1986).

The union challenged the constitutionality and legality of the revised exam, arguing that it was not an adequate measure of "merit and fitness" because of the overall high passing rate (of the 45,000 taking the exam, about 44,000 earned perfect scores). The union argued that the 1974 exam was more job-related and, hence, a better measure of potential job performance. The union believed various revisions to the test, such as allowing the job candidates (most notably the women) to drag, rather than lift garbage bags to the truck, made the exam too easy. This is an intriguing argument, in light of the fact that the agility exam was based on how incumbent male workers handled garbage.

Another noteworthy argument of the union revolves around degrees of "merit." The revised test required applicants to lift a total of 2,975 pounds in 27 minutes. The union contended that candidates who completed the test in less than the required 27 minutes should have been given higher scores. The union appeared to be looking for the "best qualified" candidates. In essence, the union was calling for a rank-ordered rather than a pass-fail scoring system, which has historically worked against women.

Interestingly, the union argued that the city inappropriately relied upon Title VII in developing a new exam. It said that the city's "reliance upon Title VII is misplaced as there are no discrimination suits presently pending against the Sanitation Department" (*Uniformed Sanitationmen's Association* 1986, 8). The union was saying that since women have not legally challenged the hiring practices of the sanitation department, there was no need to revise the exam. To support its position the union pointed to the high percentage of minority sanitation workers, which surpasses minority employment in the other uniformed services in the city. According to the union, given that at least minorities are highly represented in the sanitation department, why tamper with the status quo?

It is interesting that the union relied on minority employment statistics to defend its position because, in the early 1970s, minorities faced barriers similar to women. Indeed, a lawsuit filed by minorities against the city during the post-1972 period led the city to recruit and hire minorities into the ranks of sanitation worker (*New York Times* 5 January 1973). Thus, minorities gained access to uniformed sanitation jobs only after a legal battle.

The New York State Supreme Court ultimately ruled that the exam adequately measured the qualifications needed to perform the job of sanitation worker and, therefore, was legal and constitutional. Further, the court said that despite the statistics on minority employment, "the fact still remains that there are no female sanitation workers" (*Uniformed Sanitationmen's Association* 1986, 8). Moreover, it said that the city "is not precluded from taking into consideration the lack of women in determining whether or not [the agility exam] comports with the Constitution . . . as well as Title VII" (*Uniformed Sanitationmen's Association* 1986, 9).

The union appealed the ruling, and while on appeal, a temporary stay was granted to prevent the city from hiring new workers. When the state appellate court later refused to extend the stay, however, the city hired 137 people by lottery, two of whom were women (Johnson 1986). The appeals court eventually affirmed the lower court's ruling. The union persisted in its opposition by appealing to the highest court in New York State, the Court of Appeals. This court refused to hear the case, and so the revised exam was not dismantled. Ultimately, the two female sanitation workers kept their jobs and additional women are expected to be hired.

As discussed throughout this chapter, once women gain entry into the uniformed services, there continues to exist a great deal of resentment on the part of unions as well as male incumbents. It is not surprising, then, that the sanitation workers' union and its male constituents were not receptive to women's entry into New York City's Sanitation Department. One worker said:

We won't have to chase [the women] out, they'll chase themselves out. . . . Clerical, sure, girls can do that and they can do the brooms in the street. They can even drive a truck, I don't care what size. It's just picking up the garbage. I don't think that's possible. Men are physically built for this; they have a harder life. You know, a women [sic] does the dishes and a man does the lawn work, washes the car. I know things have changed, but not that much (Gross 1986, 1, 6).

This type of attitude presents further barriers not only to the two women out of thousands of sanitation workers in the city, but to women seeking entry into the occupation as well.

To combat these attitudes, the sanitation department is developing a program that would enable female sanitation workers to interact with women in the other uniformed services (e.g., police and fire). This would enable women to develop a support network and perhaps a mentoring system (Pecorella 1988). Such devices are critical for women in any uniformed service, particularly since they are so isolated from one another.

Women are slowly making their way into uniformed sanitation jobs throughout the country. The obstacles women face are similar to those presented in the other uniformed services. Union resistance adds to and sometimes creates the barriers. As long as unions oppose female entry into the occupation, the progress made by women in sanitation will effectively be slowed and hindered.

Conclusions

Despite legal mandates that have been in existence for almost two decades, women continue to be severely underrepresented in the uniformed services. One primary obstacle to women is resistance from unions. Notwithstanding, it is interesting that women do not place much legal pressure on unions. One could reason that, overall, women file lawsuits only against employers because they fear retaliation by unions. But, the record here seems to suggest that because of the magnitude of unions' resistance to women in the uniformed services, they will retaliate even if they are not direct parties to the lawsuit. Lawsuits may do little to change union attitudes toward women in uniformed jobs but, over time, they may be helpful in modifying union behaviors. If women are to make absolute gains, however, much more is needed.

Perhaps one of the best tools for addressing union resistance is educational and training programs for union officials and their rank-and-file. These mechanisms, too, however, will have limited value if city officials are not committed to female entry into uniformed services. As indicated in previous sections, commitment requires not only development of such programs but also implementation and evaluation. This seems prudent, else the city and perhaps the union will face legal challenges, which can be extremely costly.

These programs would also make it easier to recruit and train women. Ideally, efforts to attract females to careers in the uniformed services would be targeted not simply at adults but at young women as well. If women become aware of such career opportunities early on, they may be more apt to assert their rights to such jobs. Given the attitudes and behaviors of unions and city officials, however, expanding drives to attract women to nonclerical, uniformed service jobs may not become a reality for many years to come.

Finally, future research is needed on the actual physical strength requirements of uniformed service jobs. Without such information, even legally "valid" merit exams may not be identifying qualified job candidates.

Notes

1. See, *infra* notes 2, 3 and 4.

2. For cases dealing with minimum height and weight requirements, see, for example, *Costa v. Markey* (1982); *United States v. North Carolina* (1981); *Horace v. Pontiac* (1980); *Blake v. Los Angeles* (1979); *United States v. Buffalo* (1978); *Dothard v. Rawlinson* (1977); *Officers for Justice v. Civil Service Commission* (1975, 1979) and *Hardy v. Stumpf* (1974).

3. For cases dealing with minimum height and weight requirements see, for example, *Guardians Ass'n v. Civil Service Commission* (1980); *United States v. Buffalo* (1978); *League of United Latin American Citizens v. Santa Ana* (1976); *Lum v. New York City Civil Service Commission* (1975) and *Officers for Justice v. Civil Service Commission* (1975, 1979). For cases dealing with written exams see, for example, *Washington v. Davis* (1976); *Vulcan Society v. New York City Civil Service Commission* (1973); *Bridgeport Guardians, Inc. v. Civil Service Commission* (1973); *Officers for Justice v. Civil Service Commission* (1973); *Western Addition Community Organization v. Alioto* (1973) and *Shield Club v. Cleveland* (1972).

4. See, for example, *Berkman v. New York City* (1982, 1983, 1987), *Blake v. Los Angeles* (1979) and *Officers for Justice v. Civil Service Commission* (1975, 1979).

5. See, for example, *Firefighters Local No. 93 v. Cleveland* (1986) and *Minority Police Officers Ass'n of South Bend v. South Bend* (1983).

6. See, for example, *United States v. Paradise* (1987); *San Francisco Police Officers Ass'n v. San Francisco* (1987); *Afro-American Patrolmen's League v. Atlanta* (1987); *Firefighters Local No. 93 v. Cleveland* (1986); *Minority Police Officers Ass'n v. South Bend* (1983) and *Richards v. New York State Correctional Services* (1983).

7. See, for example, *NAACP v. Detroit Police Officers Ass'n* (1988) and *Richards v. New York State Correctional Services* (1983).

8. Also see, *Blake v. Los Angeles* (1979). It should be noted that only under certain rare circumstances have courts upheld the continued use of such requirements. For example, the Court of Appeals for the Eighth Circuit in *Boyd v. Ozark Airlines* (1977) upheld the use of minimum height as a necessary requirement for a pilot to see properly and also to reach the controls in an airplane cockpit. For a discussion, see Campion (1983).

9. See note 8, *supra*.

10. It should be noted that there have been efforts to validate physical abilities tests for some of the uniformed services (e.g., police), but the tests do not measure that *actual* strength required for the job. See, for example, Wilmore and Davis (1979).

11. The test was originally devised on the basis of a concurrent study involving incumbent male firefighters. For legal purposes, the city later sought to demonstrate the exam's concurrent validity by testing not only incumbent men (104) but also a group of the newly hired women (29). The finding of validity here leads to further questions regarding women's ability to perform the job of firefighting if training is provided or on-the-job experience is acquired.

12. See, for example, *United States v. Jefferson County* (1983); *Vulcan Society v. Fire Department of White Plains* (1981); *United States v. Buffalo* (1978) (no fire union named); *Maehren v. Seattle, cert. denied* (1981) (no fire union named), and *Brunet v. Columbus* (1986) (no fire union named). Cases are also pending in San Francisco and Cleveland.

13. I use the term "policewoman" to describe how females were classified in early years.

14. See, for example, *United States v. Chicago* (1986); *United States v. Buffalo* (1978); *United States v. Miami* (1980); *United States v. Philadelphia* (1980); *Brace v. O'Neill* (1978); *Schenectady v. State Division of Human Rights* (1975), and *United States v. Cincinnati* (1985).

15. Also see, *San Francisco Police Officers Ass'n v. San Francisco* (1987), where the police union not only negotiated a promotional exam scoring procedure that had an adverse impact on women and minorities, but filed a lawsuit against the city when it attempted to revise the scoring procedures to benefit women and minorities.

16. The emphasis here, then, is not so much on the actual bona fides of seniority systems, as was the focus in Chapter 3, but rather, on unions' use of seniority to bar women from police work.

17. *Policewomen's Endowment Association, et al. v. Civil Service Commission of the City of New York* (1981); *Policewomen's Endowment Association Against New York City Police Department* (1978).

18. There continues to be some ambiguity surrounding the BFOQ aspect of the Court's ruling. For example, in *Gunther v. Iowa State Men's Reformatory* (1980), the appellate court would not find male sex a BFOQ for the position of correctional officer because the Iowa prison did not have the "jungle atmosphere" that supposedly characterized the Alabama prison, serving as the basis for Supreme Court's decision in *Dothard.*

19. In *Mieth* (1976), Mieth charged that height and weight requirements for state trooper were discriminatory. The district court upheld her claim; the state did not appeal that decision, only that of Rawlinson.

20. This is contrary to what many criminal justice scholars as well as prison officials argue for in the way of "normalizing" the prison environment by integrating women into the work force. This would better reflect the composition of society, thereby easing the inmates' ability to readjust to societal life at some future time (Jacobs 1981).

21. In *Minnick* (1981), the Supreme Court neither upheld nor rejected the affirmative action plan in the corrections department and, so, the outcome of this case is ambiguous.

22. Beginning with *Regents of University of California v. Bakke* (1978), there has been a steady trend for courts to uphold affirmative action plans in hiring and promotions in both public and private sectors when certain conditions are met. This was recently strengthened by the Supreme Court's decision in *Johnson v. Transportation Agency* (1987). But, see the Epilogue for a brief discussion of recent Supreme Court rulings on EEO and AA.

References

Afro-American Patrolmen's League v. Atlanta 817 F. 2d 719 (11th Cir. 1987).

Anderson, Mary A. *Women in Law Enforcement: A Primer for Policewomen.* Portland, Oregon: Metropolitan Press, 1973.

Bell, Daniel J. "Policewomen: Myths and Reality." *Journal of Police Science and Administration* 10 (1982), 1:112–120.

Berkman v. New York City 536 F. Supp. 177 (1982); *aff'd.*, 705 F. 2d 584 (2d Cir. 1983).

Berkman v. New York City 580 F. Supp. 226 (1983).

Berkman v. New York City 812 F. 2d 52 (2d Cir. 1987); *cert. denied*, 108 S. Ct. 146, _U.S._ (1987).

Blake v. Los Angeles 595 F. 2d 1367 (9th Cir. 1979); *cert. denied*, 100 S.Ct. 1865, 446 U.S. 928 (1980).

Bloch, Peter and Deborah Anderson. *Policewomen on Patrol: Final Report.* Washington, D.C.: Police Foundation, 1974.

Bowersox, Michael S. "Women in Corrections." *Criminal Justice and Behavior* 8 (1981), 4:491–499.

Boyd v. Ozark Airlines 568 F. 2d 50 (8th Cir. 1977).

Brace v. O'Neill 19 FEP Cases 848 (1978).

Bridgeport Guardians, Inc. v. Civil Service Commission 482 F. 2d 1333 (2d Cir. 1973).

Brunet v. Columbus 642 F. Supp. 1214 (1986).

Bureau of National Affairs. *EEO in Public Safety Agencies*. Washington, D.C.: Bureau of National Affairs, 30 August 1982.

Burks, Edward C. "A Study of Patrols Finds Policewomen as Capable as Men." *New York Times*, 4 December 1977, 37.

By-laws. Policemen's Organization, Erie Club, Buffalo, New York, 1933–34.

Campion, Michael A. "Personnel Selection for Physically Demanding Jobs: Review and Recommendations." *Personnel Psychology* 36 (1983), 3:527–550.

Carmody, Deirdre. "2 Female Sanitation Workers Earning High Marks." *New York Times*, 31 January 1987, 29, 31.

Cayer, N. Joseph and Lee Sigelman. "Minorities and Women in State and Local Government: 1973–1975." *Public Administration Review* 40 (1980), 5:443–450.

Charles, Michael T. "Women in Policing: The Physical Aspect." *Journal of Police Science and Administration* 10 (1982), 2:194–205.

Chertos, Cynthia H. and Sarah Phillips. *Physical Training as a Strategy for Integrating Municipal Uniformed Services*. Center for Women in Government, Working Paper No. 18. State University of New York at Albany, 1986.

Colker, Ruth. "Rank-Order Physical Abilities Selection Devices for Traditionally Male Occupations as Gender-Based Employment Discrimination." *U.C. Davis Law Review* 19 (1986), 4:761–805.

Commonwealth of Pennsylvania v. AFSCME 41 FEP Cases 1564 (1986).

Considine, W., et al. "Developing a Physical Performance Test Battery for Screening Chicago Fire Fighter Applicants." *Public Personnel Management Journal* 5 (1976), 1:7–14.

Cook, Joan. "Fire Company in Basking Ridge Ordered to Open Rolls to Women." *New York Times*, 14 September 1977, 25.

Costa v. Markey 677 F. 2d 158 (1st Cir. 1982).

Daley, Suzanne. "Sex Bias Lingers in Firehouses of New York." *New York Times*, 8 December 1986, A1, B6.

Dothard v. Rawlinson 433 U.S. 321, 15 FEP Cases 10 (1977).

Dunshee, Kenneth H. *As You Pass By*. New York: Hastings House, 1952.

EEOC. *Job Patterns for Minorities and Women in State and Local Government, 1980*. Washington, D.C., April 1982.

Feinman, Clarice. *Women in the Criminal Justice System*. New York: Praeger, 1986, 2d ed.

Firefighters Local No. 93 v. Cleveland 106 S.Ct. 3063, _U.S._ (1986).

Flynn, Edith E. "Women as Criminal Justice Professionals." In Nicole Rafter and Elizabeth Stanko (eds.), *Judge, Lawyer, Victim, Thief*. Boston: Northeastern University Press, 1982.

Fried, Joseph P. "Women Win Ruling on Fire Dept. Test." *New York Times*, 6 March 1982, 1, 10.

Gordon, Kathryn. "Fighting Fire With a Woman's Hand." *Berkshire Women's News* (September/October 1986), 1.

Grondahl, Paul. "Women Bolster Firefighting." *Albany Times Union*, 31 August 1986, B1.

Gross, Jane. "2 Women Welcomed (By Some)." *New York Times*, 26 August 1986, B1, 6.

Guardians Ass'n v. Civil Service Commission 431 F. Supp. 526 (S.D.N.Y. 1977); *aff'd in relevant part* 630 F. 2d 79 (2d Cir. 1980).

Gunther v. Iowa State Men's Reformatory 612 F. 2d 1079 (8th Cir. 1980); *cert. denied*, 100 S. Ct. 2942, 446 U.S. 966 (1980).

Guyor, James R. "Spokane Learns From Experience." *Public Personnel Management* 3 (1974), 1:10–18.

Haitch, Richard. "Women Join Active Ranks of Volunteer Firefighters." *New York Times*, 23 March 1975, 61, 74.

Hardy v. Stumpf 37 Cal. App. 3d 958, 112 Cal. Rptr. 739 (1974).

Higgins, Lois. "Historical Background of Policewomen's Service." *Journal of Criminal Law, Criminology and Police Service* 41 (1951), 6:822–833.

Horace v. City of Pontiac 624 F. 2d 765 (6th Cir. 1980).

Horne, Peter. "Female Correction Officers." *Federal Probation* 49 (1985), 3:46–54.

———. "Policewomen and the Physical Aspects of Policing." *Law and Order* 28 (1980a), 9:83–88.

———. *Women in Law Enforcement.* Springfield, Illinois: Charles C. Thomas Publisher, 1980b, 2d ed.

Hubbard, Henry F., Thelma Hunt and Robert D. Krause. "Job Related Strength and Agility Tests—A Methodology." *Public Personnel Management* 4 (1975), 5:305–310.

Jacobs, James B. "The Sexual Integration of the Prison's Guard Force: A Few Comments on *Dothard v. Rawlinson*." In *Women and Corrections.* College Park, MD: American Correctional Association, 1981, 57–85.

Jacobs, James B. and Norma Meacham Crotty. *Guard Unions and the Future of the Prisons.* Ithaca, New York: New York State School of Industrial and Labor Relations, Cornell University, August 1978.

Jochnowitz, Jay. "Women Wanted as Firefighters." *Albany Times Union*, 17 July 1978a, B1, 8.

———. "Women Say Albany Resists Hiring Female Firefighters." *Albany Times Union*, 26 July 1987b, B6.

Johnson, Kirk. "Judge Allows Sanitation Hirings." *New York Times*, 13 August 1986, B1.

Johnson, Leola A. "You've Come a Long Way, Baby; Now You Can Pick Up the Trash." *Wall Street Journal*, 28 June 1985, 25.

Johnson v. Transportation Agency 107 S.Ct. 1442, _U.S._ (1987).

Kelly, Brad. "Firefighter Search Nets Women, Minorities." *Knickerbocker News*, 12 August 1987, A4.

Kennedy, Shawn G. "2 Bids Fail to Block Test by Fire Dept. for Women." *New York Times*, 8 September 1982, B3.

Koenig, Esther J. "An Overview of Attitudes Toward Women in Law Enforcement." *Public Administration Review* 38 (1979), 3:267–275.

League of United Latin American Citizens v. Santa Ana 410 F. Supp. 873 (C.D. Cal. 1976).

Local 526-M, Michigan Corrections Organization, SEIU v. Michigan 313 N.W. 2d 143 (Mich. App. 1981).

Lubasch, Arnold H. "New York City Scoring of Firefighters Rejected." *New York Times*, 18 February 1987, B3.

Lum v. New York City Civil Service Commission 10 FEP 365 (S.D.N.Y. 1975).

Maehren v. Seattle 599 P. 2d 1255 (Wash. Sup. Ct. 1979); *cert. denied*, 452 U.S. 938, 101 S.Ct. 3079 (1981).

Maitland, Leslie. "90 Women Fail Test to be Firefighters." *New York Times*, 18 March 1978, B3.

May, Clifford D. "High Court Lets Fire Dept. Keep its Physical Test." *New York Times*, 6 October 1987, A1, B7.

Melchionne, Theresa M. "The Changing Role of Policewomen." *Police Journal* 68 (1974), 4:340–358.

Mieth and Rawlinson v. Dothard 418 F. Supp. 1169 (M.D. Ala. 1976).

Minnick v. California Department of Corrections 157 Cal. Rptr. 260 (App. 1979); *cert. granted*, 100 S.Ct. 3055, 448 U.S. 910 (1980); *cert. denied*, 101 S.Ct. 2211, 452 U.S. 105 (1981).

Minority Police Officers Ass'n of South Bend v. South Bend 721 F. 2d 197 (7th Cir. 1983).

NAACP v. Detroit Police Officers Ass'n 676 F. Supp. 790 (E.D. Mich. 1988).

New York Times. "The Fitness of Firewomen." 29 August 1982, E18.

———. "Puerto Ricans Find Sanitation Job Bias." 5 January 1973, 35.

———. "Sanitation Agency Ends Recruiting." 27 July 1983, 31.

———. "State Judge's Order Prevents Hiring of Sanitation Workers." 29 June 1986, 31.

———. "The Weight of Trash, and Tradition." 30 August 1986, 24.

———. "Woman Wins the Right to Become Firefighter." 26 July 1977, A14.

———. "Women to Be Eligible to Take City Test for Sanitation Worker." 4 January 1974, 33.

Officers for Justice v. Civil Service Commission 371 F. Supp. 1328 (N.D. Cal. 1975).

Officers for Justice v. Civil Service Commission 395 F. Supp. 378 (N.D. Cal. 1975).

Officers for Justice v. Civil Service Commission 473 F. Supp. 801 (1979).

Pecorella, Robert F. "Remediation and Equity: A Case Study of Gender Integration." *Public Personnel Management Journal* 17 (1988), 1:73–81.

Policewomen's Endowment Association, et al. v. Civil Service Commission of the City of New York (81 Civ. 0537, S.D.N.Y., 1981).

Policewomen's Endowment Association Against New York City Police Department (No. 7657-EG, City of New York Commission on Human Rights, 1978).

Potts, Lee W. "Female Professionals in Corrections." *Federal Probation* 47 (1983), 1:37–44.

Regents of University of California v. Bakke 98 S.Ct. 2733, 438 U.S. 265 (1978).

Reisner, Susan L. "Balancing Inmates' Right to Privacy with Equal Employment for Prison Guards." *Women's Rights Law Reporter* 4 (Summer 1978), 4:243–251.

Riccucci, Norma M. "A Typology for Union Discrimination: A Public Sector Perspective." *Public Personnel Management Journal* 17 (1988), 1:41–51.

———. "Black Employment in Municipal Work Forces." *Public Administration Quarterly* 11 (1987), 1:76–89.

Richards v. New York State Correctional Services 572 F. Supp. 1168 (D.C.N.Y. 1983).

San Francisco Police Off. Ass'n. v. San Francisco 812 F. 2d. 1125 (9th Cir. 1987).

Schaefer v. Tannian 394 F. Supp. 1136 (1975).

Schenectady v. State Division of Human Rights 335 N.E. 2d 290 (1975).

Schick, Timothy F. "Fire Companies Gradually Admitting Women." *Albany Times Union*, 16 August 1987, B1.

Schick, Timothy F. and Rosemary O'Hara. "Volunteer Companies Lack Public Oversight." *Albany Times Union*, 12 July 1987, A1, 8.

Shield Club v. Cleveland 370 F. Supp. 251 (N.D. Ohio 1972).

Shortt v. Arlington 589 F. 2d 779 (4th Cir. 1978).

Snell v. Suffolk County 611 F. Supp. 521 (D.C.N.Y. 1985).

Syracuse Post Standard. "Hiring Settlement Generally Praised." 20 March 1980, C1.

Uniformed Sanitationmen's Association v. New York City (No. 14607/86, New York State Supreme Court, July 28, 1986).

United States v. Buffalo 457 F. Supp. 612 (1978).

United States v. Chicago 796 F. 2d 205 (7th Cir. 1986).

United States v. Cincinnati 771 F. 2d 161 (6th Cir. 1985).

United States v. Jefferson County 720 F. 2d 1511 (11th Cir. 1983).

United States v. Miami 614 F. 2d 1322 (5th Cir. 1980).

United States v. North Carolina 512 F. Supp. 968 (E.D.N.C. 1981).

United States v. Paradise 107 S.Ct. 1053, _U.S._ (1987).

United States v. Philadelphia 499 F. Supp. 1196 (1980).

Vega, Manuel and Ira J. Silverman."Female Police Officers as Viewed by Their Male Counterparts." *Police Studies* 5 (1982), 1:31–39.

Vulcan Society v. Fire Department of White Plains 505 F. Supp. 955 (1981).

Vulcan Society v. New York City Civil Service Commission 490 F. 2d 387 (2d Cir. 1973).

Washington v. Davis 96 S.Ct. 2040, 426 U.S. 229 (1976).

Weisheit, Ralph A. "Women in the State Police: Concerns of Male and Female Officers." *Journal of Police Science and Administration* 15 (1987), 2:137–144.

Western Addition Community Organization v. Alioto 369 F. Supp. 77 (N.D. Cal. 1973).

White v. Nassau County Police 15 FEP Cases 261 (1977).

Wilkerson, Isabel. "Women Share Joy in Passing Tests of Strength to be Sanitation Workers." *New York Times*, 30 July 1985a, B1, 4.

———. "Affirmative Actions Spread Through the City." *New York Times*, 13 October 1985b, 6.

Wilmore, Jack H. and James A. Davis. "Validation of a Physical Abilities Field Test for the Selection of State Traffic Officers." *Journal of Occupational Medicine* 21 (1979), 1:33–40.

Winerip, Michael. "Volunteer Fire Forces Attacked on Sex Bias." *New York Times*, 5 August 1983, B2.

Zimmer, Lynn E. *Female Guards in Men's Prisons: Creating a Role for Themselves.* Doctoral Dissertation. Ithaca, New York: Cornell University, 1982.

———. *Women Guarding Men.* Chicago: University of Chicago Press, 1986.

Zusy, Anne. "For Women Who Fight Fire, Acceptance and Frustration." *New York Times*, 12 October 1987, A1, 14.

6

UNIONS AND COMPARABLE WORTH

Wage differentials between female and male workers have not improved much within the past several decades. Today, women earn about 64 cents for every dollar earned by men.[1] This wage gap between females and males is at the heart of the pay equity or "comparable worth" debate. Unions have a considerable stake in the comparable worth issue because comparable worth seeks to restructure one of the most important considerations for unions—wage systems. The news media suggest that unions are extremely supportive of comparable worth and have taken measures to attain equal pay for comparable worth.

As several chapters in this volume have shown, however, some unions have either intentionally discriminated against women or have failed to rectify past or historical discriminations against them. Unions have frustrated women's efforts to gain access to certain jobs and have made little progress in advancing them to leadership positions within unions themselves. What, then, encourages unions to engage in the bitter and costly battle to end discrimination against women in compensation and classification systems?

There are several possible answers. One factor may be that women press their unions for protection from pay discrimination. With more women in more places in the work force, they are a force to be reckoned with by any union that expects to survive. On the more positive side of the ledger, in an era of overall dwindling union membership, unions may campaign for pay equity in hopes of attracting women. There are, in fact, specific conditions under which unions will support equal pay for comparable worth. In short, union support for pay equity policies is not unequivocal, as previous research as well as the media would have us believe. Moreover, many unions strongly oppose comparable worth measures and such opposition is rarely discussed or analyzed in any systematic fashion.

This chapter seeks to fill gaps in our existing knowledge about union involvement in comparable worth by examining the particular conditions under which some unions are willing to support comparable worth. In addition, it will point to those instances where unions are opposed or even hostile to pay equity policies.

To better determine the motivations of unions to either support or oppose comparable worth, several factors are taken into account. For example, the *type* of union is considered. More specifically, it is asked, Are industrial unions more supportive than craft unions? Also significant in determining unions' position on comparable worth is the level—federation, national or local—of unionism. Support may be evident at the federation level, for example, but not at the local. Also of interest is whether there are differences between public and private sector unions' stance on comparable worth. As we seek answers to these and other related questions, we must keep in mind the larger issue. That is, in our efforts to narrow the female-male wage gap, it is critical that we fully understand unions' motivations to either support or oppose pay equity measures in order to address union behaviors and respond accordingly.

What Is Comparable Worth?

Comparable worth differs considerably from "equal pay for equal work." The latter, which is explicitly mandated by the Equal Pay Act of 1963 for public and private employers,[2] is aimed more at pay *equality* between women and men performing similar or equal work. A female maintenance worker, for example, must be paid the same wages as a male maintenance worker, assuming the content of the jobs is equal. Equal pay may be required even if the jobs are not identical, provided that they are similar in functions and required skills (*Schultz v. Wheaton Glass Co.* 1970). Wage differences can be justified only if they are based on merit, seniority, measures of the quality or quantity of the work performed, or "any other factor other than sex."

Comparable worth, on the other hand, is aimed at pay *equity*, seeking to pay women and men equal wages for different or dissimilar jobs of comparable value to an employer. It is much more abstract as well as political in nature than pay equality, given its emphasis on measuring the intrinsic worth of jobs. Pay equity measures have been more popular in the public than private sector, perhaps because public sector jobs are not specifically linked to the "free labor market" ideology which has been a major deterrent to the implementation of pay equity in the private sector

(Kelly and Bayes, 1988). It is also important to note that comparable worth is not explicitly mandated by any federal legislation.[3] As such, the question of the ability of state or federal courts to require comparable worth consistent with, or in enforcement of, Title VII of the Civil Rights Act of 1964 is unresolved, though litigation continues to press the issue toward an eventual consideration in the Supreme Court.[4]

Because a primary mission of unions is and has been to improve the economic status of its constituents, many unions have long been heavily involved in yesterday's issue of pay equality and have more recently become involved in today's issue of pay equity.

Unions and Pay Equality

The tradition of paying women lower wages than men is endemic to both the public and private sectors. But union involvement in wage inequalities is more difficult to understand empirically in the public as compared to private sector, notwithstanding the evidence of other forms of discrimination against women by public sector unions. For one thing, private sector unions have been in existence much longer, making the record more apparent and established.

Private sector unions have negotiated red circle clauses and protective legislation, for example, which have produced intended wage disparities between females and males. One particular case involving union discrimination, *Hodgson v. Sagner* (1971), illustrates a different sort of problem.

For a two-year period following the passage of the Equal Pay Act, there were wage disparities between female and male employees of the cutting and marking department of Sagner, Inc., a clothing manufacturer. The twenty-two female cutters and markers in the department were paid 40 cents per hour less than their 100-plus male counterparts. During collective negotiations in the following year, both the employer and union, the Baltimore Regional Joint Board, Amalgamated Clothing Workers of America, agreed that female workers were paid less than male workers for the same work and, as such, that back wages were owed to the twenty-two female employees.

The amount of underpayment to the female workers for the two-year period was $29,771.36. At the union's insistence, however, this amount would not be paid to the women. Rather, the union demanded that only one-quarter of this amount be paid to them and that the remaining three-quarters be paid to the 100 male employees in the department. The union insisted on this arrangement because "the others in the cutting room would be dissatisfied and that there would be 'problems' if only the 22 female employees received the payments. . . . [A]mounts should be paid to these other employees to avoid these 'problems' " (*Hodgson v. Sagner* 1971, 639).

The company, with some trepidation, agreed to the union's proposal. Together they implemented a plan that did not rectify wage discrimination against women, but actually compounded it. Twenty-five percent of the back pay was distributed to the female employees and 75 percent was distributed to the males as a wage increase until the end of the contract year.

Interestingly, it was the union that initially called the company's attention to the wage disparities, despite the fact that the union itself had originally bargained for the 40-cent wage differential. The best case scenario to describe the union's behavior here would be that the union recognized the pay disparity and sought to correct it. This seems unlikely, however, since the union, in fact, overtly sabotaged the company's effort to redress the pay discrimination.

The worst case scenario is that the union intentionally and strategically bargained for the wage differentials between the female and male employees in an attempt to further increase the base wages of male employees, thereby perpetuating the wage imbalance between females and males. That is, the union bargains for pay differentials, then informs the company that the disparities may be in violation of the Equal Pay Act and, therefore, must be rectified. The company agrees to set aside substantial sums to correct the wage imbalance. This agreement, in essence, is an "ability to pay" statement by the employer. Once the pool of resources is established, the union insists that the majority of its constituents—males—deserves 75 percent of the back pay as a general wage increase. Whether or not the union was this specious, the union's behavior was egregious enough to warrant a finding of joint liability for monetary damages and injunctive relief.

This case points to a union's involvement in a discriminatory pay scheme, but obviously not all private sector unions have engaged in such discrimination. Indeed, locals of the International Union of Electrical Workers (IUE) have long supported pay equality between female and male employees (Wilson 1980). A landmark pay equality case, *IUE v. Westinghouse* (1980) resulted in pay adjustments for members of IUE Local 449 at a Westinghouse lamp plant in Trenton, New Jersey, most of whom were women (Portman, Grune and Johnson 1984).

Female employees have been paid lower wages than males in the public sector as well but linking the pay disparities to unions is more difficult in that setting than in the private sector. First, public sector unions are relatively new to the labor scene. Many overt or covert discriminatory wage systems predate the birth of public sector unions. Before the presence of unions, wage systems, including discriminatory programs, were set unilaterally by government employers. For example, a statute enacted in 1864 set the pay for "female clerks" in the federal service at $600 per year, or half the salary of male clerks (Van Riper 1958, 160). There is no evidence to indicate that a union was involved in this unequal pay mandate. Indeed, there is no known record of the existence of federal sector unions at this time. The first known union to have represented federal employees is the National Association of Letter Carriers (NALC), which formed in 1887.[5]

In addition, although some state, local and federal unions emerged in the late 1800s and early 1900s, public sector unions have only recently gained the formal power as well as legitimacy needed to influence wage systems. Indeed, in the federal sector, pay is excluded from the scope of bargaining for employees outside the post office. Wage systems are set by Congress. It is only through lobbying that nonpostal, federal sector unions can influence wage systems. Presumably, if a federal sector union did exist before 1887, it could have lobbied Congress for the 1864 statute described above. This, of course, is pure speculation.

It is interesting to note, however, that as early as 1917, at least one federal employee union—the National Federation of Federal Employees (NFFE)—voiced its support for the equal pay for equal work doctrine. Many editorials favoring pay equality appeared in the NFFE (originally, the Federal Employees Union) publication, *The Federal Employee.* In addition, the president of the NFFE addressed letters to the Secretaries of Labor and War protesting pay discrimination against women holding munitions' jobs. Male skilled laborers and machine operators at the time were earning between $2.24 and $2.64 an hour while women in the same job classifications earned between $1.36 and $2.24 (*The Federal Employee* 1917). The NFFE also requested the Women's Bureau of the Department of Labor to conduct a study on female employment and salaries in the federal government. That study revealed pay disparities between women and men as illustrated in Table 6.1. It is uncertain what the effects of NFFE's efforts were, but the important point is that at least one federal employee union demonstrated some support for pay equality in the early 1900s.

It has been only in the past few decades or so that unions operating at the state and local levels have gained collective bargaining rights. Their relatively short history makes it difficult to link these unions to wage schemes that promoted pay equality or that either intentionally discriminated against women or perpetuated past discriminations against them.

In sum, the record on public sector union involvement in equal pay issues is difficult to establish. Public sector union involvement in pay *equity,* on the other hand, may be easier to demonstrate given that the

Table 6.1 Federal Government Employees' Annual Salaries by Gender, 1919*

Position	Female Salary	Male Salary
Cleaning	$300-399	$600-699
Personal	300-399	300-399**
Custodial	720	700-799
Subclerical (Office Messenger)	500-599	400-499
Telephone & Telegraph	900-999	1400-1499
Typist	1000-1099	1100-1199
Stenography	1200-1299	1200-1299
Supervisor of Clerks	1200-1299	2000-2099
Scientific Lab Aid	900	1200
Statistician	1200	2300
Accountant	1400	1800
Publicity	2300	2700-3099
Biological Sciences	1800-2400	3000-3099

SOURCE: "Women in the Government Service." U.S. Department of Labor, Women's Bureau. *Bulletin of The Women's Bureau,* No. 8, Washington, D.C., 1920, pp. 30-33.

*Salary or range of salary upon entrance to federal government.
**Plus subsistence.

comparable worth movement is so new. It is also useful to determine whether private sector unions' positions on pay issues are shifting. Costly lawsuits and union liability for pay discrimination may have encouraged some unions to become more supportive of comparable worth, despite free labor market arguments.

Unions and Pay Equity

In recent years, union activity in the area of pay equity has become more pronounced. Several unions, especially those operating in the public sector, have demonstrated their support for pay equity policies. As will be seen in the following sections, however, the support is not unconditional, but rather depends upon a number of factors. Moreover, in some cases, unions simply do not support pay equity measures.

Importantly, unions have influenced comparable worth policy through a variety of means including collective bargaining, conducting wage or job evaluation studies, developing union policies, political advocacy, and litigation. Although not mutually exclusive, each strategy will be examined separately because some appear more popular than others. In addition, some have a more direct impact and, hence, are more viable than others. As will be seen, the motivations of unions to support or oppose comparable worth are tied to the specific strategies.

Collective Bargaining

Collective bargaining has been one of the most effective strategies for achieving pay equity. It certainly is the most direct, because unions that have any power at the bargaining table can immediately win pay equity increases for women for a specific time or contract period. Bargaining for pay equity appears to be more prominent in the public than private sector, despite the fact that bargaining collectively over wages is forbidden by law in many state and local governments.

The first major collectively bargained comparable worth settlement followed a 9-day strike in July of 1981 by municipal workers in San Jose, California. The agreement between the city and the Municipal Employees Association, Local 101 of the American Federation of State, County and Municipal Employees (AFSCME), called for general pay increases as well as "special equity adjustments" totalling $1.5 million for female-dominated jobs. Collective negotiations for the next contract period, covering 1983 and 1984 also called for equity adjustments totalling $375,000 (Grune and Reder 1984; Wiesenthal 1984; Cook 1983). Local 101's success led the way across the country for a number of other efforts at the bargaining table, some successful, some not. It is helpful to review some of these efforts in order to better understand unions' use of collective bargaining to support comparable worth.

Representing clerical workers in the California State University system and clerks and librarians in the City of Los Angeles, AFSCME locals have been successful in negotiating pay equity increases for females. A two and a half percent increase above the general wage increment went to clerical workers in the university system and $12 million was set aside to upgrade clerical and librarian positions in Los Angeles over a 3-year period (Cox 1985; Grune 1980).

The Maine State Employees Association (MSEA) experience illustrates a union's successful efforts to win pay equity increases in the public sector, despite legal obstacles. The MSEA, Maine's largest state employee union, has sought equity increases under a comparable worth theory since 1979. The state refuses to bargain over job classification issues, however, claiming that they are outside the scope of bargaining—that is, they are non-negotiable. Without enabling legislation, then, public employee unions in Maine will be unable to correct sex-biased job classification systems at the bargaining table (Cook 1983).

Some unions in the predominantly female health care industry have also sought pay equity increases at the bargaining table. For example, a 1981 contract between the State of Connecticut and the Health Care Employees Union, District 1199, provided for a state-established pay equity fund in the amount of one percent of the health care workers' payroll. This fund was intended to correct wage inequities among health care workers, the preponderance of whom are female.

In New York State, one of the largest government employers in this country, the Civil Service Employees Association (CSEA)—an affiliate of AFSCME—and the Public Employees Federation (PEF) negotiated settlements with the state for the 1985-1987 contract period that include $74 million to upgrade state positions held mostly by women. These negotiated raises were based on comparable worth studies recommending a new pay classification system.

Some of the few unions that have successfully negotiated pay equity increases in the private sector are the Communications Workers of America (CWA) and locals of the United Electrical Workers of America (UE) and The Newspaper Guild (TNG). The CWA's 1977 and 1980 national contracts with the telephone company provided for upgraded positions for predominantly female jobs. Guild and UE locals have also had some success in upgrading and reclassifying female jobs (Bureau of National Affairs 1984; Grune 1980).

Perhaps one of the most notable experiences in the private sector thus far involves a strike at Yale University over, among other issues, comparable worth. Local 34 of the Federation of University Employees (FUE), which represents clerical and technical workers at Yale, struck because it was unsuccessful in negotiating across-the-board wage increases for all employees as well as upgraded pay scales for women. Some 1,600 of the university's 2,500 clerical and technical workers walked the picket lines. The strike was a success, resulting in the pay raises demanded by the union (Coulson 1985; Bittman and Arnold 1984; Jacobs 1984).

These examples of pay equity increases achieved through collective bargaining and related activities (e.g., strikes) are important and certainly point to the commitment of some unions to elevate women's pay. But, what is the impetus for union support? Several factors may explain the support; one is pragmatism, defined in terms of the gender composition of the negotiating union, which is generally the union *local*.

References to union efforts and union successes convey a sense that individual unions relative to one another are either progressive or discriminatory. Unfortunately, the situation is not that simple. As is true of many facets of labor union behavior, the internal politics within and among union locals and between the national headquarters and the locals are complex indeed. Accordingly, a national union may be supportive of comparable worth, but all affiliated locals may not. For example, AFSCME at the national level has voiced its support for comparable worth, but this does not necessarily reflect the sentiment of all locals affiliated with AFSCME. Importantly, it is generally the local union through which employees deal with the employer on a day-to-day basis.

Unfortunately, information on the gender composition of union locals is virtually inaccessible. This makes it impossible to empirically link the gender composition of, for example, the Municipal Employees Association, Local 101 of AFSCME, to the Local's bargaining and strike behaviors. In certain instances, however, we do learn of a union local's gender composition. For example, approximately 85 percent of Yale University's FUE Local 34 is made up of women. That provides local officials with a very strong incentive to support pay equity for clerical and technical employees. Notwithstanding this high percentage of females in the local's unit, however, the union was unwilling to settle for only pay equity adjustments, but rather insisted upon general increases for all employees. This leads to questions as to whether the local would have struck over the pay equity demands only.

Perhaps union support for comparable worth in certain cases will be conditioned upon wage increases for male employees, even when males are the minority in the bargaining unit. This can be particularly divisive during periods of shrinking resources. Norma Briggs, coordinator of a project on women and labor, found from interviews with union members and officials that "the typical union member's firm belief in equal work for equal pay and equality of opportunity was severely modified by his belief that men were the breadwinners, the serious workers, who should therefore get the opportunities when there were not enough to go around" (Hammel 1974, 26). These attitudes reinforce the need for greater female representation in leadership positions as discussed in Chapter 2.

Statistics on gender composition are also available for the CWA. Over one half of the union consists of females employed predominantly in jobs as clerks or telephone operators (Bureau of Labor Statistics 1980).

Approximately 70 percent of the CWA's constituency in the Bell System alone is female. We would expect CWA, the national union which negotiates for clerks and telephone operators, to push for equity increases, in particular, if the females demand them. Even if the women do not demand such increases, unions, by advocating comparable worth, can demonstrate to their constituents that they are working for them. This may appease the female union members, thereby bolstering union stability.

A union's willingness to collectively bargain for pay equity may also depend on economic conditions, which tend to influence bargaining priorities. Rynes and colleagues (1984, 1985) found that during periods of economic decline, unions emphasize traditional concerns such as benefits, job security, and *general* pay increases. Conversely, during economic upswings, they are more willing to expand the agenda to include such issues as comparable worth. On the other hand, Rynes and colleagues suggest that, despite economic conditions, many unions are simply unwilling to include pay equity increases in their priorities. Sixty-eight percent of their sample responded that comparable worth would not be an issue in upcoming negotiations.

Rynes and colleagues also imply that the municipal strike in San Jose, which preceded negotiations, was an atypical union response. The study revealed that 70 percent of the unions were unwilling to strike over comparable worth. Cook (1983, 19) has also found that "not many unions have as yet been willing to strike for comparable worth or indeed to place it prominently on their bargaining agendas."

Interestingly, Rynes and colleagues' respondents were largely public sector unions (64 percent of the sample). The one union which has gained much attention for its support of comparable worth, AFSCME, was heavily represented in the responses. Their findings suggest, then, that not all public sector unions support comparable worth. The findings further tell us that not all AFSCME union officials or members share the position of the AFSCME national on comparable worth.

Then, the tendency of union locals to push for pay equity at the bargaining table may depend upon the gender composition of the local, the willingness of women to press their unions to support pay equity, how secure the local is among its constituents, and economic conditions. Some unions, however, as will be seen later in this chapter, do not and will not subscribe to comparable worth no matter what the conditions are.

Job Evaluation Studies

Job evaluation is the linchpin to pay equity. It is the foundation upon which job and, hence, pay classification systems are devised and revised. Portman, Grune and Johnson (1986, 227) note that "[t]raditional job evaluation systems have been identified as a major source of discrimination against women because they leave out or undervalue the factors that are often found in women's work."

Comparable worth advocates argue that we must reassess not only the factors we include in job evaluations but the manner in which we define or conceptualize the factors. Manual labor, for instance, which is generally considered a factor in men's work, may be comparable in value to mental fatigue, which is characteristic of many jobs performed by women. Yet, manual labor has traditionally been valued, indeed overvalued, while mental fatigue has been overlooked or undervalued. The same can be said for back strain, which is characteristic primarily of men's work and traditionally valued. On the other hand, eye strain, characteristic of clerical and secretarial work—particularly office workers in insurance companies, who are predominantly female—has been undervalued.

Job evaluation has historically been a source of tension and conflict between labor and management, because employers have traditionally sought to use job evaluation systems as the primary means for setting wages. Relying on unilaterally devised job evaluation systems precludes collective bargaining over wages and hence, from labor's perspective, results in unfair wages for all workers.

In recent years, however, many employers (mostly public) have been willing to work with unions to establish and conduct comparable worth job evaluation studies. These studies take into account job factors and attributes that have traditionally been excluded from job evaluation studies, which in turn have led to the underevaluation of women's work. The job evaluation factors that are critical for achieving pay equity include, for example, knowledge, skills, abilities, mental demands, job conditions, quality of work, education, and accountability.

The first and best-known pay equity job evaluation study was commissioned by the state of Washington in 1974 to compare female- and male-dominated jobs in state government. The study revealed pay disparities, but the state refused to correct the wage differentials. This led to the landmark case filed by AFSCME, which will be discussed later in this chapter. More typically, such studies have been commissioned or conducted jointly by labor and management. As the following examples indicate, they appear to be more common in the public as compared to private sector.

In Minnesota, a task force from the state and the AFSCME Council conducted a job evaluation study revealing wage disparities between female- and male-dominated jobs (Evans and Nelson 1986). It was found, for example, that clerical positions, predominantly filled by women, paid approximately $350 less per month than groundskeeping jobs, predominantly held by men, even though the jobs were found to be of comparable value to the employer (Wiesenthal 1984). The Minnesota study also pointed to pay disparities between LPNs, mostly women, and senior groundskeepers, mostly men. The study produced equity adjustments for these and other predominately female jobs.

By 1982, the Maine State Employees Association (MSEA) and the state of Maine developed a joint labor-management committee specifically to study comparable worth (Cook 1983). Joint committees on comparable worth are viable alternatives for unions such as the MSEA that are legally prohibited from negotiating over wages or job classification. Employers may be more willing to address the issue cooperatively rather than adversarially at the bargaining table.

Pay equity job evaluation studies have also been called for by an SEIU local in Berkeley, District 1199 of the Heath Care Workers Union (Portman, Grune and Johnson 1984), and the Connecticut State Employees Association (Johansen 1984). In Philadelphia, in Humbolt County, California and in Hennepin County, Minnesota, AFSCME locals conducted their own job evaluation and pay rate studies (*Options for Conducting a Pay Equity Study*, Hearings Before the Subcommittee 1985, Grune 1980).

There have been far fewer job evaluation studies in the private sector. District 65 of the United Auto Workers (UAW), which represents clerical workers at Boston University, has called for pay equity studies. And, the IUE has done some research on pay classification, but IUE's work has not been recognized by employers (Portman, Grune and Johnson 1984). The CWA is perhaps the most successful private sector union to have negotiated for a joint labor-management job evaluation study. The CWA and Bell Telephone established a Joint National Occupational Job Evaluation Committee comprised of CWA and AT&T officials. The committee was responsible for researching and developing a job evaluation plan aimed at correcting wage inequities resulting from technological change in the telecommunications industry. Both male and female workers benefited (Grune and Reder 1984).

The Rynes's study referred to earlier found that of the various alternatives to rectifying pay disparities, unions were most interested in job evaluation studies. Forty-four percent of the union members responded that unions should push for comparable worth study committees. Interestingly, however, union members indicated little willingness to provide financial backing for the implementation of comparable worth. Seventy-three percent said "no" to financial backing, 27 percent said "yes." So, while there may be some support for pay equity job evaluation studies, unions may not be willing to finance the most important components, that is, the outcomes of the studies.

Viewed another way, some unions may not support the ultimate findings and, hence, implementation of the study's recommendations. The recent experience in New York State provides a useful illustration of how unions, initially supportive of job evaluation studies, can potentially deter the implementation of pay equity policies.

In New York State, CSEA, which represents about one-half of the state's work force, predominantly blue-collar, negotiated a $500,000 joint pay equity study to be conducted by the Center for Women in Government in Albany, New York. The state's negotiations with PEF, which represents professional, scientific and technical employees, led to an additional, more comprehensive, study of the state's pay and classification system conducted by Arthur Young and Company. Both unions also bargained for raises recommended by the studies.

Although the state employee unions supported the comparable worth project, individual union officials from the outset were skeptical about the potential implications. One CSEA official felt, for example, that if the new classification system recommended by the studies were to consolidate various wage scales, it "would destroy the negotiating process" (*Albany Times Union* 9 November 1985, 1). There were also fears about the possibility of interunion disputes. PEF and CSEA were each looking to appease their own constituents. Thus, if pay equity adjustments were to benefit CSEA at the expense of PEF, PEF would not support the new pay classification system. Joseph Walker, PEF spokesperson, warned that "PEF would fight CSEA pay-scale adjustments designed to eliminate sex or race discrimination if they threatened PEF's pay grades. 'We're going to make sure that an LPN (licensed practical nurse, represented by CSEA) doesn't make more than an RN (registered nurse, represented by PEF)' " (*Albany Times Union* 9 November 1985, 1).

The unions were also fearful that implementation of pay equity would lower the salaries of white males, a sizable number of whom are represented by both unions. But early on, Thomas Hartnett, then Director of New York State's Office of Employee Relations (OER), the unit which represents the state at the bargaining table, assured the unions that the new classification system would not result in lower salaries for male workers. Hartnett did say, however, that it may result in lower raises for overvalued male workers in the future (*Albany Times Union* 8 November 1985).

Both studies revealed pay disparities between female and male as well as minority and nonminority workers. Over 230 job titles, filled mostly by CSEA-represented women and minorities, were deemed undervalued. It was expected that CSEA employees would reap greater benefits because CSEA represents a high percentage of clerical and maintenance employees, most of whom are women or minorities. The fact that CSEA-represented titles would receive a greater share of the funds set aside for pay equity increases than PEF-represented titles created tension, but evidently not enough to stall implementation of the plan.

A greater impediment was the recommendation by the implementation plan to downgrade at least six PEF-represented job titles filled predominantly by white males. At the same time, the plan recommended groundskeepers, mostly men. The study produced equity adjustments for these and other predominately female jobs.

By 1982, the Maine State Employees Association (MSEA) and the state of Maine developed a joint labor-management committee specifically to study comparable worth (Cook 1983). Joint committees on comparable worth are viable alternatives for unions such as the MSEA that are legally prohibited from negotiating over wages or job classification. Employers may be more willing to address the issue cooperatively rather than adversarially at the bargaining table.

Pay equity job evaluation studies have also been called for by an SEIU local in Berkeley, District 1199 of the Heath Care Workers Union (Portman, Grune and Johnson 1984), and the Connecticut State Employees Association (Johansen 1984). In Philadelphia, in Humbolt County, California and in Hennepin County, Minnesota, AFSCME locals conducted their own job evaluation and pay rate studies (*Options for Conducting a Pay Equity Study*, Hearings Before the Subcommittee 1985; Grune 1980).

There have been far fewer job evaluation studies in the private sector. District 65 of the United Auto Workers (UAW), which represents clerical workers at Boston University, has called for pay equity studies. And, the IUE has done some research on pay classification, but IUE's work has not been recognized by employers (Portman, Grune and Johnson 1984). The CWA is perhaps the most successful private sector union to have negotiated for a joint labor-management job evaluation study. The CWA and Bell Telephone established a Joint National Occupational Job Evaluation Committee comprised of CWA and AT&T officials. The committee was responsible for researching and developing a job evalua-tion plan aimed at correcting wage inequities resulting from technological change in the telecommunications industry. Both male and female workers benefited (Grune and Reder 1984).

The Rynes's study referred to earlier found that of the various alternatives to rectifying pay disparities, unions were most interested in job evaluation studies. Forty-four percent of the union members re-sponded that unions should push for comparable worth study commit-tees. Interestingly, however, union members indicated little willingness to provide financial backing for the implementation of comparable worth. Seventy-three percent said "no" to financial backing, 27 percent said "yes." So, while there may be some support for pay equity job evaluation studies, unions may not be willing to finance the most important components, that is, the outcomes of the studies.

Viewed another way, some unions may not support the ultimate findings and, hence, implementation of the study's recommendations. The recent experience in New York State provides a useful illustration of how unions, initially supportive of job evaluation studies, can potentially deter the implementation of pay equity policies.

speaking, is also a personnel issue. Historically, personnelists have evaluated and reevaluated job classification systems in order to establish appropriate wage rates. These evaluations have pointed to the need to upgrade some job titles and downgrade others. The essence of comparable worth is that some job titles are undervalued and others are overvalued and, hence, must be appropriately adjusted. This message should be conveyed clearly to unions' constituencies, in particular by unions that claim to support pay equity. Otherwise, the rank-and-file, male and female, may balk at pay equity adjustments.

CSEA ultimately approved implementation of the plan. In fact, while PEF lobbied against the appropriation of funds to implement the pay proposal, CSEA supported it. At this writing, recent contract negotiations between OER and PEF led to the withdrawal of PEF's grievance against the state. The state has not agreed to refrain from downgrading job titles in the future, however, if such action proves necessary and essential to the full implementation of pay equity in New York State. In any event, the legislature approved the comparable worth funding bill, and, consequently, at least the *first* phase of the pay equity plan has been implemented (Picchi 1987c). Some 42,000 employees represented by CSEA and 4,834 PEF-represented employees have received pay hikes.

Other unions in New York, including Council 82, an AFSCME affiliate which represents the predominantly white male corrections profession, are watching the implementation of the state pay equity policy. Although the pay grades of the employees it represents were not immediately affected, these unions are concerned about the future impact on males. These unions, however, have taken no direct actions to deter implementation.

So, it seems that some unions support comparable worth job evaluation studies, but these same unions can also deter the implementation of policies recommended by the studies. Filing grievances and lawsuits can only stall the effective implementation of pay equity. Although not as critical in New York as was initially anticipated, so, too, can interunion disputes. In addition, if female employees object strongly enough, a union may reassess its support. Even more harmful, a union can create divisions among the rank-and-file, thereby mobilizing opposition from employees who do not receive pay equity increases. All-white unions also emerge as policy participants that could potentially thwart implementation efforts. In addition, if any of the unions were then able to win the support of the general citizenry, implementation of pay equity policies would be severely jeopardized.

Unions genuinely supportive of comparable worth job evaluation studies have a responsibility to ensure the sound implementation of the studies' recommendations. This includes, for example, educating employees about the essence of comparable worth, which could serve to alleviate internal tensions among the rank-and-file. Employers, too, have a responsibility to better structure conditions so as to effectively promote implementation. For example, New York State could have included union officials in the ad hoc group in charge of developing the implementation plan. Or, the state could have proposed a *temporary* rather than permanent two-tier wage structure, which might have been more acceptable to PEF. Such steps would have allowed some differences to be addressed well in advance of the implementation stage, ultimately facilitating the realization of pay equity.

Union Organizing

Recent statistics on union membership in this country paint an unfavorable picture for labor. Between 1980 and 1984, organized labor lost a total of 2.7 million workers. In 1980, approximately 23 percent of American workers—including both public and private sector—were unionized. In 1984, only 18.8 percent of American workers carried union cards. Comparing public and private sectors, there has been greater stability in the public as compared to private sector.

Some unions have addressed the problem of declining membership by organizing women, a group of workers who have long been overlooked by unions and, as discussed in Chapter 2, are growing in number. Of course to attract female members, unions would need to appeal to their wants and needs. Advocating pay equity increases has been effective for some unions in their attempts to organize women.

Some AFSCME locals, for example, have used pay equity as an organizing tool with great success. Winn Newman, General Counsel for AFSCME, has noted that the union won two recent, very close elections by making pay equity a primary campaign issue (Aaron and Lougy 1986). AFSCME was also successful recently in winning clerical workers in Connecticut, primarily female, in a decertification election. AFSCME was able to unseat the incumbent union, an independent one, not affiliated with the AFL-CIO, by making comparable worth one of this chief areas of interest (Cook 1983).

Unions in the private sector have been far less reliant on pay equity as an organizing tool. The clerical workers union 925, an affiliate of the Service Employees International Union (SEIU), is one of the few unions to seek female members around a comparable worth campaign. In Syracuse, New York, 925 has been successful in organizing office workers of the Equitable Life Insurance Company. The union at this point, however, is attempting to gain recognition from the employer so, for the time being, 925's efforts to operationalize comparable worth support will be delayed (*Comparable Worth*, Task Force on Women's Issues 1983).

One would think that unions in the private sector would organize more around pay equity, since union membership in the private sector has fared much worse than in the public sector. In particular, the power base of unions in the manufacturing industry has been devastated due to the massive loss of jobs in manufacturing. Unions could bolster their membership by organizing and appealing to female workers in the service industry, which will experience growth in the coming decades.

Overall, however, private sector unions may be less enthusiastic about comparable worth than public sector unions because of fundamental differences between the two sectors. For example, many economists warn that market forces are too important in measuring goods produced in the private sector and, hence, in the setting of wages. They have further argued that pay equity would destroy the economic foundations of our economic system. This was a principle argument of Clarence Pendleton, former Chair of the U.S. Commission on Civil Rights, who has stated that comparable worth is the "looniest idea since Looney Tunes came on the screen" (*Public Administration Times* 15 April 1985, 4).

It would be surprising, though, if unions unquestionably accepted these arguments. For one thing, the market has never worked as freely as economists contend (Goodman 1984). Proponents of comparable worth point to several examples of where the market acts arbitrarily—for instance, the market has never responded to shortages of nurses (a predominantly female profession) the same way it has responded to shortages of doctors and engineers (both predominantly white male). The free market arguments, then, should be questioned by unions.

In addition, the research of Rynes and colleagues indicates that private sector union members are very concerned about the consequences of narrowing the earnings gap for female productivity and foreign competition. Union members feel that productivity in predominantly female occupations would rise in response to pay equity increases, thereby hurting traditionally male occupations. This seems somewhat tenuous, however, considering that the evidence on the effects of wage structures on productivity is conflicting (Aaron and Lougy 1986).

In addition, private sector union members feel that private industry in the United States would suffer from increased foreign competition. When wages in Asia, for example, are as low as 15 cents an hour, it becomes difficult for American producers, particularly in labor-intensive industries, to compete. Elevating women's wages, according to some union officials, would make it impossible. The important point to be made here is that these concerns are not typical in the public sector and, so, they tend not to dissuade public sector unions from supporting pay equity.

Of course, a deterrent to the use of comparable worth as an organizing tool in either sector is, as noted earlier, that not all women support pay equity. Hence, they would not be lured by its benefits. But, if unions seek to bolster their membership, and they recognize the potency of the pay equity issue, they can easily develop ways to generate an interest among such women. Unions may not philosophically approve of comparable worth, but overlooking its pragmatic importance in such areas as organizing seems injudicious.

Official Union Policies

Some public and private sector unions have demonstrated their support for pay equity by passing comparable worth resolutions at their national conventions. The resolutions are formal statements by the parent union regarding its position on certain policy matters. They are not mandates in any legal sense and, so, the resolutions are not necessarily reflective of union locals' positions, nor are they always implemented by the locals. Rather, they simply convey to affiliated locals, the parent union's position.

The resolutions adopted by unions take various forms. For instance, in 1972, the IUE initiated a "Title VII Compliance Program," that included an education and research effort aimed at raising staff and membership awareness of sex- and race-related problems in jobs and wages. At its 1980 convention, the CWA passed a resolution urging the EEOC to "adopt and enforce positive progressive rules on comparable worth." The National Education Association (NEA) and SEIU have passed at their conventions more general resolutions in support of comparable worth. NEA's resolution, for example, states that "all workers should be paid on the basis of the requirements, skills, and worth of their jobs and that factors such as the sex or race of the individual performing the job should never play a role in determining salary" (Bureau of National Affairs 1984, 76).

The AFL-CIO as a federation of some 100 national and international unions has adopted several comparable worth resolutions aimed at encouraging member unions to promote pay equity in a variety of ways. An AFL-CIO resolution adopted at a national convention in November of 1981 urged its affiliate unions to

- work through contract negotiations to upgrade undervalued job classifications, regardless of whether they are typically considered "male" or "female" jobs;
- initiate joint union-employer pay equity studies to identify and correct internal inequities between predominantly female and predominantly male classes;
- recognize fully their obligations to treat pay inequities resulting from sex discrimination like all other inequities which must be corrected;
- adopt the concept of "equal pay for comparable work" in contract negotiations (Grune and Reder 1984, 75).

The problem with many of these resolutions, however, is that they are expressions of support from the umbrella union only and are not enforceable among the affiliated unions or locals. In effect, support for comparable worth may exist in theory but not practice. For example, despite AFL-CIO support for comparable worth, not all of its affiliates have endorsed the national resolution and very few have developed ways to *implement* pay equity (Aaron and Lougy 1986; Cook 1983).

Police, firefighting or other craft unions either affiliated with the AFL-CIO or not, and with few or no females, have not been supportive of pay equity resolutions at national or local levels. For example, a recent effort by the city council in Princeton, Minnesota, to adopt a comparable worth policy has drawn much criticism from police and firefighting unions. Firefighters, in particular, were outraged that a librarian's job would be classified at the same level as a firefighter. One embittered firefighter remarked that a librarian's job is very dangerous, "[a] book could fall on her head" (Trost 1985, 27).

But, the type of union—craft or industrial—and the gender composition of the constituency may not always correlate with union support for pay equity resolutions. Perhaps the most glaring inconsistency is the position of the International Ladies' Garment Workers Union (ILGWU), some 85 percent of whose members are women in one of the lowest-paid industries. The ILGWU along with several AFL-CIO staff members were among the strongest opponents to AFL-CIO's resolution promoting comparable worth (*Business Week* 1979). This may be an anomaly, but one might speculate that support for pay equity is neither a function of gender composition nor the type of union but rather the fundamental beliefs and values of those in union power or leadership positions.

Another reason for ILGWU's position may be that it fears the consequences of increased foreign competition (e.g., layoffs) if female workers are given pay equity increases. In fact, Sol Chaikin, former president of the ILGWU, has often raised this concern. Although there is merit to this argument, there is an important counterpoint.

Historically, unions have supported wage increases notwithstanding the fact that higher wages, at least in labor markets where the demand for labor is highly elastic, would lead to an acceptable level of layoffs. Today, however, foreign competition poses major threats to such industries as textiles and automotive. Unions in such industries have been willing to replace general wage increases with profit-sharing formulas in an effort to withstand the loss of jobs to nonunion or foreign companies. Importantly, though, unions are willing to do so on a temporary basis. The point is that, despite foreign competition threats, the ILGWU as well as auto unions such as the UAW will continue to seek wage increases at the bargaining table for all workers. It is interesting that arguments about the effects of foreign competition are afforded relatively insufficient weight when general wage increases for all workers are at hand but are afforded insurmountable weight when the issue is increased wages for women on equity grounds.

The obvious questions presented by these ILGWU examples highlight the importance of female representation at union policy making levels. One woman in ten holding office and two females in twenty-six sitting on the union's governing board may not be enough to push for female interests in such areas as pay (Bureau of Labor Statistics 1980). Of course, female representation won't be of much help if women themselves in the garment industry hold traditional values about women's wages and pay differentials. If this is the case, the AFL-CIO in support of its resolution could produce support for educational programs. It could also put pressure on the ILGWU to inform women of the comparable worth debate.

In sum, without concrete support from the unions that are directly responsible for changes in wage policy—generally the union local—pay equity will be supported in the abstract or "on paper," but no tangible gains will be achieved. The union resolutions on comparable worth, then, have at best a symbolic value.

Political Activities

Lobbying legislative bodies has been a popular tactic among unions particularly in the public sector because of legal restrictions on various labor union activities. Unions representing nonpostal, federal employees, for instance, are prohibited from bargaining over wages and terms and conditions of employment. Hence, in order to achieve pay increases, federal employee unions must skillfully and carefully communicate their needs to Congress. Unions at the state and local levels that are legally permitted to bargain over wages also build legislative support to win better contract packages. This process is known as "double-deck bargaining."

Some unions have also relied on lobbying to rectify sex-based wage discrimination, to seek funds for comparable worth studies, and to establish funds for the implementation of pay equity policies. For example, SEIU's Local 503, representing state workers in Oregon, convinced the Oregon legislature to authorize creation of a comparable worth task force to undertake a job reclassification study (*Federal Pay Equity Act,* Hearings Before the Subcommittee 1984). In addition, the AFSCME Council in Minnesota has obtained appropriations to develop and implement a pay equity policy (Grune and Reder 1984).

Unions also lobby indirectly through various national, state and local coalitions. For example, the National Committee on Pay Equity (NCPE), comprised of some 300 individuals and organizations, including over fifteen international and national unions, has invested a great deal of energy to win pay equity legislation in Congress.

One of the more important direct techniques used to gain support for comparable worth is testimony before legislative committees. The 1984 hearings before the House Subcommittee on Compensation and Employee Benefits saw testimony from the following international and national unions: AFSCME, SEIU, NEA, the American Federation of Government Employees (AFGE), the National Federation of Federal Employees (NFFE), the National Treasury Employees Union (NTEU), the American Postal Workers Union (APWU), the American Flight Attendants (AFA), and others (*Federal Pay Equity Act*, Hearings Before the Subcommittee 1984). The testimony was in support of federal pay equity legislation and an evaluation of the position classification system in the federal government aimed at uncovering wage biases against women.

Echoing the concerns expressed in previous sections, testimony from the parent unions in support of comparable worth does not necessarily reflect the sentiment of all affiliated locals. Moreover, it seems that parent unions supporting comparable worth for the various reasons described above would continue their support through political activities. On the other hand, it seems unlikely for legal and perhaps political reasons that unions opposing pay equity measures would publicly lobby or explicitly testify against comparable worth. There are exceptions, however, as we see from at least one union president who has expressed a more subtle form of opposition.

Sol Chaikin was president of the ILGWU when he testified before a House subcommittee that "the problem of 'comparable worth' precedes the gender gap. The basic problem is less sexual than economic: the underpayment of huge sectors of the labor force that find themselves in those sectors of the economy that most closely resemble our touted ideal of a free enterprise system of open competition" (*Federal Pay Equity Act*, Hearings Before the Subcommittee 1984, 300).

Although Chaikin did allude in his testimony to the disproportionately high percentage of women in underpaid sectors of the labor force, he believes the value of women's work must be set by fundamental market powers and overseas competition rather than "pie-in-the-sky" theoretical principles such as comparable worth (*Business Week* 1979). His testimony called for more general and universally applied measures such as adjustments in federal minimum wage and reform of national labor law, making it easier for all workers to organize.

This kind of attitude has often been relied upon to disguise opposition to various types of equity policies and tends to keep workers, both female and male, supportive of customary wage differentials and, hence, general wage increases rather than pay equity increases. Ultimately, pay disparities between women and men are not rectified but perpetuated. In retrospect, it is incumbent upon the parent union, or the federation, to work with its affiliates if political support for comparable worth is to be operationalized.

Litigation

The inception of comparable worth not surprisingly has brought a new set of legal challenges to wage systems. Because the concept is so abstract, however, the courts have been reluctant to embrace it. As such, the legality of comparable worth, whether unions are involved or not, is not yet fully established. Nonetheless, if there is an interest in determining where unions stand on the issue, a review of the case law would be useful, since lawsuits represent an accurate legal account of unions' position on pay equity.

Table 6.2 summarizes the case law from the past few decades. A total of twelve cases were located where unions were involved in pay equity issues. This does not, of course, adequately reflect the incidence of union involvement in comparable worth. For example, unions may be involved in innumerable incidences of pay discrimination according to the comparable worth doctrine, but women may not file lawsuits against them because they do not recognize the discrimination, they fear reprisal, or they cannot afford the time and costs associated with filing suit.

In addition, there are AFSCME lawsuits pending in some jurisdictions, and some unions have brought pay inequity charges before the Equal Employment Opportunity Commission (EEOC) and state human rights agencies. (These same unions, however, may also be respondents to such charges.) These cases are not accounted for in this review. The important point to be made from this review of case law is that not all unions and affiliated locals, whether operating in the public or private sector, support comparable worth.

For example, Table 6.2 shows that the Teamsters have not supported pay equity measures in public or private sector work forces. Indeed, the Teamsters Union has *created* wage inequities between women and men by negotiating pay classification systems that favor white males at the expense of females. This was the case in *Taylor v. Charley Brothers*, where a federal district court found the Teamsters jointly liable with the employer for its involvement in a wage scheme that resulted in pay inequities for women.[6]

It is interesting to note that while *Taylor* was on appeal, the union and the company settled with the aggrieved female employees, agreeing to provide them with approximately $1.1 million in back pay. The union's portion amounted to $50,000, which would be distributed over a 3-year period to the female employees (Portman, Grune and Johnson 1984).

Table 6.2 shows, as we might have expected, that craft unions operating in the public sector may not strive for comparable worth. In *Power v. Barry County*, female "matrons" were paid lower salaries than male "correction

Table 6.2 Summary of Case Law on Pay Equity

Case	Employment Sector Public	Employment Sector Private	Union Type Craft	Union Type Industrial	Union Position For	Union Position Against
St. Louis Newspaper Guild v. Pulitzer Pub. Co. 618 F.Supp. 1468 (1985)		X		X	X	
AFSCME v. County of Nassau 609 F.Supp. 695 (1985)	X			X	X	
AFSCME v. City of New York 599 F.Supp. 916 (1984)	X			X	X	
Hawaii Government Employees Association, AFSCME v. State of Hawaii 38 FEP Cases 1126 (1985)	X			X	X	
AFSCME v. State of Washington 770 F.2d. 1401 (9th Cir. 1985)	X			X	X	
Connecticut State Employees Association v. State of Connecticut 31 FEP Cases 191 (1983)	X			X	X	
EEOC v. Affiliated Foods and Teamsters Union 34 FEP Cases 943 (1984)		X		X		X
Briggs v. City of Madison 536 F.Supp. 435 (1982)	X			X		X
Power v. Barry County, MI Fraternal Order of Police and Teamsters 539 F.Supp. 721 (1982)	X		X			X
Taylor v. Charley Brothers 25 FEP Cases 602 (1981)		X		X		X
Penn. Human Relations Comm. v. Hempfield Township and Teamsters 16 FEP Cases 1348 (1976)	X			X		X
American Nurses Assoc. v. State of Illinois 783 F.2d 716 (7th Cir. 1986)	X			X	X	

officers." The female matrons charged the police union, the Teamsters and the county with "devis[ing] and perpetuat[ing] a compensation scheme which underpays [female matrons] in comparison with the correction officers' jobs" (*Power* 1982, 722). The women argued that the jobs were of comparable and equal worth to the county.

The women ultimately lost the legal battle in *Power* because the district court rejected comparable worth on the grounds that Congress did not intend for Title VII to incorporate such a doctrine. The court ruled that "comparable worth is not a viable legal theory under Title VII and thus cannot be utilized by the Plaintiffs" (*Power* 1982, 722).

It is difficult to generalize about craft unions in the public sector based on this one case. But, their opposition to comparable worth here certainly comports with their history of discrimination as presented in Chapter 5. The same can be said for the Teamsters, which has an abysmal gender-relations record. Table 6.2 points to only four cases where the Teamsters was formally charged with bargaining for and maintaining discriminatory wage systems in both public and private sectors. Other incidences have no doubt occurred, but have never been brought before the courts.

Union support for pay equity in the *American Nurses Association* case is expected, given that the nursing profession is dominated by women. We would also expect support from the union in the *Connecticut State Employees Association* case, because the union represents clerical workers, predominantly female, who stood to benefit from pay equity measures (Johansen 1984). In addition, there is support for pay equity from a private sector union in *St. Louis Newspaper Guild*. In this case, the Guild's local brought a pay equity case on behalf of its female members, arguing that women are restricted to inside telephone sales positions, which pay less than male-filled outside sales positions.

This review also points to four cases where AFSCME has shown support for comparable worth. Indeed, AFSCME is to be credited for the 1983 landmark case, *AFSCME v. State of Washington*. In that case, the district court ruled that the state violated Title VII by paying lower wages to women performing comparable jobs to men (Shafritz, Hyde, and Rosenbloom 1986). The court ordered the state to elevate the wages of female workers as well as pay them back wages; however, the decision was ultimately overturned in 1985 by the Ninth Circuit Court of Appeals, which ruled that an employer would not be in violation of Title VII if it based its wages on prevailing market rates, even if the outcome means lower salaries for women. Despite the appellate court ruling, the state worked with the AFSCME local to raise the salaries of the undervalued female employees (Finn 1986; *New York Times*, 5 September 1985).

There has been much said here and elsewhere about AFSCME's support for pay equity. But, an interest in scrutinizing this support is highlighted by *Briggs v. City of Madison*. In this case, eighteen women employed by the city's Department of Public Health as public health nurses filed a Title VII suit in federal court charging that the city discriminated against them by paying higher wages to public health sanitarians, a job, they argued, requiring comparable skill, effort and responsibility. All public health nurses were female at the time of the lawsuit and all public health sanitarians were male.

Public health nurses provide health services in public schools, provide direct home health care services, instruct families in health care, operate health clinics including immunization clinics, and draft public health department policies and procedures. Public health sanitarians inspect such establishments as hotels, restaurants, and cafeterias to ensure compliance with sanitation laws and regulations. Sanitarians also monitor environmental health programs in food processing and serving, provide services at health clinics, and draft public health policies and procedures. The nurses linked the pay disparities between them and the male sanitarians to a "traditional and long-accepted devaluation of the worth of jobs done primarily by women" (*Briggs* 1982, 437).

Although unions were not named as plaintiffs or defendants in *Briggs*, they were discussed in the case because pay to both groups was based on collectively negotiated contracts. The female nurses were represented by the Madison Public Health Nurses Organization, which originally re-quested that the female nurses be classified in the male sanitarians' pay range. The union's request was denied.

The male sanitarians were affiliated with AFSCME, Local 60. It was unlikely that the AFSCME local which represented *all* males, would support a comparable worth measure to benefit all females represented by another union. Again, concerns over income redistribution and the effects of future raises to male sanitarians would be present. Also, there may have been another concern, which was in fact expressed not by the union but by the *director* of the Public Health Department. Charles Kincaid believes that male sanitarians should be paid more than female public health nurses because "society expect[s] men to be the breadwinners and protectors" (*Briggs* 1982, 440).

In sum, this case suggests that although the national level of AFSCME and AFSCME locals have demonstrated support for comparable worth, we cannot conclude that this support is uniform or unified. Rather, we must look closely at whether the constituency of the union or local stands to gain. Also, based on what we know about the leadership of the ILGWU, we must assess the attitudes and beliefs of high-level union officials.

It would appear, then, that some unions have brought legal suits against employers in support of comparable worth and others have been the objects of such lawsuits. Moreover, there is evidence that *both* public and private sector unions will support comparable worth in some instances but oppose it in others. And, while the opposition from craft unions seems consistent, it tends to vary among industrial unions for a variety of reasons.

Conclusions

Unions should be commended for their hard work, commitment and perseverance in the fight for equal pay for equal work and comparable worth. Union efforts may be some of the most important in the battle for pay equity and, therefore, it would be unjustifiable to diminish them in any way.

As suggested above, however, union support is not unequivocal. Hence, we cannot make the sweeping statement that all unions and all locals affiliated with these international and national unions are in support of pay equality and equity. If we point to examples where unions have supported pay equity and equality, we must also point to examples where these same unions as well as others have not supported, indeed have sabotaged pay policies aimed at achieving equality or equity for women.

The patterns seem to suggest that craft unions, whether operating in the public or private sector, are not very supportive of pay equity issues. However, there are inconsistencies with respect to industrial unions or locals; in some cases support is demonstrated, in others it is not. Support from industrial unions may depend on gender composition in some cases (e.g., AFSCME) but not others (e.g., ILGWU). Other factors such as economic conditions, the perceptions, consciousness and demands of female workers, and the values and beliefs of union officials may determine whether industrial unions will support comparable worth efforts.

The important point should be made that, overall, comparable worth appears to be more an economic and political rather than social issue to unions. This, of course, does not diminish the support. It simply points to the motivation of unions. It is important, in our efforts to narrow the earnings gap between female and male employees, to develop a better understanding of unions' motivations so that their support can be appropriately cultivated and their opposition overcome.

Notes

1. In solely the public sector, a somewhat different picture can be seen. For example, in the federal government women earn about 62.8 percent of men's wages, and in state and local governments women earn approximately 71.5 percent of men's salaries (Kelly and Bayes 1988, 4-5).

2. An equal pay for equal work requirement has also been read into Title VII.

3. While comparable worth is not federally mandated, several states have either passed legislation or are considering it. See, for example, Wiesenthal (1984) and Aaron and Lougy (1986).

4. It should be noted that the U.S. Supreme Court in *County of Washington v. Gunther* (1981) ruled that Title VII could sustain comparable worth suits. But the Court did not rule on its viability or legality. To date, judicial rulings on comparable worth have been inconsistent. This issue will be addressed later in this chapter. For a review, see, for example, Riccucci (1988).

5. As early as 1863, associations of letter carriers formed in New York City, but they were predominantly social organizations. See Spero (1948, 106). Also, workers in naval shipyards were organized sporadically beginning in the early 1800s (Kearney 1984).

6. It should be noted, however, that there are questions as to whether *Taylor* is actually a comparable worth case or equal pay for equal work case. See, for instance, Riccucci (1988).

References

Aaron, Henry J. and Cameran M. Lougy. *The Comparable Worth Controversy.* Washington, D.C.: Brookings Institution, 1986.

Albany Times Union. "50,000 NYS Workers Due Raises after Comparable-Worth Study." 8 November 1985, 1, 6.

———. "Overhaul of State Job System Seen." 9 November 1985, 1, 6.

Bittman, Mark and Bob Arnold. "Comparable Worth is Put to the Test at Yale." *Business Week*, 26 November 1984, 92-96.

Briggs v. City of Madison 536 F. Supp. 435 (1982).

Bureau of Labor Statistics, U.S. Department of Labor. *Directory of National Unions and Employee Associations, 1979.* Washington, D.C.: BLS, 1980.

Bureau of National Affairs. *Pay Equity and Comparable Worth.* Washington, D.C., 1984.

Business Week. "The New Pay Push for Women." 17 December 1979, 66, 69.

Comparable Worth: Every Woman's Right. Albany: New York State Assembly, Task Force on Women's Issues, May 1983.

Cook, Alice H. *Comparable Worth: The Problem and States' Approaches to Wage Equity.* Minoa, Hawaii: Industrial Relations Center, 1983.

Coulson, Crocker. "Labor Unrest in the Ivy League." *The Arbitration Journal* 40 (1985), 3:53-62.

County of Washington v. Gunther 101 S.Ct. 2242, 452 U.S. 161 (1981).

Cox, Gail Diane. "City, Unions Move to Align Pay of Women Workers." *Los Angeles Daily Journal*, 9 May 1985, 1, 20.

Evans, Sara M. and Barbara J. Nelson. "Initiating a Comparable Worth Wage Policy in Minnesota: Notes from the Field." *Policy Studies Review* 5 (1986), 4:849-862.

The Federal Employee. Publication of the National Federation of Federal Employees, March 1917, 133, 135.

Federal Pay Equity Act of 1984. Hearings Before the Subcommittee on Compensation and Employee Benefits, part 1, April 3 and 4, 1984.

Finn, Terry. "1st Comparable-Worth Dividends Due." *Albany Times Union*, 21 April 1986, D2.

Goodman, Walter. "Comparable Worth." *St. Petersburg Times*, 16 September 1984, 25, 26.

Grune, Joy Ann. *Manual on Pay Equity: Raising Wages for Women's Work.* Washington, D.C.: Committee on Pay Equity, 1980.

Grune, Joy Ann and Nancy Reder. "Pay Equity: An Innovative Public Policy Approach to Eliminating Sex-Based Wage Discrimination." *Public Personnel Management Journal* 13 (1984), 1:70-80.

Hammel, Lisa. "Why So Few Women Hold Apprenticeships." *New York Times*, 2 July 1974, 26.

Hodgson v. Sagner 326 F. Supp. 371 (D.Md. 1971), *aff'd*, 462 F. 2d 180 (4th Cir. 1972).

IUE v. Westinghouse Electric Corporation 19 FEP Cases 450 (1979), 631 F. 2d 1094 (3d Cir. 1980).

Jacobs, Sally. "Comparable Worth Becomes an Issue in Strike at Yale." *New England Business*, 19 November 1984, 43-44.

Johansen, Elaine. *Comparable Worth: The Myth and the Movement.* Boulder, Colorado: Westview Press, 1984.

Kearney, Richard C. *Labor Relations in the Public Sector.* New York: Marcel Dekker, Inc., 1984.

Kelly, Rita Mae and Jane Bayes (eds.). *Comparable Worth, Pay Equity, and Public Policy.* Westport, Connecticut: Greenwood Press, 1988.

New York Times. "Pay Equity Ruling is Upset on Appeal." 5 September 1985, B6.

Options for Conducting a Pay Equity Study of Federal Pay and Classification System. Hearings before the Subcommittee on Compensation and Employee Benefits, March 28, April 4, May 2, 30 and June 18, 1985.

Picchi, Joe. "Workers Decry State Equity Plan." *Albany Times Union*, 3 May 1987a, 1, 13.

———. "Lobbying Intensifies for Pay Equity Measure." *Albany Times Union*, 8 July 1987b, B5.

———. "State Senate Approves Pay-Equity Program." *Albany Times Union*, 10 July 1987c, A1, A16.

Portman, Lisa, Joy Ann Grune, and Eve Johnson. "The Role of Labor." In Helen Remick (ed.), *Comparable Worth and Wage Discrimination.* Philadelphia: Temple University Press, 1984, 219-237.

Public Administration Times. "Commission Rejects Comparable Worth." 15 April 1985, 1, 4.

Riccucci, Norma M. "Union Liability for Wage Disparities Between Women and Men." *University of Detroit Law Review* 65 (1988), 3:379-401.

Rynes, Sara, Thomas Mahoney and Benson Rosen. "Union Attitudes Toward Comparable Worth." *Pay Equity and Comparable Worth.* Washington, D.C.: Bureau of National Affairs, 1984, 110-117.

Rynes, Sara, Benson Rosen and Thomas Mahoney. "Evaluating Comparable Worth: Three Perspectives." *Business Horizons* July/August 1985, 82-86.

Salpukas, Agis. "The 2-Tier Wage System is Found to be 2-Edged Sword by Industry." *New York Times*, 21 July 1987, A1, D22.

Schultz v. Wheaton Glass Co. 421 F. 2d 259, 9 FEP Cases 502 and 508 (3d Cir. 1970).

Shafritz, Jay M., Albert C. Hyde and David H. Rosenbloom. *Personnel Management in Government.* New York: Marcel Dekker, Inc., 1986. 3d ed.

Spero, Sterling D. *Government as Employer.* New York: Remsen Press, 1948.

Trost, Cathy. "In Minnesota, 'Pay Equity' Passes Test, but Foes See Trouble Ahead." *Wall Street Journal,* 10 May 1985, 27.

Van Riper, Paul P. *History of the United States Civil Service.* Evanston, Illinois: Row, Peterson & Co., 1958.

Wiesenthal, Eric. "Comparable Worth: Issue of the '80s." *Public Administration Times,* 15 April 1984, 1, 5.

Wilson, Carole. "The IUE's Approach to Comparable Worth." In Joy Ann Grune (ed.), *Manual on Pay Equity: Raising Wages for Women's Work.* Washington, D.C.: Committee on Pay Equity, 1980, 89-90.

7

CONCLUSIONS AND SUMMARY

Unions operating in the public sector are important components in the policy processes affecting female and minority employment. In some cases, and for a variety of reasons, unions will facilitate such policies. In other cases, however, unions will not only oppose such policies but, despite legal mandates, overtly sabotage them.

Notwithstanding the potential impact, union involvement in female and minority employment in the public sector has received relatively little attention by policy makers and researchers. This book was intended to describe the importance of union involvement so that the role of unions in the policy-making process may be more clearly defined. In particular, as described in this book, unions that support equal employment opportunity (EEO) and affirmative action (AA) measures may prove instrumental in the EEO and AA policy-making processes. This appears evident in the participation of certain unions in the development and implementation of pay equity policies, as discussed in Chapter 6. On the other hand, union opposition to EEO and AA policies and programs should not be ignored by policy analysts nor women and minorities who choose to challenge discriminatory employment practices and policies.

It would appear that, on the whole, craft unions operating in the public sector tend to oppose measures aimed at promoting equal employment as well as pay equity for women and minorities.[1] Craft unions, for example, have resisted the entry of women and minorities into certain apprenticeship training programs, which has severely limited the employment opportunities of such groups in the high-paying, skilled crafts. Other craft unions such as police, firefighting, corrections and sanitation also continue to oppose policies and programs aimed at hiring, promoting and/or retaining women in uniformed service jobs.

The record for industrial unions operating in the public sector appears mixed.[2] Some unions, or more specifically, union locals, have demonstrated support for EEO and AA, while others have not. The motivations for their positions were examined in this book. In particular, some industrial unions may be responding to the increase of at least women in certain public sector work forces by advocating, in a host of arenas, such measures as pay equity or comparable worth. The projected growth in employment of women by labor economists may encourage more unions in the next decade or so to push for certain programs that would attract these workers to union ranks. This would be mutually beneficial to the workers and the unions.

In sum, because craft unions and some industrial unions cannot be relied upon to promote EEO and AA measures, their role in the policy processes aimed at enhancing the employment status of women and minorities should be limited. Indeed, their behaviors and actions must be closely monitored and, when necessary, circumscribed in order to prevent unions from thwarting the development and effective implementation of policies and programs aimed at promoting EEO and AA.

It is important to note that one union practice that may not be successfully curbed or challenged in the near future is the use of seniority in employment decisions. Because women and minorities systematically lack seniority, employment decisions which take into account length of service will adversely affect them. The U.S. Supreme Court has said in recent decisions that seniority systems which do not intentionally discriminate against women and minorities are "bona fide" and, hence, legal under Title VII. The Court's treatment of seniority systems represents a serious blow to EEO and AA measures.

The Court has, however, recently upheld the legality and constitutionality of AA in hiring and promotion decisions and, so, unions' challenges to as well as efforts to dismantle AA programs and policies may prove unsuccessful.[3] In any event, union behaviors and attitudes toward women and minorities in public sector work forces should not escape the attention of policy makers and researchers.

Directions for Future Research

It was pointed out at the beginning of this book that very little research has been conducted on the role of public sector unions in the employment practices and policies affecting women and minorities. Yet, there is a plethora of research on the involvement of private sector unions in female and minority employment issues and policies. The body of literature here can provide directions for much-needed future studies on public sector unions and female and minority employment. In particular, the works of Hill (1985), Foner (1980), Kenneally (1978), Gould (1977), Wertheimer and Nelson (1975), Marshall (1965), Northrup (1944) and many others can provide rich insights into such studies.

One area requiring further research, which was addressed in a preliminary fashion in Chapter 4, is the effect of unions on females' and minorities' attempts to gain entry into public sector apprenticeship programs. This would be extremely timely in light of the growing popularity of jointly sponsored apprenticeship training for certain job titles in the public sector. Research in this area may enable public sector employers to avoid the problems as well as litigation encountered by private sector employers as a result of union discrimination.

The role of federal sector unions, both postal and nonpostal, in female and minority employment patterns has also been neglected. In particular, the ability of women and minorities to sue postal unions as well as other federal sector unions for their discriminatory behaviors and practices deserves further attention. This topic was addressed briefly in Chapter 3.

Studies on the role of unions in the employment patterns of several overlooked protected class members are also needed. There is virtually no research on unions and Hispanic workers, older workers and disabled workers in the public sector. Union involvement in the employment issues germane to these special workers requires attention. If older workers become a growing part of public sector work forces in the 1990s, for example, job retraining programs will be necessary. What will the role of unions be here? And, how will unions respond to other special needs of the older worker?

Also of importance would be a study of the various alternatives to effectively combat union discrimination against women and minorities. It would appear that legal and in some cases judicial mandates have had limited success. Other strategies such as education must be studied, tested, and documented (Riccucci 1988).

There are a good many unanswered questions regarding the role of unions in female and minority employment in the public sector. This book attempted to answer some of these questions, but much more research on this topic is needed. Such research will better enable us to address and respond to union behaviors and attitudes toward women and minorities in state, local and federal government work forces.

Notes

1. This is also the case in the private sector. For a discussion, see, for example, Gould (1977).

2. Industrial unions operating in the private sector also appear to have a mixed record. For a discussion, see Gould (1977).

3. But, see Epilogue.

References

Foner, Philip S. *Women and the American Labor Movement.* New York: The Free Press, 1980.

Gould, William B. *Black Workers in White Unions.* Ithaca, New York: Cornell University Press, 1977.

Hill, Herbert. *Black Labor and the American Legal System.* Madison, Wisconsin: University of Wisconsin Press, 1985.

Kenneally, James J. *Women and American Trade Unions.* St. Albans, Vermont: Eden Press Women's Publications, Inc., 1978.

Marshall, F. Ray. *The Negro and Organized Labor.* New York: John Wiley & Sons, Inc., 1965.

Northrup, Herbert. *Organized Labor and the Negro.* New York: Harper, 1944.

Riccucci, Norma M. "A Typology for Union Discrimination: A Public Sector Perspective." *Public Personnel Management Journal* 17 (1988), 1:41-51.

Wertheimer, Barbara M. and Anne H. Nelson. *Trade Union Women: A Study of Their Participation in New York City Locals.* New York: Praeger, 1975.

EPILOGUE

While this book was in press, the U.S. Supreme Court issued several rulings[1] which have implications for employment discrimination law and affirmative action. The rulings do not directly affect the thesis of this book, but it is important to note that they may influence the future employment of women and minorities. For example, the decisions suggest that it may be more difficult for women and minorities to bring certain types of employment discrimination suits (see, *Patterson v. Mclean Credit Union,* 1989), more difficult to win them (see, *Wards Cove v. Atonio,* 1989) and, if they do win, the remedies may be more vulnerable to attack (see, *Martin v. Wilks,* 1989).

In effect, women and minorities may face greater obstacles in filing certain types of discrimination suits against their unions. If women and minorities are successful in their suits, the rulings further suggest that unions will have greater opportunities to challenge the remedies awarded to the protected class groups by the courts. As the case law continues to unfold in the coming years, greater analysis of the decisions and their significance to unions is needed.

Note

1. See, for example, *City of Richmond v. Croson Company* (1989), *Wards Cove v. Atonio* (1989), *Lorance v. AT&T* (1989), *Patterson v. McLean Credit Union* (1989), and *Martin v. Wilks* (1989).

References

City of Richmond v. Croson Company 57 *Law Week* 4132, 24 January 1989.
Lorance v. AT&T 57 *Law Week* 4654, 13 June 1989.
Martin v. Wilks 57 *Law Week* 4616, 13 June 1989.
Patterson v. McLean Credit Union 57 *Law Week* 4705, 13 June 1989.
Wards Cove v. Atonio 57 *Law Week* 4583, 5 June 1989.

TABLE OF CASES

Afro-American Patrolmen's League v. Atlanta 817 F.2d 719 (11th Cir. 1987), 135n, 136

AFSCME v. City of New York 599 F. Supp. 916 (1984), 163

AFSCME v. County of Nassau 609 F. Supp. 695 (1985), 163

AFSCME v. State of Washington 770 F.2d 1401 (9th Cir. 1985), 163, 164

Albemarle Paper Co. v. Moody 95 S.Ct. 2362, 422 U.S. 405 (1975), 47, 64

Allen v. Butz 390 F. Supp. 836 (E.D. Pa. 1975), 41, 64

Allen v. Seattle Police Officers' Guild 645 P.2d 1113 (Wash. App. 1982), 38, 64

Allen v. Seattle Police Officers' Guild 670 P.2d 246 (Wash. 1983), 38, 39, 64

American Nurses Assoc. v. State of Illinois 783 F.2d 716 (7th Cir. 1986), 163, 164

American Tobacco Co. v. Patterson 102 S.Ct. 1534, 456 U.S. 63 (1982), 51, 56, 64n, 64

Berkman v. New York City 536 F. Supp. 177 (1982); *aff'd.*, 705 F.2d 584 (2d Cir. 1983), 110, 111, 134n, 136

Berkman v. New York City 580 F. Supp. 226 (1983), 111, 112, 134n, 136

Berkman v. New York City 812 F.2d 52 (2d Cir. 1987); *cert. denied*, 108 S.Ct. 146, _U.S._ 1987, 113, 134n, 136

Blake v. City of Los Angeles 595 F.2d 1367 (9th Cir. 1979); *cert. denied*, 100 S.Ct. 1865, 446 U.S. 928 (1980), 134n, 135n, 136

Boston Chapter, NAACP v. Beecher and Boston Firefighters and Boston Police Patrolmen's Assoc. 679 F.2d 965 (1st Cir. 1982), 54, 55, 56, 57, 65

Bowen v. U.S. Postal Service 103 S.Ct. 588, 459 U.S. 212 (1983), 40, 62n, 63n, 65

Boyd v. Ozark Airlines 568 F.2d 50 (8th Cir. 1977), 135n, 136

Brace v. O'Neill 19 FEP Cases 848 (1978), 117, 135n, 136

Bridgeport Guardians, Inc. v. Civil Service Commission 482 F.2d 1333 (2d Cir. 1973), 134n, 136

Briggs v. City of Madison 536 F. Supp. 435 (1982), 163, 165, 167

Brown v. General Services Administration 96 S.Ct. 1961, 425 U.S. 820 (1976), 41, 42, 63n, 65

Brown v. Neeb and Fire Fighters Local Union 92 644 F.2d 551 (6th Cir. 1981), 55, 56, 57, 65

Brunet v. City of Columbus 642 F. Supp. 1214 (S.D. Ohio 1986); *appeal dismissed* 826 F.2d 1062 (6th Cir. 1987); *cert. denied*, 108 S.Ct. 1593, _U.S._ (1988), 135n, 137

City of Richmond v. Croson Company 57 *Law Week* 4132, January 24, 1989, 7n, 8, 64n, 65, 175n, 176

Commonwealth of Pennsylvania v. AFSCME 41 FEP Cases 1564 (1986), 128, 137

Connecticut State Employees Assoc. v. State of Connecticut 31 FEP Cases 191 (1983), 163, 164

Costa v. Markey 677 F.2d 158 (1st Cir. 1982), 134n, 137

County of Washington v. Gunther 101 S.Ct. 2242, 452 U.S. 161 (1981), 167n, 167

Dothard v. Rawlinson 433 U.S. 321, 15 FEP Cases 10 (1977), 105, 125, 126, 134n, 137

EEOC v. Affiliated Foods and Teamsters Union 34 FEP Cases 943 (1984), 163

Firefighters Local No. 93 v. Cleveland 106 S. Ct. 3063, _U.S._ (1986), 7n, 8, 61, 65, 135n, 137

Firefighters Local Union No. 1784 v. Stotts, Memphis v. Stotts 104 S.Ct. 2576, 467 U.S. 561 (1984), 58, 59, 61, 64n, 65

Ford v. University of Montana 598 P.2d 604 (1979), 63n, 65

Franks v. Bowman Transportation Co. 495 F.2d 398 (5th Cir. 1974), *rev'd and remanded*, 96 S.Ct. 1251, 424 U.S. 747 (1976), 47, 56, 58, 63n, 65

Fulenwider v. Firefighters Assn. Local Union 1784 649 S.W. 2d 268 (1982), 57, 65

Gaynor v. Rockefeller 256 N.Y.S. 2d 584 (1965), 99n, 100

Golden v. Local 55, Firefighters 633 F.2d 817 (9th Cir. 1980), 39, 63n, 65

Goodman v. Lukens Steel Co. 107 S.Ct. 2617, _U.S._ (1987), 43, 65

Griggs v. Duke Power Co. 91 S.Ct. 849, 401 U.S. 424 (1971), 49, 50, 52, 65

Guardians Ass'n v. Civil Service Commission 431 F. Supp. 526 (S.D.N.Y. 1977); *aff'd in relevant part*, 630 F.2d 79 (2d Cir. 1980), 134n, 138

Gunther v. Iowa State Men's Reformatory 612 F.2d 1079 (8th Cir. 1980), *cert. denied*, 100 S.Ct. 2942, 446 U.S. 966 (1980), 125, 136n, 138

Hardy v. Stumpf 37 Cal. App. 3d 958, 112 Cal. Rptr. (1974), 134n, 138

Hawaii Government Employees Assoc., AFSCME v. State of Hawaii 38 FEP Cases 1126 (1985), 163

Hodgson v. Sagner 326 F. Supp. 371 (D. Md. 1971), *aff'd*, 462 F.2d 180 (4th Cir. 1972), 143, 144, 168

Horace v. City of Pontiac 624 F.2d 765 (6th Cir. 1980), 134n, 138

International Brotherhood of Teamsters v. United States 97 S.Ct. 1843, 431 U.S. 324 (1977), 48, 50, 51, 52, 53, 55, 56, 58, 59, 61, 63n, 64n, 65

IUE v. Westinghouse Electric Corporation 631 F.2d 1094 (1980), 144, 168

James v. Stockham Valves & Fittings Co. 394 F. Supp. 434 (N.D. Ala. 1975), *rev'd and remanded*, 559 F.2d 310 (5th Cir. 1977), *cert. denied*, 98 S.Ct. 767, 434 U.S. 1034 (1978), 51, 64n, 65

Jennings v. American Postal Workers Union 672 F.2d 712 (8th Cir. 1982), 41, 42, 43, 65

Jersey Central Power & Light Co. v. I.B.E.W. 508 F.2d 687 (3d Cir. 1975), 49, 50, 52, 65

Johnson v. Transportation Agency, Santa Clara County, California 107 S.Ct. 1442, _U.S._ (1987), 7n, 8, 61, 65, 108, 127, 136n, 138

Karahalios v. National Federation of Federal Employees 57 Law Week 4311, March 7, 1989, 40, 63n, 65

League of United Latin American Citizens v. Santa Ana 410 F. Supp. 873 (C.D. Cal. 1976), 134n, 138

Local 12, United Rubber Workers v. NLRB 368 F.2d 12 912 (5th Cir. 1966), 62n, 65

Local 526-M, Michigan Corrections Organization, SEIU v. Michigan 313 N.W. 2d 143 (Mich. App. 1981), 127, 138

Lorance v. AT&T 57 Law Week 4654, 13 June 1989, 52, 64n, 65, 175n, 176

Lum v. New York City Civil Service Commission 10 FEP Cases 365 (S.D.N.Y. 1975), 134n, 138

Maehren v. Seattle 599 P.2d 1255 (Wash. Sup. Ct. 1979), *cert. denied*, 452 U.S. 938, 101 S.Ct. 3079 (1981), 135n, 139

Martin v. Wilks 57 Law Week 4616, 13 June 1989, 175, 175n, 176

Mieth and Rawlinson v. Dothard 418 F. Supp. 1169 (M.D. Ala. 1976), 126, 136n, 139

Minnick v. California Department of Corrections 157 Cal. Rptr. 260 (app. 1979); *cert. granted*, 100 S.Ct. 3055, 448 U.S. 910 (1980); *cert. denied*, 101 S.Ct. 2211, 452 U.S. 105 (1981), 127, 136n, 139

Minority Police Officers Ass'n of South Bend v. South Bend 721 F.2d 197 (7th Cir. 1983), 135n, 139

Moore v. City of San Jose 615 F.2d 1265 (9th Cir. 1980), 63n, 65

NAACP v. Detroit Police Officers Ass'n 676 F. Supp. 790 (E.D. Mich. 1988), 135n, 139

Newbold v. U.S. Postal Service 614 F.2d 46 (5th Cir. 1980), *cert. denied*, 101 S.Ct. 225, 449 U.S. 878 (1980), 41, 42, 43

Officers for Justice v. Civil Service Commission 371 F. Supp. 1328 (N.D. Cal.

1973), 134n, 139

Officers for Justice v. Civil Service Commission 371 F. Supp. 378 (N.D. Cal. 1975), 134n, 135n, 139

Officers for Justice v. Civil Service Commission 473 F. Supp. 801 (1979), 134n, 135n, 139

Papermakers, Local 189 v. United States 416 F.2d 980 (5th Cir. 1969), *cert. denied*, 90 S.Ct. 926, 397 U.S. 919 (1970), 46, 47, 66

Patterson v. McLean Credit Union 57 *Law Week* 4705, 13 June 1989, 175, 175n, 176

Pennsylvania Human Relations Comm. v. Hempfield Township and Teamsters 16 FEP Cases 1348 (1976), 163

Policewomen's Endowment Association, et al. v. Civil Service Commission of the City of New York (81 Civ. 0537, S.N.Y. 1981), 135n, 139

Policewomen's Endowment Association Against New York City Police Department (No. 7657-EG, City of New York Commission on Human Rights, 1978), 135n, 139

Power v. Barry County, MI, Fraternal Order of Police and Teamsters 539 F. Supp. 721 (1982), 162, 163, 164

Pullman-Standard v. Swint 102 S.Ct. 1781, 456 U.S. 273 (1982), 64n, 66

Quarles v. Philip Morris, Inc. 279 F. Supp. 505 (E.D. Va. 1968), 46, 47, 49, 52, 66

Regents v. Bakke 98 S.Ct. 2733, 438 U.S. 265 (1978), 1, 9, 136n, 139

Richards v. New York State Correctional Services 572 F. Supp. 1168 (D.C.N.Y. 1983), 135n, 139

San Francisco Police Officers Ass'n. v. San Francisco 812 F.2d 1125 (9th Cir. 1987), 135n, 139

St. Louis Newspaper Guild v. Pulitzer Pub. Co. 618 F. Supp. 1468 (1985), 163, 164

Schaefer v. Tannian 394 F. Supp. 1136 (1975), 120, 121, 139

Schenectady v. State Division of Human Rights 335 N.E. 2d 290 (1975), 119, 121, 135n, 139

Schultz v. Wheaton Glass Co. 421 F.2d 259 (3d Cir. 1970), 142, 168

Sheet Metal Workers Local 28 v. EEOC 106 S.Ct. 3019, _U.S._ (1986), 7n, 9, 61, 66, 81, 82, 83, 99n, 101

Shield Club v. Cleveland 370 F. Supp. 251 (N.D. Ohio 1972), 134n, 139

Shortt v. Arlington 589 F.2d 779 (4th Cir. 1978), 119, 122, 123, 139

Snell v. Suffolk County 611 F. Supp. 521 (D.C.N.Y. 1985), 104, 139

Steele v. Louisville & Nashville Railroad Co. 65 S.Ct. 226, 323 U.S. 192 (1944), 35, 36, 66

Stotts v. Memphis Fire Department 679 F.2d 541 (6th Cir. 1982), 55, 56, 57, 66

Taylor v. Charley Brothers 25 FEP Cases 602 (1981), 162, 163

Uniformed Sanitationmen's Association v. New York City (No. 14607/86, New York State Sup. Court, July 28, 1986), 131, 132, 139

United Air Lines v. Evans 97 S.Ct. 1885, 431 U.S. 553 (1977), 51, 66

United States v. Buffalo 457 F. Supp. 612 (1978), 134n, 135n, 139

United States v. Chicago 796 F.2d 205 (7th Cir. 1986), 135n, 139

United States v. Cincinnati 771 F.2d 161 (6th Cir. 1985), 119, 121, 122, 135n, 139

United States v. Jefferson County 720 F.2d 1511 (11th Cir. 1983), 135n, 139

United States v. Miami 614 F.2d 1322 (5th Cir. 1980), 118, 135n, 139

United States v. North Carolina 512 F. Supp. 968 (E.D.N.C. 1981), 134n, 139

United States v. Paradise 107 S.Ct. 1053, _U.S._ (1987), 7n, 9, 61, 66, 135n, 139

United States v. Philadelphia 499 F. Supp. 1196 (1980), 118, 119, 135n, 139

United States v. T.I.M.E.-D.C., Inc. 6 FEP Cases 690 (1974), 51, 66

United Steelworkers v. Weber 99 S.Ct. 2721, 443 U.S. 193 (1979), 1, 9, 80, 101

Vaca v. Sipes 87 S.Ct. 903, 386 U.S. 171 (1967), 36, 39, 66

Vulcan Society v. Fire Department of White Plains 505 F. Supp. 955 (1981), 135n, 139

Vulcan Society v. New York City Civil Service Commission 490 F.2d 387 (2d Cir. 1973), 134n, 139

Wallace Corp. v. National Labor Relations Board 65 S.Ct. 238, 323 U.S. 248 (1944), 36, 66

Wards Cove v. Atonio 57 Law Week 4583, 5 June 1989, 175, 175n, 176

Washington v. Davis 96 S.Ct. 2040, 426 U.S. 229 (1976), 134n, 139

Waters v. Wisconsin Steel Works 502 F.2d 1309 (7th Cir. 1974), 49, 50, 66

Watkins v. Steelworkers, Local 2369 369 F. Supp. 1221 (E.D. La. 1974), 516 F.2d 41 (5th Cir. 1975), 48, 49, 66

Western Addition Community Organization v. Alioto 369 F. Supp. 77 (N.D. Cal. 1973), 134n, 139

White v. Nassau County Police 15 FEP Cases 261 (1977), 106, 139

Wygant v. Jackson Board of Education 106 S.Ct. 1842, _U.S._ (1986), 7n, 9, 59, 60, 61, 66

INDEX

Aaron, Benjamin, 36, 40, 64
Aaron, Henry J., 156, 157, 159, 167n, 167
Abbott, Grace, 75, 99
adverse impact, 38, 43, 50, 62, 110, 113, 135n
affirmative action (AA), 1-7, 7n, 39, 53-55, 57-62, 64, 67, 69-74, 78, 81, 96-97, 118-119, 127, 136n, 171, 175
Albany Permanent Professional Firefighters Association, 114
Amalgamated Clothing Workers of America, 143
Amalgamated Transit Union (ATU), 27
American Federation of Government Employees (AFGE), 27, 41, 71, 161
American Federation of Labor-Congress of Industrial Organizations (AFL-CIO), 30n, 156, 158, 159, 160
American Federation of State, County and Municipal Employees (AFSCME), 3, 8, 128, 147-152, 155-156, 160-162, 164-166
American Federation of Teachers

(AFT), 26
American Flight Attendants (AFA), 161
American Nurses Association (ANA), 26
American Postal Workers Union (APWU), 26, 41, 42, 161
Anderson, Deborah, 117, 136
Anderson, Mary A., 116, 136
antidiscrimination clauses, 70
Arnold, Bob, 148, 167
Ashmore, R.D., 27, 30
attorney's fees, 36

back pay, 36, 43, 44, 144, 162
Baker, Elizabeth F., 76, 99
Ban, Carolyn, 37, 66
bargaining agent, 34, 38, 44
bargaining unit, 34, 35, 39, 72, 73, 94
Baxandall, Rosalyn, 11, 30
Bayes, Jane, 143, 166n, 168
Bell, Daniel J., 116, 136
Bell, John, 98, 100
Bent, Alan Edward, 2, 8
Berkman, Brenda, 110, 111, 112, 116
Beyer, Janice M., 8n, 8
Bittman, Mark, 148, 167
Bloch, Peter, 117, 136

blue-collar worker, 153
bona fide occupational qualification
    (BFOQ), 6, 126, 128, 129, 136n
Bowersox, Michael S., 103, 126, 136
Bradburn, Pamela G., 62, 63n, 65
Braxton, Lillian, 123
Breitenbeck, Joseph T., 43, 66
Briggs, Norma, 79, 99n, 100
Briggs, Vernon M., 78, 79, 80, 85, 100
Brown, Clair, 30
Brown, Roxanne, 29n, 30
Bureau of Apprenticeship and Training
    (BAT), 76, 85, 94, 96, 97, 99n
Burks, Edward C., 117, 137
business necessity, 126

California Correction Officers'
    Association (CCOA), 127
Campion, Michael A., 107, 108, 135n,
    137
Carmody, Deirdre, 130, 137
Cayer, N. Joseph, 15, 30, 103, 137
Chaikin, Sol C., 159, 161
Charles, Michael T., 107, 108, 137
Chertos, Cynthia H., 109, 137
Chicago Firefighters Union, 113
Civil Rights Act of 1866, 34, 40
Civil Rights Act of 1964, 33, 70, 81,
    98n, 143
Civil Service Employees Association,
    New York State (CSEA), 148,
    153-155
Civil Service Reform Act (CSRA) of
    1978, 40
closed shop, 80, 82
Coalition of Black Trade Unionists
    (CBTU), 28
Coalition of Labor Union Women
    (CLUW), 28
Coffman, T., 27, 30
Colker, Ruth, 103-105, 110, 137
Collins, B.E., 30
Communication Workers of America
    (CWA), 148-150, 152, 158
compensatory damages, 62n, 63n
competitive status seniority, 50
Connecticut State Employees
    Association, 152

Considine, W., 108, 137
construction unions, 82
constructive seniority, 47, 48, 63n,
    118
Cook, Alice H., 12, 14, 31, 147, 148,
    150, 152, 156, 159, 167
Cook, Joan, 115, 137
cooptation, 68
Coulson, Crocker, 148, 167
Council 82, 128, 155
Cowan, Ruth S., 76, 100
Cox, Gail Diane, 148, 167
craft unions, 3, 4, 63n, 81, 83, 97,
    142, 159, 162, 164, 166, 171,
    172
Crotty, Norma Meacham, 128, 129,
    138

Daley, Suzanne, 112, 137
Davis, Charles, 8n, 8
Davis, James A., 135n, 140
Department of Labor, 76, 86, 87, 96,
    98, 145
departmental seniority, 46, 47, 49,
    51, 54, 119, 120, 121
Detroit Police Lieutenants' and
    Sergeants' Association (DPLSA),
    121
DiMarco, Nicholas, 27, 31
disabled workers, 72, 173
discriminatory intent, intent to
    discriminate, 50, 122
disparate impact, 50, 104
distributive bargaining, 69
District 1199, 148, 152
double-deck bargaining, 160
Drescher, Nuala McGann, 72
Dubinsky, Irwin, 80, 100
Dunshee, Kenneth H., 109, 137
duty of fair representation (DFR), 6,
    34, 35, 36, 37, 38, 39, 40, 41,
    42, 61, 62n

Ebony, 30
educational unions, 5
equal employment opportunity
    (EEO), 2-7, 7n, 36, 50, 62, 67,
    70, 71, 99, 105, 125, 171

Equal Employment Opportunity Act of 1972, 33, 54, 103
Equal Employment Opportunity Commission (EEOC), 7, 9, 49, 76, 105, 114, 137, 162
Equal Pay Act of 1963, 142-144, 154
equal pay for equal work, 142, 145, 166, 167n
Equal Protection Clause, 60, 61
Evans, Sara M., 151, 167
exclusive recognition, 34, 35
Executive Order 11246, 96, 98n
Executive Order 11375, 96, 98n
Exum, William H., 5, 8

fair employment practices' laws, 37, 99n
Farmers Home Administration (FHA), 70
Federal Employees Union, 145
Federation of University Employees (FUE), 148, 149
Feinman, Clarice, 105, 124, 137
fictional seniority, 47, 118
Fifth Amendment, 99n
Fine, Howard F., 50, 63n, 65
Finn, Terry, 164, 167
Fire Academy, 111
Fitzgerald Act, 76
Flynn, Edith H., 127, 137
Foner, Philip S., 173, 174
Fossum, John A., 40, 65, 80, 100
Fourteenth Amendment, 60, 118
Fraternal Order of Police (FOP), 26, 116, 118, 119, 121
"freedom now" theory, 47
Freeman, Richard B., 11, 30
Fried, Joseph P., 110, 137

gender-conscious remedies, 61
General Services Administration (GSA), 70, 87
Gerhart, Paul F., 2, 8
goals, 59, 60, 61, 69, 71, 118, 127
Gonzalez, Zaida, 111, 112
good faith, 34, 39, 43, 44, 70
Goodman, Walter, 157, 168
Gordon, Kathryn, 114, 137
Gordon, Linda, 11, 30

Gould, William B., 3, 8, 12, 26-28, 29n, 30, 90, 100, 173, 173n, 174
grievances, 34, 39, 41, 43, 62n, 84, 119, 154, 155
Grondahl, Paul, 114, 137
Gross, Jane, 130, 133, 137
Grossman, Paul, 34, 36, 40, 43, 62n, 63n, 66
Grune, Joy Ann, 144, 147, 148, 150, 152, 158, 160, 162, 168, 169
guilds, 75
Guyor, James, 108, 138

Haitch, Richard, 115, 138
Hammel, Lisa, 149, 168
Harris, Abram L., 76, 101
height requirements, 103, 105-107, 119, 125, 128, 134n, 135n, 136n
Higgins, Lois, 116, 138
Hill, Herbert, 90, 100, 173, 174
hiring halls, 63n
Horne, Peter, 107, 116, 117, 123, 126, 127, 129, 138
Hough, Joseph C., Jr., 27, 31
Howard, Lauren, 113
Hunt, Richard, 8n, 8
Hyde, Albert C., 57, 66, 164, 168

industrial unions, 4, 91, 142, 166, 172, 174n
injunctive relief, 36, 43, 44, 144
integrative bargaining, 69
International Association of Fire Fighters (IAFF), 26, 107
International Association of Policewomen, 123
International Association of Women Police, 123
International Ladies Garment Workers Union (ILGWU), 29n, 159, 160, 161, 165, 166
International Union of Electrical, Radio and Machine Workers (IUE), 144, 152, 158

Jackson, John H., 80, 100
Jacobs, James B., 126, 128, 129, 136n, 138

Jacobs, Sally, 148, 168
Jerdee, Thomas H., 27, 31
job classification, 145, 148, 152, 155, 158
job evaluation, 147, 150-152, 155
job seniority, 46, 48, 120, 121
Jochnowitz, Jay, 114, 138
Johansen, Elaine, 152, 164, 168
Johnson, Eve, 144, 150, 152, 162, 168
Johnson, Kirk, 132, 138
Johnson, Leola A., 126, 138
Joint Apprenticeship Committee (JAC), 6, 7, 68, 69, 74, 80-83, 88, 89, 91, 92, 94, 96, 97, 99

Karlins, M., 27, 30
Kearney, Richard C., 2, 8, 57, 65, 89, 100, 167n, 168
Kelly, Brad, 114, 138
Kelly, Rita Mae, 143, 166n, 168
Kenneally, James J., 11, 30n, 30, 173, 174
Kennedy, Shawn G., 110, 138
Klingner, Donald E., 2, 8
Knights of Labor (KL), 12
Koenig, Esther J., 117, 138
Koziara, Karen S., 27, 30
Krause, Robert D., 138
Krislov, Samuel, 28, 31
Kursh, Harry, 78, 80, 100

Labor Agreement Information Retrieval System (LAIRS), 70
Labor Council on Latin American Advancement, 28
Labor Management Relations Act (LMRA), 34, 36, 40, 42, 62n, 63n
last hired, first fired, 48
last-in, first-out (LIFO), 54, 55, 59
Law Enforcement Assistance Administration (LEAA), 105
layoffs, 7, 45, 48, 50, 54, 55, 56, 58-61, 64n, 106, 116, 120, 121, 159
Leonard, Jonathan S., 8n, 11, 30
Levine, Susan, 76, 100
liability (of unions), 6, 34, 43, 44, 46, 62n, 63n, 144, 146

Lougy, Cameran M., 156, 157, 159, 167n, 167
Lubasch, Arnold H., 113, 138
Lucy, William, 27, 31

Mahoney, Thomas, 168
Maine State Employees Association (MSEA), 148, 152
Maitland, Leslie, 110, 139
Mancuso, Nicholas, 110, 113
Marshall, F. Ray, 12, 31, 78, 79, 80, 85, 100, 173, 174
Masengill, Douglas, 27, 31
May, Clifford D., 113, 139
McConahay, John B., 27, 31
McDaniel, Ann, 97, 100
McKelvey, Jean T., 36, 64, 65, 66
McKersie, Robert B., 69, 101
Melchionne, Theresa M., 116, 139
Menges, Robert J., 5, 8
merit, 6, 45, 84, 85, 107, 108, 110, 114, 115, 121, 130-132, 134, 142
Methé, David T., 3, 9
monetary damages, 43, 44, 144
moot, mootness, 58
Mosher, Frederick C., 28, 31
Municipal Employees Association, 147, 149

Nalbandian, John, 2, 7n, 8, 9, 64n, 65
National Alliance of Postal Employees, 12
National Alliance of Postal and Federal Employees, 29n
National Apprenticeship Act of 1937, 76
National Association of Government Employees (NAGE), 26
National Association of Letter Carriers (NALC), 12, 13, 26, 29, 31, 145
National Center for Productivity and Quality of Working Life, 67
National Committee on Pay Equity (NCPE), 160
National Education Association

(NEA), 26, 158, 161
National Federation of Federal
Employees (NFFE), 26, 70, 145,
161
National Labor Relations Act (NLRA)
of 1935, 34, 36, 38, 40, 62n
National Labor Relations Board
(NLRB), 37, 62n, 63n
National Labor Union (NLU), 11
National Treasury Employees Union
(NTEU), 71, 161
National Women's Trade Union League
(WTUL), 31n
Negro American Labor Council, 28
Nelson, Anne H., 173, 174
Nelson, Barbara J., 151, 167
New York State Commission Against
Discrimination, 75, 80
Newman, Harold R., 37, 66
Newman, Winn, 156
Newspaper Guild, The (TNG), 148
nepotism, 78, 79
Nigro, Felix A., 2, 9
Nigro, Lloyd G., 2, 9
925, 156
Northrup, Herbert, 173, 174

Office of Employee Relations (OER),
New York State, 153, 155
Office of Federal Contract Compliance
Programs (OFCCP), 96
O'Hara, Rosemary, 114, 140
older workers, 173
outreach programs, 83, 97

Patrolmen's Benevolent Association
(PBA), 116, 118, 121
pay equality, 142, 143, 144, 145, 166
pay equity, 6, 141, 142, 143, 145, 147,
148, 149, 150, 151, 152, 153, 155,
156, 157, 158, 159, 160, 161, 162,
164, 166, 171, 172
Pechman, Joseph A., 30
Pecorella, Robert F., 133, 139
Pendleton Act of 1883, 84
Pendleton, Clarence, 157
perpetuation of past discrimination
into the present, 46, 51

Perry, James L., 2, 4, 9
Phillips, Sarah, 109, 137
physical agility exams, 6, 104, 105,
107, 108, 109, 110, 112, 114,
115, 119, 125, 130, 131, 132
Picchi, Joe, 154, 155, 168
Pierson, David A., 27, 30
plant, plantwide seniority, 45, 46,
47, 48, 49, 50, 119
Policewomen's Endowment
Association (PEA), 123, 124
Portman, Lisa, 144, 150, 152, 162,
168
Postal Alliance, 12, 13, 17, 29n
postal employees/workers, 36, 37,
40, 41, 42, 63n
Postal Record, 12, 13, 31
Postal Reorganization Act of 1970,
17, 29n, 63n
Potter, Joan, 8n, 9
Potts, Lee W., 117, 125, 139
"preferred means" theory, 56
PREP, Inc., 97
Press, Aric, 97, 100
prison guards, 124, 125, 126
privacy rights, 125
progression-line seniority, 45, 46
Public Employees Federation (PEF),
148, 153, 154, 155, 156
Public Employment Relations Board
(PERB), New York State, 37
punitive damages, 62n, 63n

quotas, 61, 118

race-conscious relief, remedies, 61,
81, 83
racism, 12, 127
Railway Labor Act (RLA), 34, 35,
36
Railway Mail Association, 12
Reder, Nancy, 147, 152, 158, 160,
168
reductions-in-force (RIFS), 54
Reeves, T. Zane, 2, 8
referral systems, 63n
Reisner, Susan, 125, 139
retroactive seniority, 47, 48, 118

Reverby, Susan, 11, 30
Reynolds, Stacia E., 38, 39, 66
Riccucci, Norma M., 3, 8n, 9, 37, 66,
 103, 106, 139, 167n, 168, 173, 174
"rightful place" theory, 47
Roberts, Robert N., 54, 66
Rorabaugh, W.J., 75, 76, 100
Rosen, Benson, 27, 31, 168
Rosenbloom, David H., 2, 9, 28, 31, 40,
 57, 63n, 66, 89, 98n, 100, 164, 168
Rowan, Richard L., 76, 80, 81, 100
Ruben, Lester, 76, 80, 81, 100
Rust-Tierney, Diann, 78, 79, 80, 84, 96,
 97, 101
Rynes, Sara, 150, 152, 157, 168

Salpukas, Agis, 154, 168
Scales-Trent, Judy, 8n, 9
Schein, Virginia E., 27, 31
Schell, George K. H., 52, 66
Schick, Timothy F., 114, 115, 139, 140
Schlei, Barbara L., 34, 36, 40, 43, 62n,
 63n, 66
scope of bargaining, 44, 145, 148
Section 703 (c), Title VII, 33, 34, 41, 42
Section 703 (h), Title VII, 45, 46, 49,
 51, 52, 53, 56, 58, 64n, 121, 122
Section 717, Title VII, 40, 41, 42, 63n
Section 1981, 42 U.S.C., 34, 36, 37, 38,
 40, 41, 42, 43, 62n, 63n
Section 1983, 42 U.S.C., 56
segregation, 12, 26, 79, 92, 97, 126
Senator Case of New Jersey, 45, 52, 53
Senator Clark of Pennsylvania, 45, 52,
 53
seniority, 6, 34, 44, 45, 46, 47, 48, 49,
 50, 51, 52, 53, 54, 55, 56, 57, 58,
 59, 60, 61, 62, 63n, 64n, 70, 106,
 118, 119, 120, 121, 122, 129, 135n,
 142, 154, 172
Service Employees International Union
 (SEIU), 92, 152, 156, 158, 160, 161
"settlement" theory, 56
sexism, 127
sexual harassment, 84, 111, 112, 129
Shafritz, Jay M., 2, 9, 40, 57, 63n, 66,
 89, 98n, 100, 164, 168
Sigelman, Lee, 15, 30, 103, 137

Silver, Marc L., 83, 84, 101
Silverman, Ira J., 117, 140
Simon, David Offen, 34, 35, 36, 66
slavery, 12, 76, 109
social representativeness, 28
socialization, 28, 79, 111
sovereignty, 2
Sovern, Michael I., 37
Spero, Sterling Denhard, 12, 31,
 63n, 66, 76, 101, 167n, 169
Stanko, Elizabeth, 137
State Apprenticeship Council (SAC),
 85, 94, 96, 97, 99n
"status-quo" theory, 47
Steinberg, Ronnie, 12, 14, 31
stereotyping, stereotypes, 27, 79,
 116, 126
strike, 2, 40, 113, 147, 148, 149, 150
strikebreakers, 113
Sulzner, George T., 70, 101
super-seniority, 47
Swoboda, Frank, 30n, 31
Sylvis, William, 11, 31

Taft-Hartley Act of 1947, 80
Teamsters, 162, 164
Tennessee Valley Authority (TVA),
 67
Tennessee Valley Trades and Labor
 Council, 67
Thompson, Frank J., 28, 31
"time and motion" studies, 131
Title VII, Civil Rights Act of 1964, 6,
 33, 34, 36, 37, 38, 40, 41, 42,
 43, 44, 45, 46, 47, 48, 49, 52,
 53, 54, 56, 59, 61, 62, 63n, 64n,
 81, 82, 83, 96, 103, 105, 114,
 118, 120, 121, 122, 125, 126,
 132, 143, 158, 164, 165, 167n,
 172
Title 29, Part 30, 98n
tokens, 72
Trescott, Martha M., 100
Trice, Harrison M., 8n, 8
Trost, Cathy, 159
trowel crafts, 81
Turner, Renee D., 29n, 31
Twentieth Century Fund, 27, 31

two-tier wage system, 154, 156

unfair labor practice, 36, 37, 40, 62n, 63n
Uniformed Firefighters Association (UFA), 110, 111, 112, 113
Uniformed Sanitationmen's Association, 131
union leadership position, 13, 26, 27, 30n
United Auto Workers (UAW), 152, 159
United Electrical Workers of America (UE), 148
United Steelworkers of America, 80
United University Professions (UUP), 72, 73, 96
United Women Firefighters, 115
Urban League, 97
urban transit, 91, 92
U.S. Commission on Civil Rights, 26, 27, 28, 30n, 31, 99n, 101, 157

Van Riper, Paul, 145, 169
Vega, Manuel, 117, 140
Volz, William H., 43, 66

wage gap, 141, 142
Walters, G., 27, 30
Walton, Richard E., 69, 101
weight requirements, 103, 105, 106, 107, 119, 125, 128, 134n, 136n
Weisheit, Ralph A., 103, 140
Wellington, Harry H., 2, 9
Wertheimer, Barbara Mayer, 11, 26, 31, 173, 174
white-collar workers, 67
Wiesenthal, Eric, 147, 151, 167, 169
Wilkerson, Isabel, 123, 130, 140
Willenborg, Eileen, 43, 66
Wilmore, Jack H., 135n, 140
Wilson, Carole, 169
Winerip, Michael, 114, 115, 140
Winter, Ralph K., 2, 9
Women's Bureau, 145
Wood, Stephen L., 40, 63n, 66

Yale University, 148, 149

Zagoria, Sam, 30
Zimmer, Lynn E., 127, 128, 129, 140
"zone of reasonableness," 36
Zusy, Anne, 113, 140

About the Author

NORMA M. RICCUCCI is Assistant Professor in the Department of Public Administration and Policy at the State University of New York, Albany. She has written articles on public sector labor relations, equal employment opportunity, and affirmative action for *Review of Public Personnel Administration, Public Administration Quarterly, Policy Studies Journal,* and the *University of Detroit Law Review,* among others.